STUDIES IN ECONOMIC AND SOC

This series, specially commissioned by
provides a guide to the current interpretations of the key themes of
economic and social history in which advances have recently been made or
in which there has been significant debate.

Originally entitled 'Studies in Economic History', in 1974 the series had its
scope extended to include topics in social history, and the new series titles,
'Studies in Economic and Social History', signalises this development.

The series gives readers access to the best work done, helps them to draw
their own conclusions in major fields of study, and by means of the critical
bibliography in each book guides them in the selection of further reading.
The aim is to provide a springboard to further work rather than a set of
pre-packaged conclusions or short-cuts.

ECONOMIC HISTORY SOCIETY

The Economic History Society, which numbers around 3000 members,
publishes the *Economic History Review* four times a year (free to members)
and holds an annual conference. Enquiries about membership should be
addressed to the Assistant Secretary, Economic History Society, PO Box
70, Kingswood, Bristol BS15 5FB. Full-time students may join at special
rates.

CURRENT ISSUES IN ECONOMICS

General Editor: David Greenaway, University of Nottingham

Current Issues in Industrial Economics
Edited by John Cable

Current Issues in Microeconomics
Edited by John D. Hey

Current Issues in Macroeconomics
Edited by David Greenaway

Current Issues in Labour Economics
Edited by David Sapsford and Zafiris Tzannatos

Current Issues in International Monetary Economics
Edited by David T. Llewellyn and Chris Milner

Current Issues in Development Economics
Edited by V. N. Balasubramanyam and S. Lall

Current Issues in Financial and Monetary Economics
Edited by Kevin Dowd and M. K. Lewis

Current Issues in Public Sector Economics
Edited by Peter Jackson

Current Issues in the Economics of Welfare
Edited by Nicholas Barr and David Whynes

Current Issues in Agricultural Economics
Edited by A. J. Rayner and David Colman

Series Standing Order
If you would like to receive future titles in this series as they are
published, you can make use of our standing order facility. To place a
standing order please contact your bookseller or, in case of difficulty,
write to us at the address below with your name and address and the
name of the series. Please state with which title you wish to begin your
standing order. (If you live outside the United Kingdom we may not
have the rights for your area, in which case we will forward your order
to the publisher concerned.)

Customer Services Department, Macmillan Distribution Ltd
Houndmills, Basingstoke, Hampshire, RG21 2XS, England.

Current Issues in Microeconomics

Edited by
John D. Hey
Professor of Economics and Statistics
University of York

MACMILLAN

First published 1989 by
THE MACMILLAN PRESS LTD
Houndmills, Basingstoke, Hampshire RG21 2XS
and London
Companies and representatives
throughout the world

ISBN 0–333–45472–3 hardcover
ISBN 0–333–45473–1 paperback

A catalogue record for this book is available
from the British Library.

Printed in Hong Kong

Reprinted 1991, 1993

Contents

List of Figures

List of Tables

Series Editor's Preface

The *Current Issues* series has slightly unusual origins. *Current Issues in International Trade*, which Macmillan published in 1987 and which turned out to be the pilot for the series was in fact 'conceived' in the Horton Hospital, Banbury, and 'delivered' (in the sense of completed) in the Hilton International in Nicosia! The reader may be struck by the thought that a more worthwhile and enjoyable production process would start and finish the other way around. I agree! Be that as it may, that is how the series started.

As I said in the Preface to *Current Issues in International Trade* the reason for its creation was the difficulty of finding suitable references on 'frontier' subjects for undergraduate students. Many of the issues which excite professional economists and which dominate the journal literature take quite a time to percolate down into texts, hence the need for a volume of *Current Issues*. The reception which *Current Issues in International Trade* received persuaded me that it may be worth doing something similar for the other subject areas we teach. Macmillan agreed with my judgement, hence the series. Thus each volume in this series is intended to take readers to the 'frontier' of the particular subject area. Each volume contains ten essays, nine of which deal with specific current issues, and one which provides a general overview, setting the relevant current issues in the context of other recent developments.

As series editor the main challenge I faced was finding suitable editors for each of the volumes – the best people are generally the busiest! I believe, however, that I have been fortunate in having such an impressive and experienced team of editors with the necessary skills and reputation to persuade first-class authors to participate. I would like to thank all of them for their cooperation and assistance in the development of the series. Like me, all of them will, I am sure, hope that this series provides a useful service to undergraduate and postgraduate students as well as faculty.

Microeconomics is the point of embarkation for almost all students of economics. Being at the core of the discipline, it is also an area to which most of us return from time to time, whatever our specialism. In this volume John Hey has selected nine issues which have been at the centre of recent developments in economics, issues which include: choice under uncertainty; microeconometrics; experimental economics; game theory; macroeconomics, and a number of others besides. He has persuaded a group of distinguished authors from the United Kingdom and North America to contribute. The result is a volume which should prove to be challenging, stimulating, and rewarding (in that order).

As well as being a first-rate economist, John Hey has considerable editorial skills. The combination of the two has resulted in what I think is a very fine volume. He himself provides a skilful overview of the chapters in his introductory chapter and it is unnecessary for me to comment on the detail of the chapters. I hope readers find the essays as interesting and rewarding as I have.

University of Nottingham   DAVID GREENAWAY

Notes on the Contributors

John Broome is Reader in Economics, University of Bristol.

Melvyn Coles is Assistant Professor of Economics, Princeton University.

John D. Hey is Professor of Economics and Statistics, University of York.

Graham Loomes is Senior Lecturer in Economics, University of York.

Bruce Lyons is Lecturer in Economics, University of East Anglia.

Mark J. Machina is Associate Professor of Economics, University of California, San Diego.

Paul Madden is Senior Lecturer in Econometrics and Social Statistics, University of Manchester.

James M. Malcomson is Professor of Economics, University of Southampton.

Ray Rees is Professor of Economics, University of Guelph.

Robert A. Solo is Professor of Economics, Michigan State University.

Yanis Varoufakis is Lecturer in Economics, University of East Anglia.

Ian Walker is Professor of Economics, Keele University.

1 Introduction: Recent Developments in Microeconomics

JOHN D. HEY

This Series of books is aimed at students of economics and non-specialist economists interested in learning about recent developments in economics. Usually, such recent developments first see the light of day in one of the academic journals, and take some time to filter through to the general economist. This process often takes several years. At the same time, however, the developments are assimilated – often in an informal (and sometimes mistaken) fashion by the leading economists, and are implicit in various pedagogical activities carried out within the profession. This puts the non-specialist at a considerable disadvantage. Unfortunately, there is usually no easy way for the non-specialist to make him-/or her-self aware of these recent developments, given that they are typically communicated in specialist language in high-level journals, from one highbrow economist to another. Often, advanced mathematics is used, and much – in the way of prior knowledge – is taken for granted in the exposition. Nevertheless, knowledge of such recent developments is of great importance: the greater the degree of dissemination of such developments, the more likely it is that those elements which are of practical importance for economics will eventually be put to use.

It is the purpose of this series of books – and of this book in particular – to help to close this information gap: to enable non-specialists to become acquainted with recent developments in the

1

subject; to communicate in non-specialist language to non-specialists. We hope that this series will be of immense value to students as well as economists in all walks of life who like to keep up with what is happening at the frontier.

This particular book is concerned with recent developments in *microeconomics*. I would contend that such developments lie at the very heart of economics – certainly given the way that economics is currently practised by the majority of the profession. It is increasingly recognised that all areas of economics rely on a central *core* of microtheory. This is true even in *macroeconomics*, where it is now widely agreed – in sharp contradistinction to the situation of twenty years ago – that theory must have a firm micro base. (This is not to imply that I agree with this: it is simply a comment on the situation as it exists at present.) So developments in microeconomics have possible implications well outside the narrow confines of micro itself. Conversely, developments in microeconomics – as we will see in the course of this book – have often been motivated by inadequacies in other areas of economics. This is particularly true of the ongoing macroeconomic quest to provide a satisfying theoretical explanation of various allegedly disequilibrium phenomena such as unemployment and inflation. We will find echoes of this particularly in Chapter 7 (which discusses the microfoundations of macroeconomics) but also in Chapters 4 and 5.

The recent history of microtheory can distinguish three broad phases (within the now-dominant mathematical neoclassical paradigm): first, the theory of the maximising agent (or agents) in a certain world; second – based on the triumphant rise of the Neumann–Morgenstern (now normally referred to as SEU – subjective expected utility) theory of behaviour under uncertainty – the theory of the maximising agent (or agents) in a (Neumann–Morgenstern) uncertain world; third, and most recently, the behaviour of agents in one we might call a post-SEU (post-Neumann–Morgenstern) world. It is with these latter two phases that this book is mainly concerned. (As will be or will become apparent, different parts of the subject are at different phases in their development: some are still absorbing the implications of the [SEU] theory of the rational agent in an uncertain world; others have moved on from there – for one reason or another.)

Much of this book is concerned with the treatment and effect of uncertainty – though there are deeper (methodological) issues to which I shall come in a minute. The SEU theory of rational behaviour under uncertainty (of which I hope most readers are aware) fits in most satisfyingly with mainstream neoclassical economics in that it provides a logical (and rather elegant) description of how rational people *ought* to behave in an uncertain world. The application of this theory to economic problems has led to many satisfying predictions, which have, in many instances, been borne out by the facts. A number of illuminating examples can be found in Chapters 3 and 5. There is now a veritable cottage industry applying SEU theory across the whole range of economics. Although these are 'recent developments' in one sense, we do not include much discussion of such developments in this volume – for the simple reason that they do not describe 'current issues' at the frontier; in R&D terminology, recent applications of SEU theory are *developments* while the current issues discussed in this volume are *research*.

While SEU theory has proved a godsend in many areas of economics, there are other areas in which it has either proved 'unusable' and yet other areas in which it has proved empirically unsound. Accordingly, in these areas the literature has moved on, with current issues being concerned with alternatives to, or generalisations of, SEU theory.

Chapter 2 is concerned with some of these issues. Written by Mark Machina, this chapter is concerned, first, with the evidence casting doubt on SEU theory, and second, with the various alternative theories that have been put forward over the past few years. This is a very vigorous area of current research. To give a simple example which motivates the material of that chapter, consider (one variant of) the famous Allais Paradox: let A denote getting \$3000 with certainty, and let B denote a gamble which gives you \$4000 with probability 0.8 and \$0 with probability 0.2. If you were given a choice between A and B here and now, which would you choose? Now, consider the choice between C and D defined as follows: with C you would get \$3000 with probability 0.25 and \$0 with probability 0.75; with D you would get \$4000 with probability 0.2 and \$0 with probability 0.8. If you were given a choice between C and D here and now, which would you choose? Now, the conventional wisdom (SEU theory) requires that if you chose A (B) in the first problem you should choose C (D) in the second. Did you in fact do this? (To see why the conventional wisdom says that you 'should' have this pattern of choice, consider the following: precede both A and B in the first problem by a piece of preliminary risk – in each case a 25 per cent chance of getting to the initial starting-point and a 75 per cent chance of simply getting $0; does this change your choice? Now note that A preceded by the preliminary piece of risk is simply C, while B preceded by the preliminary risk is simply D.) In practice, it is frequently observed that many people make choices that go against this prediction/prescription of the conventional wisdom. Moreover, many of these people continue to hold to their 'irrational' choices even after the error of their ways is pointed out to them. This is but one example of many which provide evidence to suggest that many people have preferences, and hence behaviour, which is inconsistent with the conventional wisdom in economics. Mark Machina describes this evidence, explains in what ways it departs from that indicated by SEU theory, and discusses the implications. In essence, these are two-fold: either the recommendation that we embark on a programme of education, so that 'irrational' people are taught the error of their ways; or the recommendation that economists produce some new theory to explain this apparently irrational behaviour. Naturally, this chapter is mainly concerned with this latter. Machina introduces us to a number of new theories – including Prospect theory, Regret theory, Disappointment theory and Machina's own generalised Subjective expected utility (SEU) theory ('SEU theory without the independence axiom').

In Chapter 3, we return to the conventional wisdom. Under the guidance of Ray Rees, we explore what SEU theory has to tell us about the impact of uncertainty on the behaviour of individuals and on the behaviour of markets. As might be anticipated, uncertainty not only affects behaviour but it also has adverse effects on individuals' welfare. Thus ways of evading or avoiding uncertainty are likely to prove of value (unless, of course, the evasion or avoidance is excessively costly). It is not surprising, therefore, that we see in the real world numerous instruments for avoiding risk: for example, various forms of futures markets; various price stabilisation schemes; various risk-sharing contracts; and so on. But, of course, the example *par excellence* is that of insurance. This is one of the main elements in Ray Rees's chapter. To begin with, Rees shows that a risk-averse agent would always choose to be fully insured if offered actuarially-fair insurance. A problem, however, arises in a market situation if what is an 'actuarially-fair price' cannot be identified. This arises when the risk which the individual faces cannot be observed by the other side of the market. This is a classic example of what has now come to be termed the problem of *asymmetrical information* – when one side of any potential transaction has less information than the other side. Effectively, this means that (at least) one side of the market is uncertain about the nature of the good being traded. This problem frequently surfaces in economics – and resurfaces in later chapters of this book. When it arises, all sorts of problems can occur – at the worst trade may not take place ('the market ceases to exist'); at the best contracts are redefined in anticipation of the uncertainty (though this presupposes a critical amount of information available to market participants); in between, various suboptimal outcomes may result. This chapter discusses these issues – which are of crucial importance for the appropriate operation of economic policy.

Subjective expected utility theory is essentially aimed at the description of the behaviour of economic agents facing essentially exogenous uncertainty – uncertainty generated by Nature, rather than by the behaviour of other interested (possibly competing) agents. Crucially, in such 'games against nature', the nature of the uncertainty – although possibly modified by the agent's behaviour – is not essentially determined by it. In contrast, when there are other interested agents involved, the very essence of the uncertainty is affected (or perhaps can be affected) by the agents' behaviour. The most obvious example is that of duopoly. Consider the simple (mineral springs) model of duopoly used by Cournot in his classic study. In this each of the two duopolists must choose output in ignorance of the choice made by the other. So there is uncertainty – uncertainty about what the rival will do. But this is a different form of uncertainty from that encountered in games against nature: there is no exogenous probability distribution over the rivals' choices. But there is something else. This is seen in starkest form when the two duopolists are identical in all respects. In this case each duopolist can observe that the rival is identical and, in particular, must share the same reasoning about the appropriate solution to the choice problem. Thus, one duopolist can decide what to do by assuming that his or her rival is going through exactly the same mental process. In this way, possibly, the uncertainty can be resolved. The analysis of whether this is indeed the case is the subject matter of Chapter 4, written jointly by Bruce Lyons and Yanis Varoufakis. They use the Cournot duopoly model and the famous 'prisoner's dilemma' as introductory motivation for their analysis. The latter is a classic example: it examines the decision problems faced by two criminals who are caught and interrogated in separate rooms. If both confess, the police will be able to prosecute successfully a major charge, but will recommend leniency. If neither confess, the police will only be able to make a minor charge stick. If only one confesses while the other does not, then the one confessing will get an extremely light sentence while the other will 'get the book thrown at him' (to use the words of Lyons and Varoufakis). Game theory analyses the solution to the prisoners' decision problem; clearly, whether it is 'one-off' or repeated is of crucial significance. Playing a key role in the analysis is the concept of a *Nash equilibrium*: in this each prisoner is choosing what is for him or her the best choice given the choice made by the other prisoner. As will be demonstrated in Chapter 4 the Nash equilibrium in the one-off prisoner's dilemma is where both prisoners confess. (Note that this is Pareto-dominated by the situation in which neither confess – but this is not a Nash equilibrium.) Lyons and Varoufakis discuss these issues in some detail, before applying them to some important topics in economics: the theory of price competition in homogeneous goods and in differentiated products, both in static (one-off) situations and in repeated games; private contributions to public goods; and the provision of family bequests.

The final part of the chapter turns to bargaining theory; in many ways this is the same as game theory, but there is one crucial difference: the individuals (or groups) are allowed to make binding contracts (the enforcement of which will be ensured by some third part – possibly the courts). This, for example, could enable the prisoners in the prisoner's dilemma to escape the Pareto suboptimality of the Nash equilibrium. Lyons and Varoufakis show how such bargaining theory can be used, for example, to 'explain' bargaining between firms and unions over pay and employment.

There is, unfortunately, a problem with all of this. The theory always predicts that any conflict will always be bargained away, and that strikes or lockouts, for example, will never be more than threatened. This does not appear to accord too well with the facts!

Therefore, the final part of this chapter turns to attempts to explain such phenomena. Some of these attempts revolve around the notion of 'bounded rationality', a concept made familiar by Herbert Simon, which has already figured in the material of Chapter 2 – explaining departures of actual behaviour from fully optimal (fully 'rational') behaviour.

One of the recurring themes of Chapter 4 is that there may be several (indeed perhaps a very large number) of possible equilibria of a game or a bargaining problem. Moreover, it is also possible that some of these equilibria may be Pareto-inefficient. So, for example, all the parties to a bargain may find themselves bargaining to an outcome that would be less preferred by all than some other outcome. In this case, one might be led to think about redefining the rules of the bargaining – or decision – process. This is one of the concerns of Chapter 5 on contract theory. Written by Melvyn Coles and Jim Malcomson, this chapter partly returns to some of the concerns of Chapter 3, though from a different perspective. Here again, the prisoner's dilemma is used as an *entrée*, but then the analysis turns to what is now termed the *theory of principal and agent*. The essential concern is, as I noted above, the question of whether an appropriate contract between principal and agent can be drawn up that leads to a 'mutually satisfactory' outcome. (Clearly there is conflict between the two other parties – otherwise there would not be a problem to discuss – so 'mutual satisfaction' must be a relative concept.) Examples of principal-agent problems abound in the real world and in the literature: doctor and patient; supervisor and supervisee; manager and worker; contractor and subcontractor; and so on. Rather interestingly, Coles and Malcomson employ the same example as that used by Ray Rees in Chapter 3 – namely, the contract between insurer and insured in an insurance contract. Consider a feature of such markets analysed in Chapter 3, though from a different perspective: the problem of moral hazard. If an individual is completely insured against some eventuality, then the individual no longer has any incentive to control the probability of that eventuality happening. Indeed, if the probability is affected by the level of effort or money expended by the individual, then he or she has every incentive to reduce the expenditure to a minimum. Thus, the taking-out of complete insurance almost inevitably implies an increase in the probability of the thing being insured against happening; this is the moral hazard problem. But this is not the end of the story: if the initial price of the insurance was actuarially fair, and if it is to remain fair after the occurrence of the moral hazard effect, then the price must rise because of the moral hazard. In this final position we may found ourselves in a position which is Pareto-inefficient: the insurer may find his profit margins reduced because the price has had to rise; the insured may find himself worse off in the sense that he or she would prefer the original price combined with the appropriate expenditure to keep the probability at its original value to the final price (combined with zero expenditure). One of the major concerns of Chapter 5 is the design of a contract which gets round this problem: in modern jargon, it is concerned with the design of an *incentive-compatible* contract; the contract provides the appropriate incentive for both (all) parties to behave in such a way that leads to a 'mutually-satisfactory' outcome. Coles and Malcomson provide a thorough analysis of this problem; the overlaps with Chapters 3 and 4 are illuminating. Of particular importance, once again, is the issue of whether the contract is one-off or repeated. In addition, the issue of *verifiability* – whether the terms and conditions of the contract can be verified by both parties – is seen to be of considerable importance. Clearly, Chapters 4 and 5 differ in that the former analyses the outcome of some pre-specified game, while the latter analyses the question of whether a game can be designed to achieve a required outcome. The issue, therefore, as to whether the analysis of Chapter 5 is realistic does not arise in the same way as it did in Chapter 4.

However, we come back to questions of realism in Chapter 6. Moreover, we return to some of the concerns of Chapter 2, though now from a different perspective. Written by Graham Loomes, Chapter 6 is concerned with experimental economics – one of the main growth areas of economics. This chapter dispels the myth – possibly perpetuated by econometricians! – that economics is a non-experimental subject. To natural scientists, long used to generating data experimentally, this must be a strange myth. Before the growth of experimental methods, economists would rely on data generated by others – invoking a random-error term to account for the transition from the *ceteris paribus* world of the theory to the real world. But with experimental methods, this is not necessary – the economist can design his or her experiment in such a way that control is exercised over those factors which are held constant in the theory. In this way, direct tests of the theory can be implemented. Graham Loomes describes such tests. One of the areas he examines takes us back to SEU theory and to the direct testing of the various components of that theory. He also examines experimental tests of the various new theories, and shows how such controlled tests shed new light on economic decision-making processes that are used by real people in real life.

Loomes also discusses a second area in which experimental methods play an important role: in shedding light on the solutions to problems for which economic theory is of relatively little help. Good examples include the outcome of market processes of various types – such as auctions and bidding – and the outcome in oligopolistic markets. As Chapter 4 shows, economic theory may not indicate a unique outcome (indeed it could suggest an infinity of equilibria); in such situations, experimental methods – by actually replicating the market in an experimental setting – can shed light on the subset of equilibria that merit further investigation. Crucial to the whole operation of such experiments is the feature that participants in the experiments receive payment related to their performance in their particular economic role. In contrast to the situation with psychology experiments, in economics there is usually a natural target variable on which to base such payment.

In Chapter 7, we return to more familiar ground. Here, Paul Madden examines recent developments in the construction of 'proper' microfoundations for macroeconomics. Although now firmly established as an intellectual discipline, it was not too long ago that macro- and microeconomics were regarded as quite separate disciplines. The 'merger' was motivated mainly by the desire to provide more satisfactory theoretical underpinnings to the macro theory of unemployment – earlier Keynesian-type explanations having been proved unappealing. One of the early realisations was that any such explanation would necessarily involve some disequilibrium features. This line of enquiry has now led to a large literature, which is described and evaluated by Madden. Ironically, perhaps, one of the distinguishing features of this literature is that it employs equilibrium methods, with the disequilibrium being modelled by uncertainty or by some exogenous frictions. I suppose one should not be too surprised by this given the current paradigm in economics – which relies crucially on the twin concepts of optimality and equilibrium – but it leaves one wondering whether the literature is moving in the right direction.

Chapter 8 is also concerned with the link between microeconomics and macroeconomics. In addition it is concerned with the empirical testing and estimation of microeconomic theories of household behaviour. Recent major advances in computing power and a significant improvement in recent years of the (electronic) availability of large-scale micro data sets have transformed the possibilities open to the applied microeconometrician. Chapter 8, written by Ian Walker, describes the current exciting position. Even as recently as ten years ago, the testing and estimation of micro theories of household behaviour was fraught with difficulties: so much so that most such testing was carried out at a very aggregative level – using macro time-series data. For many reasons this procedure was unsatisfactory. However, over the past ten years or so there has been a tremendous improvement in computing power – nowadays computations can be performed on desk-top microcomputers that would have been difficult ten years ago even on mainframe computers – while at the same time, many central statistical offices have improved out of all recognition the quantity, quality and availability of large-scale micro (household) data sets. Of particular importance in the UK are the *Family Expenditure Survey* and the *General Household Survey* – subsets of which can now be downloaded electronically to desk-top micros. These developments have dramatically enlarged the range of possible tests of micro theories of behaviour. Ian Walker describes some of these tests. His chapter begins by discussing the important issue of the *translation* of the theory into testable form – with an emphasis on the theory of labour supply and the theory of the (household) demand for commodities. Of particular importance in this translation is the question of *separability* – across commodities and across time. Walker shows how various assumptions about separability lead to simplifications in testing and estimation.

But the implications spread beyond testing and estimation: the use of large-scale data sets and powerful computing software combined with detailed theoretical specifications can address important *policy* questions. For example, how will a suggested alteration to the income tax schedule affect labour supply decisions and hence welfare? Will introducing transferable personal tax allowances (say from spouse to spouse) increase or decrease labour supply and welfare? Will the new EC proposals for changing VAT regulations harm or benefit the low-income groups in the UK? Walker illustrates the power of microsimulation techniques in helping to answer these questions.

The final two substantive chapters take us into rather different territory. Chapter 9 by John Broome, takes us into welfare economics. The current issue with which he is concerned is one which has attracted many great thinkers – that of equality. He considers different distributions of income (across some population or subset of some population) and asks how one might decide whether one distribution is worse than another in some sense. Crucial to the answer is the closely related question of whether the inequality in one distribution is worse than that in another. Other issues discussed in this chapter relate to the definition and measurement of poverty.

So far virtually all the chapters have come from an essentially neoclassical base. In contradistinction, the final chapter, written by Robert Solo is concerned with institutional economics. This is largely a quite separate branch of economics – with a paradigm and methodology of its own. Most mainstream economists will be unfamiliar with this branch, and it is for this reason that the chapter is more descriptive. When pressed to include more explicit discussion of 'current issues' Solo replied that current activity was taking place across the whole spectrum of issues described in the chapter. A glance at the *Journal of Economic Issues*, the leading journal for institutionalists, will confirm this reply. This may well be connected with the prevailing methodology in this branch.

2 Choice under Uncertainty: Problems Solved and Unsolved*

MARK J. MACHINA

2.1 INTRODUCTION

Fifteen years ago, the theory of choice under uncertainty could be considered one of the 'success stories' of economic analysis: it rested on solid axiomatic foundations, it had seen important breakthroughs in the analytics of risk, risk aversion and their applications to economic issues, and it stood ready to provide the theoretical underpinnings for the newly emerging 'information revolution' in economics.[1] Today choice under uncertainty is a field in flux: the standard theory is being challenged on several grounds from both within and outside economics. The nature of these challenges, and of economists' responses to them, is the topic of this chapter.

The following section gives a description of the economist's classical model of choice under uncertainty, the *expected utility* model of preferences over random prospects. I shall present this model from two different perspectives. The first perspective is the most familiar, and has traditionally been the most useful for addressing standard economic questions. However, the second, more modern perspective will be the most useful for illustrating some of the problems which have beset the model, as well as some of the proposed responses.

Each of the subsequent sections is devoted to one of these

problems. All are important, some are more completely 'solved' than others. In each case I shall begin with an example or description of the phenomenon in question. I shall then review the empirical evidence regarding the uniformity and extent of the phenomenon. Finally, I shall report on how these findings have changed, or are likely to change, or *ought* to change, the way we view and model economic behaviour under uncertainty. On this last topic, the disclaimer that 'my opinions are my own' has more than the usual significance.[2]

2.2 THE EXPECTED UTILITY MODEL

The classical perspective: cardinal utility and attitudes towards risk

In light of current trends towards generalising this model, it is useful to note that the expected utility hypothesis was itself first proposed as an alternative to an earlier, more restrictive theory of risk-bearing. During the development of modern probability theory in the seventeenth century, mathematicians such as Blaise Pascal and Pierre de Fermat assumed that the attractiveness of a gamble offering the pay-offs $(x_1,\ldots,x_n)$ with the probabilities $(p_1,\ldots,p_n)$ was given by its *expected value* $\bar{x}=\sum x_i p_i$. The fact that individuals consider more than just expected value, however, was dramatically illustrated by an example posed by Nicholas Bernoulli in 1728 and now known as the *St Petersburg paradox*. In modern monetary units it may be phrased as:

> Suppose someone offers to toss a fair coin repeatedly until it comes up heads, and to pay you $1 if this happens on the first toss, $2 if it takes two tosses to land a head, $4 if it takes three tosses, $8 if it takes four tosses, etc. What is the largest sure gain you would be willing to forgo in order to undertake a *single* play of this game?

Since this game offers a one-in-two chance of winning $1, a one-in-four chance of winning $2, etc., its expected value is $(1/2)\cdot\$1+(1/4)\cdot\$2+(1/8)\cdot\$4+\ldots=\$1/2+\$1/2+/1/2+\ldots=\infty$, so it should be preferred to any finite sure gain. However, few individuals would forgo more than a moderate amount for a one-shot play. Although the unlimited financial backing needed actually to make this offer is unrealistic, it is not essential for the point: limiting the game to one million tosses will still lead to a striking discrepancy between most individuals' valuations of the gamble and its expected value of $500 000.

The resolution of this paradox was offered independently by Gabriel Cramer and Nicholas's cousin Daniel Bernoulli (Bernoulli, 1738/1954). Noting that a gain of $200 was not necessarily 'worth' twice as much as a gain of $100, they hypothesised that the individual possesses what we now term a *von Neumann–Morgenstern utility function* $U(\cdot)$, and rather than using value $\bar{x} = \sum x_i p_i$, will evaluate gambles on the basis of *expected utility* $\bar{u} = \sum U(x_i) p_i$. Thus the sure gain ξ which would yield the same utility as the Petersburg gamble, i.e. the *certainty equivalent* of this gamble, is given by the equation

$$U(W + \xi) = (1/2) \cdot U(W + 1) + (1/4) \cdot U(W + 2)$$

$$+ (1/8) \cdot U(W + 4) + \ldots \tag{2.1}$$

where W is the individual's current wealth. If utility took the logarithmic form $U(x) \equiv \ln(x)$ and $W = \$50\,000$, for example, the certainty equivalent ξ would only be about $9, even though the gamble has an infinite expected value.

Although it shares the name 'utility', $U(\cdot)$ is quite distinct from the ordinal utility function of standard consumer theory. While the latter can be subjected to any monotonic transformation, a von Neumann–Morgenstern utility function is *cardinal* in that it can only be subjected to transformations of the form $a \cdot U(x) + b$ $(a > 0)$, i.e. transformations which change the origin and/or scale of the vertical axis, but do not affect the 'shape' of the function.[3]

To see how this shape determines risk attitudes, consider Figures 2.1 and 2.2. The monotonicity of $U_a(\cdot)$ and $U_b(\cdot)$ in the figures reflects the property of stochastic dominance preference, where one lottery is said *stochastically to dominate* another one if it can be obtained from it by shifting probability from lower to higher outcome levels.[4] Stochastic dominance preference is thus the probabilistic analogue of the attitude that 'more is better'.

Consider a gamble offering a 2/3:1/3 chance of either x' or x''. The point $\bar{x} = (2/3) \cdot x' + (1/3) \cdot x''$ in the figures give the expected

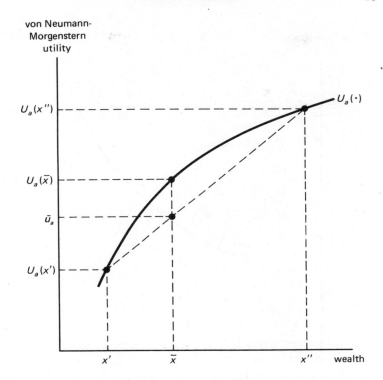

FIGURE 2.1   Concave utility function of a risk averter

value of this gamble, and $\bar{u}_a = (2/3) \cdot U_a(x') + (1/3) \cdot U_a(x'')$ and $\bar{u}_b = (2/3) \cdot U_b(x') + (1/3) \cdot U_b(x'')$ give its *expected utilities* for $U_a(\cdot)$ and $U_b(\cdot)$. For the concave utility function $U_a(\cdot)$ we have $U_a(\bar{x}) > \bar{u}_a$, which implies that this individual would prefer a sure gain of $\bar{x}$ (yielding utility $U_a(\bar{x})$) to the gamble. Since someone with a concave utility function will in fact *always* prefer receiving the expected value of a gamble to the gamble itself, concave utility functions are termed *risk averse*. For the convex function $U_b(\cdot)$ we have $\bar{u}_b > U_b(\bar{x})$, and since this preference for bearing the risk rather than receiving the expected value will also extend to all gambles, $U_b(\cdot)$ is termed risk loving. In their famous article, Friedman and Savage (1948) showed how a utility function which was concave at low wealth levels and convex at high wealth levels could explain the

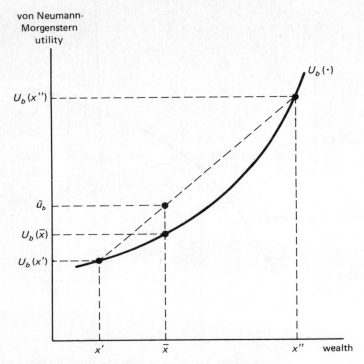

FIGURE 2.2   **Convex utility function of a risk lover**

behaviour of individuals who both *incur* risk by purchasing lottery tickets as well as *avoid* risk by purchasing insurance.

Since a knowledge of $U(\cdot)$ would allow us to predict behaviour in any risky situation, experimenters are frequently interested in eliciting or *recovering* subjects' von Neumann–Morgenstern utility functions. One way of doing so is termed the *fractile method*. This begins by adopting the normalisation $U(0) = 0$ and $U(M) = 1$ (see Note 3), and fixing a 'mixture probability' $\bar{p}$, say $\bar{p} = 1/2$. The next step involves finding the individual's certainty equivalent ξ_1 of a 1/2:1/2 chance of M or 0, which implies

$$U(\xi_1) = 1/2 \cdot U(M) + 1/2 \cdot U(0) = 1/2$$

Finding the certainty equivalents of the $1/2:1/2$ chances of ξ_1 or 0 and of M or ξ_1 gives the values ξ_2 and ξ_3 which solve $U(\xi_2) = 1/4$ and $U(\xi_3) = 3/4$. By repeating this procedure (i.e. $1/8, 3/8, 5/8, 7/8, 1/16, 3/16$, etc.) the utility function can (in the limit) be completely assessed.

Our discussion so far has paralleled the economic literature of the 1960s and 1970s by emphasising the *flexibility* of the expected utility model compared with the Pascal–Fermat expected value approach. However, the need to analyse and respond to growing empirical challenges has led economists in the 1980s to concentrate on the *behavioural restrictions* implied by the expected utility hypothesis. It is to these restrictions that we now turn.

A modern perspective: linearity in the probabilities as a testable hypothesis

As a theory of individual behaviour, the expected utility model shares many of the underlying assumptions of standard consumer theory. In each case we assume that

(a) the objects of choice can be unambiguously and objectively described;
(b) situations which ultimately imply the same set of availabilities will lead to the same choice;
(c) the individual is able to perform the mathematical operations necessary to determine the set of availabilities;
(d) preferences are *transitive*.

We shall examine the validity of these assumptions for choice under uncertainty in some of the following sections.

However, the strongest implication of the expected utility hypothesis stems from the form of the expected utility maximand or *preference function* $\sum U(x_i)p_i$. Although this function generalises the expected value form $\sum x_i p_i$ by dropping the property of linearity in the *pay-offs* (the x_is), it retains the other key property of this form, namely *linearity in the probabilities*.

Graphically, we can illustrate the property of linearity in the probabilities by considering the set of all lotteries or prospects over the fixed outcome levels $x_1 < x_2 < x_3$, which can be represented by the set of all probability triples of the form $P = (p_1, p_2, p_3)$ where $p_i = \text{prob}(x_i)$ and $\sum p_i = 1$. Since $p_2 = 1 - p_1 - p_3$, we can represent

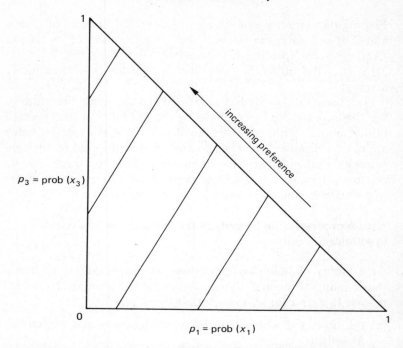

FIGURE 2.3 **Expected utility indifference curves in the triangle diagram**

these lotteries by the points in the unit triangle in the (p_1,p_3) plane, as in Figure 2.3.[5] Since upward movements in the triangle increase p_3 at the expense of p_2 (i.e. shift probability from the outcome x_2 up to x_3) and leftward movements reduce p_1 to the benefit of p_2 (shift probability from x_1 up to x_2), these movements (and more generally, all north-west movements) lead to stochastically dominating lotteries and would accordingly be preferred. Finally, since the individual's indifference curves in the (p_1,p_3) diagram are given by the solutions to the linear equation

$$\bar{u} = \sum_{i=1}^{3} U(x_i)p_i = U(x_1)p_1 + U(x_2)(1 - p_1 - p_3)$$

$$+ U(x_3)p_3 = \text{constant} \tag{2.2}$$

they consist of parallel straight lines of slope $[U(x_2) - U(x_1)]/[U(x_3) - U(x_2)]$, with more preferred indifference curves lying to the north-west. Thus in order to know an expected utility maximiser's preferences over the entire triangle, it suffices to know the slope of a single indifference curve.

To see how this diagram can be used to illustrate attitudes towards risk, consider Figures 2.4 and 2.5. The broken lines in these figures are not indifference curves but rather *iso-expected value lines*, i.e. solutions to

$$\bar{u} = \sum_{i=1}^{3} x_i p_i = x_1 p_1 + x_2 (1 - p_1 - p_3) + x_3 p_3 = \text{constant} \tag{2.3}$$

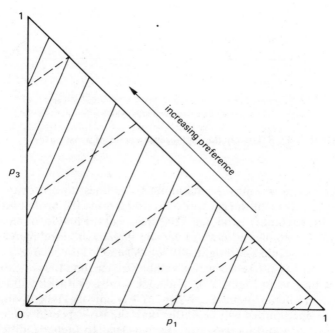

(solid lines are expected utility indifference curves)
(broken lines are iso-expected value lines)

FIGURE 2.4 Relatively steep indifference curves of a risk averter

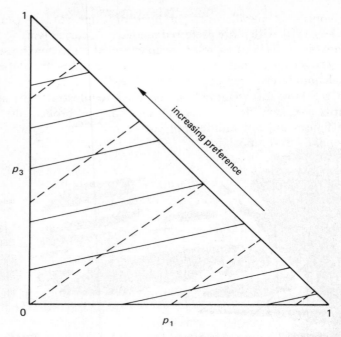

(solid lines are expected utility indifference curves;
broken lines are iso-expected value lines)

FIGURE 2.5   Relatively flat indifference curves of a risk lover

Since north-east movements along these lines do not change the
expected value of the prospect but do increase the probabilities of
the tail outcomes x_1 and x_3 at the expense of the middle outcome x_2,
they are examples of *mean preserving spreads* or 'pure' increases in
risk (Rothschild and Stiglitz, 1970). When $U(\cdot)$ is concave (i.e. risk
averse), its indifference curves will be steeper than the iso-expected
value lines as in Figure 2.4,[6] and such increases in risk will lead to
lower indifference curves. When $U(\cdot)$ is convex (risk loving), its
indifference curves will be flatter than the iso-expected value lines
(Figure 2.5) and increases in risk will lead to higher indifference
curves. If we compare two utility functions, the one which is more
risk averse in the Arrow–Pratt sense will possess the steeper
indifference curves.

Behaviourally, we can view the property of linearity in the probabilities as a restriction on the individual's preferences over *probability mixtures* of lotteries. If $P^* = (p_1^*,...,p_n^*)$ and $P = (p_1,...,p_n)$ are two lotteries over a common outcome set $\{x_1,...,x_n\}$, the $\alpha{:}(1-\alpha)$ probability mixture of P^* and P is the lottery $\alpha P^* + (1-\alpha)P = (\alpha p_1^* + (1-\alpha)p_1,...,\alpha p_n^* + (1-\alpha)p_n)$. This may be thought of as that prospect which yields the same ultimate probabilities over $\{x_1,...,x_n\}$ as a two-stage lottery offering an $\alpha{:}(1-\alpha)$ chance of either P^* or P. Since linearity in the probabilities implies

$$\sum U(x_i)(\alpha p_i^* + (1-\alpha)p_i) = \alpha \cdot \sum U(x_i)p_i^* +$$

$$+ (1-\alpha) \cdot \sum U(x_i)p_i$$

expected utility maximisers will exhibit the following property, known as the *independence axiom* (Samuelson, 1952):

If the lottery P^* is preferred (resp. indifferent) to the lottery P, then the mixture $\alpha P^* + (1-\alpha)P^{**}$ will be preferred (resp. indifferent) to the mixture $\alpha P + (1-\alpha)P^{**}$ for all $\alpha > 0$ and P^{**}.

This property, which is in fact *equivalent* to linearity in the probabilities, can be interpreted as follows:

In terms of the ultimate probabilities over the outcomes $\{x_1,...,x_n\}$, choosing between the mixtures $\alpha P^* + (1-\alpha)P^{**}$ and $\alpha P + (1-\alpha)P^{**}$ is the same as being offered a coin with a probability $1-\alpha$ of landing tails, in which case you will obtain the lottery P^{**}, and being asked *before the flip* whether you would rather have P^* or P in the event of a head. Now either the coin will land tails, in which case your choice won't have mattered, or else it will land heads, in which case you are 'in effect' back to a choice between P^* or P, and it is only 'rational' to make the same choice as you would before.

Although this is a *prescriptive* argument, it has played a key role in economists' adoption of expected utility as a *descriptive* theory of choice under uncertainty. As the evidence against the model mounts, this has led to a growing tension between those who view

economic analysis as the description and prediction of 'rational'
behaviour and those who view it as the description and prediction
of *observed* behaviour. We turn now to this evidence.

2.3   VIOLATIONS OF LINEARITY IN THE PROBABILITIES

The Allais paradox and 'fanning out'

One of the earliest and best-known examples of systematic violation of linearity in the probabilities (or equivalently, of the independence axiom) is the well-known *Allais paradox* (Allais, 1953,
1979). This problem involves obtaining the individual's preferred
option from each of the following two pairs of gambles (readers
who have never seen this problem may want to circle their own
choice from each pair before proceeding):

a_1:   1.00 chance of $1 000 000
           versus
           0.10 chance of $5 000 000
a_2:   0.89 chance of $1 000 000
           0.01 chance of $0

and

a_3:   0.01 chance of $5 000 000
           0.90 chance of $0
           versus
           0.11 chance of $1 000 000
a_4:   0.89 chance of $0

Defining $\{x_1, x_2, x_3\} = \{\$0; \$1\,000\,000; \$5\,000\,000\}$, these four gambles
are seen to form a parallelogram in the (p_1, p_3) triangle, as in
Figures 2.6 and 2.7. Under the expected utility hypothesis, therefore, a preference for a_1 in the first pair would indicate that the
individual's indifference curves were relatively steep (as in Figure
2.6) and hence a preference for a_4 in the second pair. In the
alternative case of relatively flat indifference curves, the gambles a_2
and a_3 would be preferred.[7] However, researchers such as Allais

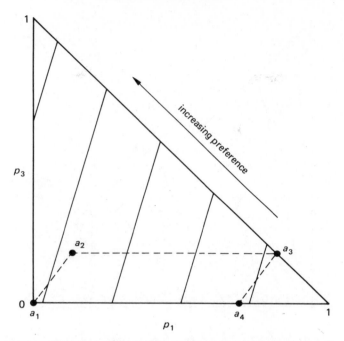

FIGURE 2.6   Expected utility indifference curves and the Allais paradox

(1953), Morrison (1967), Raiffa (1968) and Slovic and Tversky (1974) have found that the modal if not majority preferences of subjects has been for a_1 in the first pair and a_3 in the second, which implies that indifference curves are not parallel but rather *fan out* as in Figure 2.7.

Additional evidence of fanning out

Although the Allais paradox was first dismissed as an isolated example, it is now known to be a special case of a general pattern termed the *common consequence effect*. This involves pairs of probability mixtures of the form:

$$b_1: \alpha\delta_x + (1-\alpha)P^{**} \quad versus \quad b_2: \alpha P + (1-\alpha)P^{**}$$

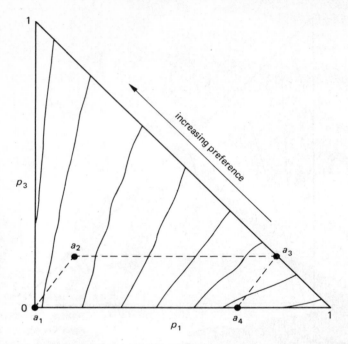

FIGURE 2.7 Indifference curves which 'fan out' and the Allais paradox

and

$$b_3: \alpha\delta_x + (1-\alpha)P^* \quad versus \quad b_4: \alpha P + (1-\alpha)P^*$$

where δ_x denotes the prospect which yields x with certainty, P involves outcomes both greater and less than x, and P^{**} stochastically dominates P^*.[8] Although the independence axiom implies choices of either b_1 and b_3 (if δ_x is preferred to P) or else b_2 and b_4 (if P is preferred to δ_x), researchers have found a tendency for subjects to choose b_1 in the first pair and b_4 in the second (MacCrimmon, 1968; MacCrimmon and Larsson, 1979; Kahneman and Tversky, 1979; Chew and Waller, 1986). When the distributions δ_x, P, P^* and P^{**} are each over a common outcome set $\{x_1, x_2, x_3\}$, the prospects b_1, b_2, b_3, and b_4 will again form a parallelogram in the (p_1, p_3) triangle, and a choice of b_1 and b_4 again implies indifference curves which fan out, as in Figure 2.7.

The intuition behind this effect can be described in terms of the above 'coin-flip' scenario. According to the independence axiom, preferences over what would occur in the event of a head should not depend upon what would occur in the event of a tail. In fact, however, they *may well* depend upon what would otherwise happen.[9] The common consequence effect states that the *better off* individuals would be in the event of a tail, the *more risk averse* they become over what they would receive in the event of a head. Intuitively, if the distribution P^{**} in the pair $\{b_1, b_2\}$ involves very high outcomes, I may prefer not to bear further risk in the unlucky event that I do not receive it, and prefer the sure outcome x over the distribution P in this event (i.e. choose b_1 rather than b_2). But if P^* in $\{b_3, b_4\}$ involves very low outcomes, I may be more willing to bear risk in the (lucky) event that I do not receive it, and prefer the lottery P to the outcome x in this case (i.e. choose b_4 rather than b_3). Note that it is not my *beliefs* regarding the probabilities in P which are affected here, merely my willingness to bear them.[10]

A second class of systematic violations, stemming from another early example of Allais (1953), is known as the *common ratio effect*. This phenomenon involves pairs of prospects of the form:

$$c_1: \quad \begin{array}{l} p \text{ chance of } \$X \\ 1-p \text{ chance of } \$0 \end{array}$$

versus

$$c_2: \quad \begin{array}{l} q \text{ chance of } \$Y \\ 1-q \text{ chance of } \$0 \end{array}$$

and

$$c_3: \quad \begin{array}{l} rp \text{ chance of } \$X \\ 1-rp \text{ chance of } \$0 \end{array}$$

versus

$$c_4: \quad \begin{array}{l} rq \text{ chance of } \$Y \\ 1-rq \text{ chance of } \$0 \end{array}$$

where $p > q$, $0 < X < Y$ and r lies between 0 and 1. This includes the 'certainty effect' of Kahneman and Tversky (1979) and the ingenious 'Bergen paradox' of Hagen (1979) as special cases.[11] Setting $\{x_1, x_2, x_3\} = \{0, X, Y\}$ and plotting in the (p_1, p_3) triangle, the segments $\overline{c_1 c_2}$ and $\overline{c_3 c_4}$ are seen to be parallel (as in Figure 2.8), so that the

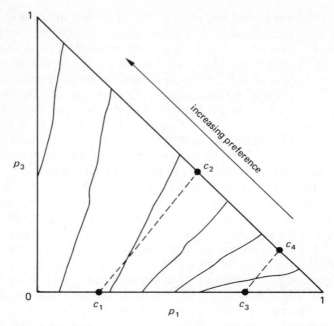

FIGURE 2.8   Indifference curves which fan out and the common ratio effect

expected utility model again predicts choices of c_1 and c_3 (if the individual's indifference curves are steep) or else c_2 and c_4 (if they are flat). However, studies have found a tendency for choices to depart from these predictions in the direction of preferring c_1 and c_4, which again suggests that indifference curves fan out, as in the figure (Tversky, 1975; MacCrimmon and Larsson, 1979; Chew and Waller, 1986). In a variation on this approach, Kahneman and Tversky (1979) replaced the gains of X and Y in the above gambles with losses of these magnitudes, and found a tendency to depart from expected utility in the direction of c_2 and c_3. Defining $\{x_1, x_2, x_3\}$ as $\{-Y, -X, 0\}$ (to maintain the condition $x_1 < x_2 < x_3$) and plotting these gambles in Figure 2.9, a choice of c_2 and c_3 is again seen to imply that indifference curves fan out. Finally, Battalio, Kagel and MacDonald (1985) found that laboratory rats choosing among gambles which involved substantial variations in their actual daily food intake also exhibited this pattern of choices.

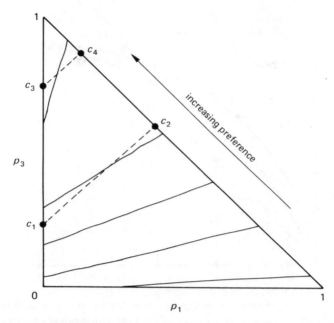

FIGURE 2.9   Indifference curves which fan out and the common ratio effect for negative pay-offs

A third class of evidence stems from the elicitation method described in the previous section. In particular, note that there is no reason why the mixture probability $\bar{p}$ *must* be 1/2 in this procedure. Picking any other $\bar{p}$ and defining ξ_1^*, ξ_2^* and ξ_3^* as the certainty equivalents of the $\bar{p}:(1-\bar{p})$ chances of M or 0, ξ_1^* or 0, and M or ξ_1^* yields the equations $U(\xi_1^*)=\bar{p}$, $U(\xi_2^*)=\bar{p}^2$, $U(\xi_3^*)=\bar{p}+(1-\bar{p})\bar{p}$, etc., and such a procedure can also be used to recover $U(\cdot)$.

Although this procedure should recover the same (normalised) utility function for any mixture probability $\bar{p}$, researchers such as Karmarkar (1974, 1978) and McCord and de Neufville (1983, 1984) have found a tendency for higher values of $\bar{p}$ to lead to the 'recovery' of higher valued utility functions, as in Figure 2.10. By illustrating the gambles used to obtain the values ξ_1, ξ_2 and ξ_3 for $\bar{p}=1/2$, ξ_1^* for $\bar{p}=1/4$ and ξ_1^{**} for $\bar{p}=3/4$, Figure 2.11 shows that, as with the common consequence and common ratio effects, this

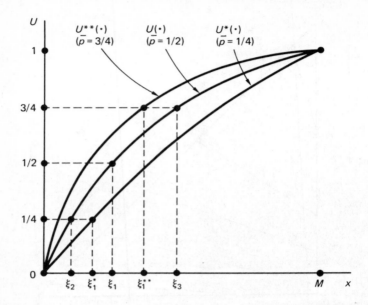

FIGURE 2.10   'Recovered' utility functions for mixture probabilities 1/4, 1/2 and 3/4

utility evaluation effect is precisely what would be expected from an individual whose indifference curves departed from expected utility by fanning out.[12]

Non-expected utility models of preferences

The above violations of linearity in the probabilities have led researchers to generalise the expected utility model by positing *non-linear* functional forms for the individual preference function. Examples include:

$$\sum v(x_i)\pi(p_i) \quad \begin{matrix} \text{Edwards (1955)} \\ \text{Kahneman and Tversky (1979)} \end{matrix} \tag{2.4}$$

$$\frac{\sum v(x_i)\pi(p_i)}{\sum \pi(p_i)} \quad \text{Karmarkar (1978)} \tag{2.5}$$

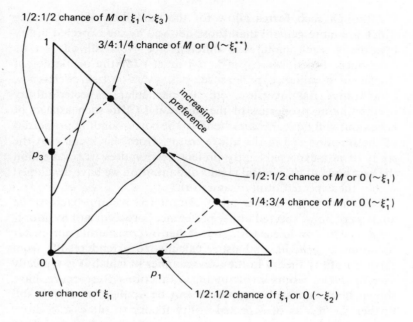

(~ denotes indifference)

FIGURE 2.11   Fanning out indifference curves which generate the responses of Figure 2.10

$$\frac{\sum v(x_i)p_i}{\sum \tau(x_i)p_i} \quad \begin{array}{l}\text{Chew (1983)}\\ \text{Fishburn (1983)}\end{array} \tag{2.6}$$

$$\sum v(x_i)[g(p_1+\ldots+p_i)-g(p_1+\ldots+p_{i-1})] \text{ Quiggin (1982)} \tag{2.7}$$

$$\sum v(x_i)p_i+[\sum \tau(x_i)p_i]^2 \quad \text{Machina (1982)} \tag{2.8}$$

$$\sum v(x_i)g(p_i;x_1,\ldots,x_n) \quad \text{Hey (1984)} \tag{2.9}$$

Many (though not all) of these forms are flexible enough to exhibit the properties of stochastic dominance preference, risk aversion/risk preference and fanning out, and have proven to be useful both theoretically and empirically. Additional analyses of these forms can be found in Chew, Karni and Safra (1987), Fishburn (1984), Segal (1984) and Yaari (1987a).

Although such forms allow for the modelling of preferences which are more general than those allowed by the expected utility hypothesis, each requires a different set of conditions on its component functions $v(\cdot)$, $\pi(\cdot)$, $\tau(\cdot)$ or $g(\cdot)$ for the properties of stochastic dominance preference, risk aversion/risk preference, comparative risk aversion, etc. In particular, expected utility results linking properties of the function $U(\cdot)$ to such aspects of behaviour will typically *not* extend to the corresponding properties of the function $v(\cdot)$ in the above forms. Does this mean that the study of non-expected utility preferences requires us to abandon the vast body of theoretical results and intuition we have developed within the expected utility framework?

Fortunately, the answer is no. An alternative approach to the analysis of non-expected utility preferences proceeds not by adopting a *specific* non-linear form, but rather by considering non-linear functions *in general*, and using calculus to extend results from expected utility theory in the same manner in which it is typically used to extend results involving linear functions. Researchers have shown how that such techniques can be applied to extend still further the results of expected utility theory to the case of non-expected utility preferences, to characterise and explore the implications of preferences which 'fan out', and to conduct new and more general analyses of economic behaviour under uncertainty (Machina, 1982; Chew, 1983; Fishburn, 1984; Hey, 1984; Epstein, 1985; Allen, 1987; Chew, Karni and Safra, 1987). However, while they constitute a promising response to the phenomenon of non-linearities in the probabilities, these models do *not* provide solutions to the more problematic empirical phenomena of the following sections.

2.4   THE PREFERENCE REVERSAL PHENOMENON

The evidence

The finding now known as the *preference reversal phenomenon* was first reported by psychologists Slovic and Lichtenstein (1971). In this study, subjects were first presented with a number of pairs of bets and asked to choose one bet out of each pair. Each of these pairs took the following form:

$$P\text{-bet:} \quad \begin{matrix} p \text{ chance of } \$X \\ 1-p \text{ chance of } \$x \end{matrix}$$

versus

$$\$\text{-bet:} \quad \begin{matrix} q \text{ chance of } \$Y \\ 1-q \text{ chance of } \$y \end{matrix}$$

where X and Y are respectively greater than x and y, p is greater than q, and Y is greater than X (the names 'P-bet' and '$\$$-bet' come from the greater probability of winning in the first bet and greater possible gain in the second). In some cases, x and y took on small negative values. The subjects were next asked to 'value' (state certainty equivalents for) each of these bets. The different valuation methods used consisted of:

(a) asking subjects to state their minimum selling price for each bet if they were to own it;
(b) asking them to state their maximum bid price for each bet if they were to buy it;
(c) the elicitation procedure of Becker, DeGroot and Marschak (1964), in which it is in a subject's best interest to reveal his or her true certainty equivalent.[13]

In case (c) real money was used.

The expected utility model, and each of the *non*-expected utility models of the previous section, clearly implies that the bet which is chosen out of each pair will also be the one which is assigned the higher certainty equivalent.[14] However, Slovic and Lichtenstein found a systematic tendency for subjects to violate this prediction by choosing the P-bet in a direct choice but assigning a higher value to the $\$$-bet. In one experiment, 127 out of 173 subjects assigned a higher sell price to the $\$$-bet in *every* pair in which the P-bet was chosen. Similar results were obtained by Lindman (1971), and in an interesting variation on the usual experimental setting, by Slovic and Lichtenstein (1973) in a Las Vegas casino where customers actually staked (and sometimes lost) their own money. In another real-money experiment, Mowen and Gentry (1980) found that groups who could discuss their joint decisions were, if anything, *more* likely than individuals to exhibit the phenomenon.

Although these studies involved deliberate variations in design in order to check for the robustness of the phenomenon, they were, none the less, received sceptically by economists, who perhaps felt they had more at stake than psychologists in such a finding. In an admitted attempt to 'discredit' this work, economists Grether and Plott (1979) designed a pair of experiments which, by correcting for issues of incentives, income effects, strategic considerations, and ability to indicate indifference, would presumably eliminate the phenomenon. None the less, they found it in both experiments. Further experiments by Pommerehne, Schneider and Zweifel (1982) and Reilly (1982) yielded the same results. The phenomenon has been found to persist (although in mitigated form) even when subjects were allowed to engage in experimental market transactions involving the gambles (Knez and Smith, 1986), or when the experimenter could act as an arbitrageur and make money from such reversals (Berg, Dickhaut and O'Brien, 1983).

Two interpretations of this phenomenon

How you interpret these findings depends on whether you adopt the world-view of an economist or a psychologist. An economist would reason as follows: each individual possesses a well-defined *preference relation* over lotteries, and information about this relation can be gleaned from either direct choice questions or (properly designed) valuation questions. Someone exhibiting the preference reversal phenomenon is therefore telling us that he or she:

(a) is indifferent between the P-bet and some sure amount ξp;
(b) strictly prefers the P-bet to the $-bet;
(c) is indifferent between the $-bet and an amount $\xi\$$ *greater than* ξp.

Assuming they prefer $\xi\$$ to the lesser amount ξp, this implies that their preferences over these objects are cyclic or *intransitive*.

Psychologists, on the other hand, would deny the premise of a common mechanism generating both choice and valuation behaviour. Rather, they view choice and valuation as distinct processes, subject to possibly different influences. In other words, individuals exhibit what are termed *response mode effects*. (Discussions of such effects and their implications for the elicitation of probabilities and utility functions appear in Hogarth (1975), Slovic, Fischhoff and Lichtenstein (1982), Hershey and Schoemaker (1985) and MacCrimmon and Wehrung (1986).)

Implications of the economic world-view

The issue of intransitivity is new neither to economics nor to choice under uncertainty. May (1954), for example, observed intransitivities in pair-wise rankings of three alternative marriage partners, where each candidate was rated highly in two of three attributes (intelligence, looks, wealth) and low in the third. Besides the preference reversal phenomenon, Edwards (1954, pp. 404–5) and Tversky (1969) also observed intransitivities in preferences over risky prospects. On the other hand, researchers have shown that many aspects of economic theory, such as the existence of demand functions or of general equilibrium, are robust to failures of transitivity (Sonnenschein, 1971; Mas-Colell, 1974; Shafer, 1974).

In any event, economists have begun to develop and analyse models of non-transitive preferences over lotteries. The leading example of this is the 'expected regret' model developed independently by Bell (1982), Fishburn (1982) and Loomes and Sugden (1982). In this model of pair-wise choice, the von Neumann–Morgenstern utility function $U(x)$ is replaced by a *regret/rejoice function* $r(x,y)$ which represents the level of satisfaction (or if negative, dissatisfaction) the individual would experience if he or she were to receive the outcome x when the alternative choice would have yielded the outcome y (this function is assumed to satisfy $r(x,y) \equiv -r(y,x)$). In choosing between statistically independent gambles $P^* = (p_1^*, \ldots, p_n^*)$ and $P = (p_1, \ldots, p_n)$ over a common outcome set $\{x_1, \ldots, x_n\}$, the individual will choose P^* if the expectation

$$\sum_i \sum_j r(x_i, x_j) p_i^* p_j$$

is positive, and P if it is negative.

Note that when the regret/rejoice function takes the special form

$$r(x,y) \equiv U(x) - U(y)$$

this model reduces to the expected utility model, since we have

$$\sum_i \sum_j r(x_i, x_j) p_i^* p_j \equiv \sum_i \sum_j [U(x_i) - U(x_j)] p_i^* p_j \equiv$$

$$\sum_i U(x_i)p_i^* - \sum_j U(x_j)p_j \qquad\qquad (2.10)$$

so that the individual will prefer P^* to P if and only if

$$\sum_i U(x_i)p_i^* > \sum_j U(x_j)p_j.[15]$$

However, in general such an individual will neither be an expected utility maximiser nor have transitive preferences.

However, this intransitivity does not prevent us from graphing such preferences, nor even from applying 'expected utility' analysis to them. To see this, consider the case when the individual is facing alternative independent lotteries over an outcome set $\{x_1,x_2,x_3\}$, so that we may again use the triangle diagram to illustrate their 'indifference curves', as in Figure 2.12. In such a case it is important to understand what is and is not still true of these indifference curves. The curve through P will still correspond to the set of lotteries that are indifferent to P, and it will still divide the set of lotteries that are strictly preferred to P (the points in the direction of the arrow) from the ones to which P is preferred. Furthermore, if (as in the figure) P^* lies above the indifference curve through P, then P will lie below the curve through P^* (i.e. the individual's ranking of P and P^* will be unambiguous). However, unlike indifference curves for transitive preferences, these curves will cross,[16] and preferences over the lotteries P, P^* and P^{**} are seen to form an intransitive cycle. But in regions where the indifference curves do *not* cross (e.g. near the origin) these preferences will be indistinguishable from transitive (albeit non-expected utility) preferences.

To see how expected utility results can be extended to this nontransitive framework, fix a lottery $P = (p_1,\ldots,p_n)$ and consider the question of when an (independent) lottery $P^* = (p_1^*,\ldots,p_n^*)$ will be preferred or not preferred to P. Since $r(x,y) \equiv -r(y,x)$ implies

$$\sum_i \sum_j r(x_i,x_j)p_i p_j \equiv 0$$

we have that P^* will be preferred to P if and only if:

$$0 < \sum_i \sum_j r(x_i,x_j)p_i^* p_j = \sum_j \sum_j r(x_i,x_j)p_i^* p_j - \sum_i \sum_j r(x_i,x_j)p_i p_j$$

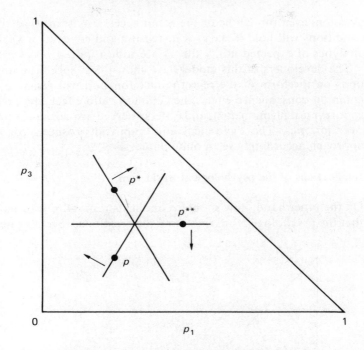

FIGURE 2.12 'Indifference curves' for the expected regret model

$$= \sum_i \left[\sum_j r(x_i, x_j) p_j \right] p_i^* - \sum_i \left[\sum_j r(x_i, x_j) p_j \right] p_i$$

$$= \sum_i \varphi(x_i; P) p_i^* - \sum_i \varphi(x_i; P) p_i \qquad (2.11)$$

in other words, P^* will be preferred to P if and only if it implies a higher expectation of the 'utility function'

$$\varphi(x_i; P) \equiv \sum_j r(x_i, x_j) p_j$$

than P. Thus if $\varphi(x_i; P)$ is increasing in x_i for all P the individual will exhibit global stochastic dominance preference, and if $\varphi(x_i; P)$ is concave in x_i for all P the individual will exhibit global risk aversion, even though he or she is not necessarily transitive (these conditions will hold if $r(x,y)$ is increasing and concave in x). The analytics of expected utility theory are robust indeed.

The developers of this model have shown how specific assumptions on the form of the regret/rejoice function will generate the common consequence effect, the common ratio effect, the preference reversal phenomenon, and other observed properties of choice over lotteries. The theoretical and empirical prospects for this approach accordingly seem quite impressive.

Implications of the psychological world-view

On the other hand, how should economists respond if it turns out that the psychologists are right, and the preference reversal pheno-

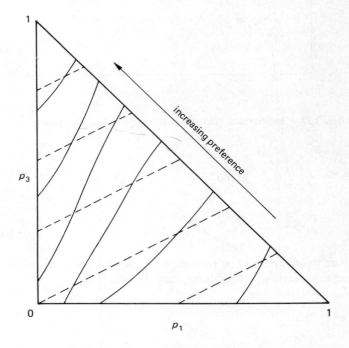

(broken lines are iso-expected value lines)

FIGURE 2.13   Risk aversion of every local expected utility approximation is equivalent to global risk aversion

menon *really is* generated by some form of response mode effect (or effects)? In that case, the first thing to do would be to try to determine if there were analogues of such effects in real-world economic situations. Will individuals behave differently when determining their valuation of an object (e.g. a bid on a used car) than when reacting to a fixed and non-negotiable price for the same differences in choice? An early example of this phenomenon was reported by Slovic (1969), who found that offering a gain or loss contingent on the joint occurrence of four independent events with probability *p* elicited different responses than offering it on the occurrence of a single event with probability *p* (all probabilities were stated explicitly).[17] In comparison with the single-event case, making a gain contingent on the joint occurrence of events was found to make it more attractive, and making a loss contingent on the joint occurrence of events made it more unattractive.

In another study, Payne and Braunstein (1971) used pairs of gambles of the type illustrated in Figure 2.14. Each of these gambles, known as a *duplex gamble*, involves spinning the pointers on both a 'gain wheel' (on the left) and a 'loss wheel' (on the right), with the individual receiving the sum of the two amounts. Thus Gamble A yields a gain of $0.40 with probability 0.3 (if the pointer in the gain wheel landed up and the pointer in the loss wheel landed down), a loss of $0.40 with probability 0.2 (if the pointers landed in the opposite positions), and no change with probability 0.5 (if the pointers landed either both up or both down). An examination of Gamble B reveals that it has an identical distribution, so that subjects should be indifferent between the two gambles regardless of their risk attitudes. However, these researchers found that subjects' preferences between such gambles were systematically affected by the attributes of the component wheels. When the probability of winning in the gain wheel was greater than the probability of losing in the loss wheel for each gamble (as in the figure), they tended to choose the gamble whose gain wheel yielded the greater probability of a gain (Gamble A). When the probabilities of losing in the loss wheels were greater than the probabilities of winning in the gain wheels, they tended towards the gamble with the lower probability of losing in the loss wheel.

Finally, although the gambles in Figure 2.14 possess identical underlying distributions, continuity suggests that a slight worsening of the terms of the preferred gamble could yield a pair of non-

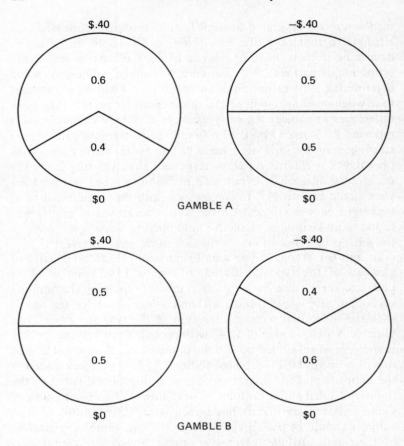

FIGURE 2.14   Duplex gambles with identical underlying distributions

equivalent duplex gambles in which the individual will actually choose the one with the *stochastically dominated* underlying distribution. In an experiment where subjects were allowed to construct their own duplex gambles by choosing one from a pair of prospects involving gains and one from a pair of prospects involving losses, dominated prospects were indeed chosen (Tversky and Kahneman, 1981).[18]

A second class of framing effects involves the phenomenon of a *reference point*. Theoretically, the variable which enters an individual's von Neumann–Morgenstern utility function should be final wealth, and gambles phrased in terms of gains and losses should be added to current wealth and re-expressed as distributions over final wealth levels before being evaluated. However, economists since Markowitz (1952) have observed that risk attitudes over gains and losses are more stable than can be explained by a fixed utility function over final wealth, and have suggested that the utility function might be best defined in terms of *changes* from the 'reference point' of current wealth. This stability of risk attitudes in the face of wealth variations has also been observed in several experimental studies (see Machina, 1982).

Markowitz (1952, p. 155) also suggested that certain circumstances may cause the individual's reference point to deviate temporarily from current wealth. If these circumstances include the manner in which a given problem is verbally described, then differing risk attitudes over gains and losses can lead to different choices depending upon the exact description. A simple example of this, from Kahneman and Tversky (1979), involves the following two questions:

1. In addition to whatever you own, you have been given 1000 (Israeli pounds). You are now asked to choose between a 1/2:1/2 chance of a gain of 1000 or 0 or a sure gain of 500.
2. In addition to whatever you own, you have been given 2000. You are now asked to choose between a 1/2:1/2 chance of a loss of 1000 or 0 or a sure loss of 500.

These two problems involve identical distributions over final wealth. However, when put to two different groups of subjects, 84 per cent chose the sure gain in the first problem but 69 per cent chose the 1/2:1/2 gamble in the second. A non-monetary version of this type of example, from Tversky and Kahneman (1981, 1986), posits the following scenario:

Imagine that the US is preparing for the outbreak of an unusual Asian disease, which is expected to kill 600 people. Two alternative programs to combat the disease have been proposed. Assume that the exact scientific estimate of the consequence of the programs are as follows:

If Program A is adopted, 200 people will be saved.

If Program B is adopted, there is 1/3 probability that 600 people will be saved, and 2/3 probability that no people will be saved.

Seventy-two per cent of the subjects who were presented with this form of the question chose Program A. A second group was given the same initial information, but the descriptions of the programs were changed to read:

If Program C is adopted 400 people will die.
If Program D is adopted there is 1/3 probability that nobody will die, and 2/3 probability that 600 people will die.

Although this statement of the problem is once again identical to the former one, 78 per cent of the respondents chose Program D.

In other studies, Schoemaker and Kunreuther (1979), Hershey and Schoemaker (1980), McNeil, Pauker, Sox and Tversky (1982) and Slovic, Fischhoff and Lichtenstein (1982) have found the subjects' choices in otherwise identical problems will depend upon whether they are phrased as decisions whether or not to gamble or whether or not to insure; whether the statistical information for different therapies is presented in terms of cumulative survival probabilities or cumulative mortality probabilities, etc. For similar examples of this phenomenon in non-stochastic situations, see Thaler (1980).

In a final class of examples, not based on reference point effects, Moskowitz (1974) and Keller (1982) found that the proportion of subjects choosing in conformance with or in violation of the independence axiom in examples like the Allais paradox was affected by whether the problems were described in the standard matrix form (e.g. Raiffa, 1968, p. 7), decision-tree form, or as minimally structured written statements. Interestingly enough, the form which was judged the 'clearest representation' by the majority of Moskowitz's subjects (the tree form) led to the lowest degree of consistency with the independence axiom, the highest proportion of fanning-out choices, and the highest persistency rate of these choices (Moskowitz, 1974, pp. 234, 237–38).

Two issues regarding framing

The replicability and pervasiveness of the above types of examples is indisputable. However, before being able to assess their implications for economic modelling we need to resolve two issues.

The first issue is whether these experimental observations possess any analogue outside the laboratory. Since real-world decision problems do not present themselves as neatly as the ones on experimental questionnaires, monitoring such effects would not be as straightforward. However, this does not mean that they do not exist, or that they cannot be objectively observed or quantitatively measured. The real-world example which comes most quickly to mind, and is presumably of no small importance to the involved parties, is whether gasoline price differentials should be represented as 'cash discounts' or 'credit surcharges'. Similarly, Russo, Krieser and Miyashita (1975) and Russo (1977) found that the practice, and even method, of displaying unit-price information in supermarkets (information which consumers could calculate for themselves) affected both the level and distribution of consumer expenditures. The empirical marketing literature is no doubt replete with findings that we could legitimately interpret as real-world framing effects.

The second, more difficult, issue is that of the independent observability of the particular frame that an individual will adopt in a given problem. In the duplex gamble and matrix/decision tree/ written statement examples of the previous section, the different frames seem unambiguously determined by the form of presentation. However, in instances where framing involves the choice of a reference point, which presumably include the majority of real-world cases, this point might not be objectively determined by the form of presentation, and might be chosen differently, and what is worse, *unobservably*, by each individual. In a particularly thorough and insightful study, Fischhoff (1983) presented subjects with a written decision problem which allowed for different choices of a reference point, and explored different ways of predicting which frame individuals would adopt, in order to be able to predict their actual choices. While the majority choice of subjects was consistent with what would appear to be the most appropriate frame, Fischhoff noted 'the absence of any relation within those studies between [separately elicited] frame preference and option preference'. Indeed to the extent that frame preferences varied across his experiments, they did so *inversely* to the incidence of the predicted choice.[19] If such problems can occur in predicting responses to specific written questions in the laboratory, imagine how they could plague the modelling of real-world choice behaviour.

Framing effects and economic analysis: have we already solved this problem?

How should we respond if it turns out that framing actually is a real-world phenomenon of economic relevance, and in particular, if individuals' frames cannot always be observed? I would argue that the means of responding to this issue can already be found in the 'tool box' of economic analysis.

Consider first the case where the frame of a decision problem, even though it should not matter according to standard theory, can at least be independently observed. I believe that economists have already solved such a problem in their treatment of the concept of 'uninformative advertising'. Although it is hard to give a formal definition of this term, it is widely felt that economic theory is hard put to explain a large proportion of current advertising in terms of traditional informational considerations.[20] However, this has hardly led economists to abandon consumer theory. Rather, models of uninformative advertising proceed by quantifying this variable (e.g. air time) and treating it as an additional independent variable in the utility and/or demand function. Standard results like the Slutsky equation need not be abandoned, but rather reinterpreted as properties of demand functions *holding this new variable constant*. The amount of advertising is then determined as a maximising variable on the part of the firm given some cost curve, and can be subjected to standard comparative static analysis.

In the case when decision frames can be observed, framing effects could presumably be modelled in an analogous manner. To do so, we would begin by attempting to quantify, or at least categorise, frames. The second step would be to study both the effect of this new variable, holding standard economic variables constant, and conversely, to retest standard economic theories in conditions where we held the frame fixed. With any luck we would find that, holding the frame constant, the Slutsky equation still held.

The next step is to ask 'who determines the frame?' If (as with advertising) it is the firm, then the effect of the frame upon consumer demand, and hence upon firm profits, can be incorporated into the firm's maximisation problem, and the choice of the frame as well as prices, quantities, etc. can be simultaneously determined and subjected to comparative static analysis, just as in the case of uninformative advertising.

A more difficult case is when the individual chooses the frame (such as with a reference point) and this choice *cannot* be observed. Although we should not forget the findings of Fischhoff (1983), assume that this choice is at least systematic in the sense that the consumer will jointly choose the frame and make the subsequent decision in a manner which maximises a 'utility function' which depends both on the decision *and* the choice of frame. In other words, assume individuals make choices as part of a *joint maximisation problem*, the other component of which (the choice of frame or reference point) cannot be observed. In this case the *theory of induced preferences*, which has proved useful in several other branches of economic analysis, could be used to derive testable implications on an individual's choice behaviour (see Milne, 1981 and Machina, 1984).

The above remarks should *not* be taken as implying that we have already solved the problem of framing in economics or that there is no need to adapt, and if need be abandon, existing models in light of this phenomenon. Rather, they reflect the view that when psychologists have collected enough evidence on how these effects operate, economists will be able to respond accordingly.

2.5   OTHER ISSUES: IS PROBABILITY THEORY RELEVANT?

The manipulation of subjective probabilities

The evidence discussed so far has consisted of cases where subjects have been presented with explicit or 'objective' probabilities as part of their decision problems, and the models which have addressed these phenomena have accordingly been defined over objective probability distributions. However, there is extensive evidence that when individuals have to estimate or revise probabilities for themselves they will make systematic mistakes in doing so.

The psychological literature on the handling of probabilistic information is too large to summarise here. However, it is worth noting that researchers have uncovered several 'heuristics' used by subjects which lead to predictable errors in the formation and use of subjective probabilities. Kahneman and Tversky (1973), Bar-Hillel (1974) and Grether (1980), for example, have found that probability updating systematically departs from Bayes's law in the direction of underweighting prior information and overweighting the 'representativeness' of current data. In a phenomenon termed the 'law of small numbers', Tversky and Kahneman (1971) found that individuals overestimate the probability of drawing a perfectly representative sample out of a heterogeneous population. Bar-Hillel (1973), Tversky and Kahneman (1983) and others have found systematic biases in the formation of the probabilities of conjunctions of both independent and non-independent events. For additional studies of the formation and handling of probabilities see Edwards, Lindman and Savage (1963), Slovic and Lichtenstein (1971), Tversky and Kahneman (1974) and the papers in Kahneman, Slovic and Tversky (1982) and Arkes and Hammond (1986). For examples of how economists have responded to some of these issues, see Arrow (1982) and Viscusi (1985).

The existence of subjective probabilities

The evidence referred to above indicates that when individuals are asked to formulate probabilities they do not do it correctly. However, these findings may be rendered moot by evidence which suggests that when individuals making decisions under uncertainty are *not* explicitly asked to form subjective probabilities, they might not do it (or even act as if doing it) *at all*.

In an example given by Ellsberg (1961), subjects were presented with a pair of urns, the first containing fifty red balls and fifty black balls and the second also containing 100 red and black balls but in an unknown proportion. When faced with the choice of staking a prize on: (R_1) drawing a red ball from the first urn; (R_2) drawing a red ball from the second urn; (B_1) drawing a black ball from the first urn, or (B_2) drawing a black ball from the second urn, a majority of subjects strictly preferred (R_1) to (R_2) *and* strictly preferred (B_1) to (B_2). It is clear that there can exist no subjectively assigned probabilities $p:(1-p)$ of drawing a red rather than black ball from the second urn, even $1/2:1/2$, which can simultaneously generate *both* these strict preferences. Similar behaviour has been observed by Raiffa (1961), Becker and Brownson (1964), Slovic and Tversky (1974) and MacCrimmon and Larsson (1979).

2.6 CONCLUDING COMMENT

Life (and economic analysis) without probability theory

One response to this phenomenon has been to suppose that individuals 'slant' subjective probabilities in a manner which reflects the amount of confidence associated with them (Fellner, 1961; Becker and Brownson, 1964; Fishburn, 1986; Hogarth and Kunreuther, 1986). In the case of *complete* ignorance regarding probabilities, Arrow and Hurwicz (1972), Maskin (1979) and others have presented axioms which imply principles such as ranking options solely on the basis of their worst and/or best outcomes (e.g. maximin, maximax), the unweighted average of their outcomes ('principle of insufficient reason'), or similar criteria (see Arrow, 1951). Finally, generalisations of expected utility theory which drop the standard additivity and/or compounding laws of probability theory have been developed by Schmeidler (1986) and Segal (1987).

An approach which allows for the analysis of behaviour under uncertainty without the use of probabilities at all is the *state-preference* model of Arrow (1953/1964). Debreu (1959), Hirshleifer (1966), Yaari (1969) and Diamond and Yaari (1972). Uncertainty in this model is represented by a set of mutually exclusive and exhaustive *states of nature* $S = \{s_i\}$. Depending upon the application, this partition of all possible futures could be very coarse, such as the pair of states (it rains here tomorrow, it doesn't rain here tomorrow) or else very fine, so that the definition of a state might read 'it rains here tomorrow *and* the temperature at Gibraltar is 75° at noon *and* the price of gold in New York is below \$700.00/ounce'. The objects of choice consist of *state–pay-off bundles* of the form $(c_1,\ldots,c_n)$, each of which specifies the pay-off c_i the individual would receive should state *i* occur. In the case of two states, we can represent these bundles in the (c_1, c_2) plane, and the individual's preferences over them by indifference curves in this plane. These authors have used this approach to derive results from individual demand through general equilibrium in a context which requires neither the expected utility hypothesis nor the existence of subjective probabilities. In other words, life without probabilities does not imply life without economic analysis.

2.7 A FINAL THOUGHT

The evidence and theories reported in this chapter have taken us a long way from the classical expected utility approach presented at the outset. To what extent will these new models be incorporated into mainstream economic thought and practice? I believe the answer will depend upon a single factor: the extent to which they can address the important issues in the economics of uncertainty, such as search, investment, bargaining or auctions, to which the expected utility model has been so usefully applied.

3 Uncertainty, Information and Insurance*

RAY REES

3.1 INTRODUCTION

Insurance is a form of economic activity which can only exist in a world of uncertainty. By entering into an insurance contract, an individual gives up some amount of wealth – the premium – for certain in exchange for a payment if and only if some specified set of uncertain events occurs. A rigorous economic analysis of insurance markets could not have been contemplated until the theory of individual choice under uncertainty had been developed, and the results of this analysis are one of the major achievements of the application of expected utility theory.

This chapter is organised as follows. We first consider the individual insurance decision as a problem of choice under uncertainty, and show that insurance can essentially be viewed as trade in claims to wealth in different states of the world. We pay particular attention to the case in which an individual may take out insurance for full compensation of the loss he may suffer; on average, the amount paid out by the insurance company equals the amount received in premiums.

Next, we consider the question of the interaction of the risks different individuals face in determining the existence of 'social risk' – uncertainty about aggregate wealth. In order to make it at least *a priori* feasible that individuals can take out full insurance, we must assume away social risk. We also assume that the insurance market will be perfectly competitive in the usual sense. The reason for this is to allow the analysis to focus on the consequences of information asymmetry: in particular *adverse selection* where insurers do not know the probability of occurrence of the insured event that any particular buyer of insurance faces; and *moral hazard*, where insurers cannot observe the extent of the costs the buyer may incur in reducing the probability of the insured event. These help us to understand and explain many commonly-observed features of real insurance contracts. They give us insights into the way in which incomplete information – in this case the information which insurers possess about some attributes of insurance-buyers – can cause markets to fail to achieve an efficient allocation of resources under uncertainty. The nature and consequences of this kind of market failure have general interest and significance in all aspects of the economics of uncertainty, but in the analysis of insurance markets they can be identified with particular clarity.

3.2   THE INDIVIDUAL CHOICE PROBLEM

We assume that an individual is faced with two possible states of the world. In state 1, his wealth will be W_1^0, and in state 2 it will be $W_2^0 = W_1^0 - L$, where $L > 0$ is the loss which will result from the occurrence of some unhappy event (sickness, unemployment, burglary, motor accident, fire, etc.). The probability of the loss occurring is denoted by p, and so $1 - p$ is the probability that wealth will be W_1^0. The expected value of the individual's wealth is then

$$\overline{W}^0 = (1 - p)W_1^0 + pW_2^0 = W_1^0 - pL \tag{3.1}$$

The individual's expected utility in the initial situation is

$$\overline{u}^0 = (1 - p)u(W_1^0) + pu(W_2^0) \tag{3.2}$$

where $u(\cdot)$ is his von Neuman–Morgenstern utility function.

We now regard $W_1 \geqslant 0$ and $W_2 \geqslant 0$ as variable amounts of state-contingent wealth, of which W_1^0 and W_2^0 can be regarded as initial endowments. Our individual can achieve some state-contingent wealth distribution (W_1, W_2) other than (W_1^0, W_2^0) by buying insurance. Thus suppose that the insurance market offers a contract $\alpha = (r, C)$, under which the individual pays a premium r for sure, and then receives an amount of compensation C if and only if the unhappy event that defines state 2 occurs. Then, if he buys insurance, he faces the state-contingent income distribution $(W_1^0 - r, W_2^0 + C - r)$, which has the expected value

$$\overline{W}^a = (1 - p)(W_1^0 - r) + p(W_2^0 + C - r) = W_1^0 - p(L - C) - r \quad (3.3)$$

and yields the expected utility

$$\overline{u}^a = (1 - p)u(W_1^0 - r) + pu(W_2^0 + C - r) \quad (3.4)$$

Then he would accept the insurance contract α only if $\overline{u}^a \geqslant \overline{u}^0$.

Now we define a *full insurance* contract as one in which $L = C$, so the individual is just compensated for the loss, no more, no less (of course, in general an insurance contract need not be for full insurance). Also, define a *fair insurance contract* as one in which $r = pC$, so that the premium is simply the expected value of the compensation to be paid. This premium is called a *fair* premium. Then, the *full and fair insurance contract* $\alpha = (pL, L)$, with compensation equal to loss and a fair premium $r = pL$, implies an expected wealth value of

$$\overline{W}^{\bar{a}} = (1 - p)(W_1^0 - \overline{r}) + p(W_2^0 + C - \overline{r}) = W_1^0 - \overline{r} = \overline{W}^0 \quad (3.5)$$

Thus, the full and fair insurance contract allows the individual to exchange the uncertain wealth distribution (W_1^0, W_2^0) for the certain wealth $\overline{W}^0$, the expected value of the initial distribution. If the individual is risk averse, we can safely predict that the contract $\overline{\alpha}$ will always be preferred to the initial (uninsured) situation, since risk aversion implies $u(\overline{W}^0) > \overline{u}^0$. Moreover, we shall shortly show that $\overline{\alpha}$ is the preferred contract in any set of fair insurance contracts, i.e. if allowed to choose among contracts offering varying amounts of compensation C, each with the appropriate fair premium pC, the individual, if risk averse, would always choose that contract offering full insurance.

All this is illustrated in Figure 3.1. The 45°-line OC will be called

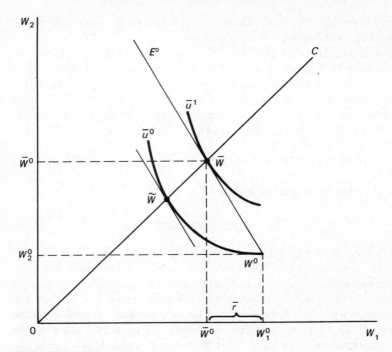

FIGURE 3.1   Fair insurance

the *certainty line*, because it shows the set of (W_1, W_2) pairs such that $W_1 = W_2$. The initial endowment point $W^0 = (W_1^0, W_2^0)$ lies below the certainty line. The negatively sloped line E^0 shows the set of (W_1, W_2) pairs that satisfy the expected value condition

$$(1-p)W_1 + pW_2 = \overline{W}^0 = (1-p)W_1^0 + pW_2^0 \qquad (3.6)$$

i.e. that have the same expected value as the initial endowment distribution (which must then of course lie on the line). For obvious reasons we call E^0 an *expected value line*. Note that as we move along this line from W^0 toward OC, the dispersion of the values of W_1 and W_1 about the mean $\overline{W}^0$ decreases, but then starts increasing again when we pass through point $\overline{W}^0$ and move away from OC. From (3.6) it is clear that the slope of this line must equal $-(1-p)/p$.[1] It is natural to interpret E^0 as a kind of budget line. *If* the individual is offered an insurance contract under which he may choose the compensation C and then has to pay the fair premium pC, he is in fact being offered all the points on the line E^0. As he moves along E^0, he is trading off wealth in State 1 for wealth in State 2 at the rate $\Delta W_2/\Delta W_1 = -(1-p)/p$, i.e., giving up \$1 of wealth contingent on State 1 gives him \$$(1-p)/p$ if State 2 occurs. Since this is the way gambling odds are usually expressed,[2] the slope of E^0 is often referred to as the 'odds ratio', or, more precisely, the 'fair odds ratio'. Thus, if the insurance market makes the budget line E^0 available to the individual, he is being offered insurance at fair odds.

So much for the budget constraint; now let us consider preferences. The individual's expected utility is in general terms

$$\bar{u} = (1-p)u(W_1) + pu(W_2) \tag{3.7}$$

Setting this equal to a given value defines a set of (W_1, W_2) pairs among which the individual is indifferent (*given* the probabilities p and $(1-p)$), and so defines an indifference curve in (W_1, W_2)-space. Examples of these are shown as $\bar{u}^0$ and $\bar{u}^1$ in the figure. The two properties of these indifference curves which are central to our purposes are:

Property (i) They are convex to the origin (as are the indifference curves of standard consumer theory). This can be shown to be a direct implication of the assumption that the individual is risk averse.[3] Intuitively, moving along the line E^0 *from* W^0 toward OC, since it reduces the dispersion of wealth around a given mean, makes a risk-averse individual strictly better off. Since this is true whatever the (unequal) wealth distribution from which we start, the indifference curves must be convex to the origin.

Property (ii) At the point at which an indifference curve cuts the certainty line OC, its slope is exactly equal to the odds ratio $-(1-p)/p$.[4] Thus for example in Figure 3.1 the indifference curve $\bar{u}^0$ has a slope of $-(1-p)/p$ at point $\tilde{W}$, and $\bar{u}^1$ has the same slope at point $\overline{W}^0$. This is essentially because if wealth is the same in each state then the marginal utility of wealth is also equal in each state. For example suppose that the two states were equally probable. Then the reduction in expected utility resulting from losing a small amount of wealth in one state would be equal to the gain in expected utility resulting from gaining the same (small) amount of wealth in the other, i.e., $p = \frac{1}{2}$ implies an odds ratio of 1, equal to the marginal rate of substitution between W_1 and W_2 at a point on the certainty line. If $p \neq \frac{1}{2}$, then, say, a small loss of wealth in State 1 would require a gain in wealth in State 2 of $(1-p)/p$ times as much if expected utility is to remain unchanged. Note that in general, the marginal rate of substitution – slope of an indifference curve – depends on *both* the odds ratio and the marginal utilities of wealth in the two states. If we change the probability p, therefore, the whole family of indifference curves would correspondingly have to change their slopes at every point.

Before using these properties of the individual's preferences to consider the choice problem, notice that the certain wealth $\tilde{W}$ in Figure 3.1 has the same expected utility as the initial wealth distribution (W_1^0, W_2^0), i.e. $u(\tilde{W}) = \bar{u}_0$. Hence we call $\tilde{W}$ the *certainty equivalent* of the initial wealth distribution and note that $\tilde{W} < \overline{W}^0$, as must of course be true by the definition of risk aversion. The difference, $\tilde{r} = \overline{W}^0 - \tilde{W}$, is called the individual's risk premium, since it can be interpreted as the maximum excess over the fair premium $\bar{r}$ the individual would be prepared to pay to exchange the risky distribution (W_1^0, W_2^0) for a certain wealth, and so $\bar{r} + \tilde{r}$ is the maximum insurance premium the individual would pay. The fact that $\tilde{r} > 0$ follows from the convexity of the indifference curve, and indeed the value of $\tilde{r}$ is a measure of this convexity, thus reinforcing the idea of the equivalence between risk aversion and the convexity of the indifference curves. Figure 3.1 demonstrates that a risk-averse individual will always be willing to pay more than the fair premium for insurance.

Figure 3.1 also shows that an individual offered insurance at fair odds, with an initial endowment at W^0 would always choose full insurance with $C = L$, paying the fair premium $\bar{r}$ and this follows directly from property (ii) above. The offer of fair insurance makes available to the individual the expected value of his wealth distribution and, since he always prefers this wealth value for certain to any uncertain wealth distribution with the same expected value, he maximises expected utility by choosing to insure fully. Thus, interpreting E^0 as a budget constraint, we have a standard tangency solution for the choice problem, and the nature of the expected utility function is such that this must be at a point on the certainty line.

What happens to this solution, however, if the individual is not offered fair insurance? Let us suppose that he is offered a contract in which C can take any value he chooses, at the premium $r = \pi C$, with $\pi \neq p$. In effect, the insurer is setting a probability on the event being insured against, which need not be the same as that perceived by the individual himself. Since the individual's wealth in each state, if he insures, will now be, respectively:

$$W_1 = W_1^0 - \pi C \tag{3.8}$$

$$W_2 = W_2^0 + C - \pi C = W_2^0 + (1 - \pi)C \tag{3.9}$$

the insurance contract is effectively offering him a budget constraint of the form

$$(1 - \pi)W_1 + \pi W_2 = W^\pi \equiv (1 - \pi)W_1^0 + \pi W_2^0 \tag{3.10}$$

This implies that he can trade wealth in State 1 for wealth in State 2 at the rate $-(1 - \pi)/\pi$. Thus the implied budget constraint will be flatter than that shown in Figure 3.1 if $\pi > p$, and steeper if $\pi < p$. This is illustrated in Figure 3.2, where the line E^H corresponds to the case in which $\pi > p$, and E^L to that in which $\pi < p$. Along E^H, the insurer is implicitly treating the individual as if he were a 'higher risk' than he is in fact, while along E^L he is implicitly being treated as a lower risk. Figure 3.2 illustrates two basic results:

1. When $\pi > p$, so the individual is paying more than his fair premium, he will 'under-insure' or 'co-insure', by choosing a value of C which leaves him below the certainty line, as illustrated by point b in the figure. That the solution must be of this kind can be seen by noting that at point c, where E^H cuts OC, the indifference curve (not shown) is tangent to the dotted line (parallel to E^0) and so is *intersected* from the right by E^H at that point. Some points to the right of c on E^H must therefore be preferred to c itself, and b is the best of such points. The interpretation of this solution is that because the individual is being charged more than the fair premium he prefers to carry some of the risk himself.

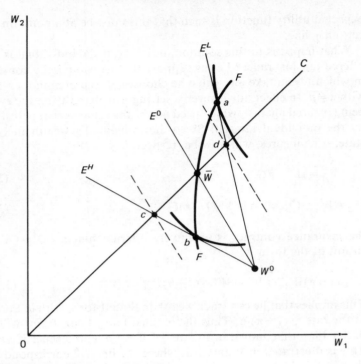

FIGURE 3.2   Insurance in general

2. When $\pi < p$, so the individual is paying less than the fair
   premium, he will 'over-insure', by choosing a value of C
   which leaves him above the certainty line, as illustrated by
   point a in the figure. At point d, where E^L cuts OC, the
   indifference curve (not shown) is tangent to the dotted line
   (parallel to E^0) and so is intersected from below by E^L at that
   point. Some points to the left of d on E^L must therefore be
   preferred, and a is the best of these. Because the individual is
   being offered better than fair odds, he is actually taking a
   gamble on the occurrence of the event against which he is
   insuring.

Thus the broad nature of the insurance contract the individual
chooses depends on a comparison of the 'true' probability (for that

individual) p with the implied probability π defined by the insurance contract, given of course the assumption that he is able to choose whatever level of compensation he prefers. The analysis makes it clear that insurance is essentially the exchange of wealth in the high wealth state for wealth in the low wealth state, and we could think of the individual's 'demand for insurance' as the amount of wealth he wishes to have finally in the low-wealth state. This demand will be a function of the value of π: as Figure 3.2 shows, as π falls, defining a sequence of budget constraints say from F^H, through E^0 to E^L, we will obtain a sequence of tangencies which define an *offer curve*, *FF* in the figure. Any point on this offer curve shows the exchange of State 1 for State 2 wealth the individual is prepared to make at the implied value of π.

3.3   THE SUPPLY OF INSURANCE

Insurance is an example of an economic activity which generates benefits without actually adding to total wealth: it is a process of pure exchange which increases economic welfare *ex ante*. In the following sections of this chapter we take a very simplistic view of the 'supply side' of the insurance market: an 'insurer' is simply an agent who costlessly arranges mutual insurance amongst a large group of individuals, rather than a firm with its own identity and objectives, as is the case in the usual analysis of markets. It will be useful at this point therefore to clarify what is involved in this simplification. We begin by considering some simple two-person economics, and examine what insurance means in this context.

Suppose first that we have two individuals of the type considered in the previous section, facing identical but independent risks. Each individual will have wealth with probability W_1^0 with probability $1 - p$, and wealth $W_2^0 = W_1^0 - L$ with probability p. Since these risks are independent, there are four possible states of the world for the economy: i.e. four possible "social states", which are set out in Table 3.1.

The first thing we note about this economy is that social risk exists, i.e. total wealth is uncertain. The implication of this is that it is either impossible or undesirable to provide full insurance at a fair premium to each individual in the economy. This is because, as we saw in the previous section, full insurance at a fair premium would

TABLE 3.1 Individual versus social risk

		Individual wealth		Total wealth	Probability
		1	2		
	1	W_1^0	W_1^0	$2W_1^0$	$(1-p)^2$
Social state	2	$W_1^0 - L$	W_1^0	$2W_1^0 - L$	$p(1-p)$
	3	W_1^0	$W_1^0 - L$	$2W_1^0 - L$	$p(1-p)$
	4	$W_1^0 - L$	$W_1^0 - L$	$2(W_1^0 - L)$	p^2

imply that each individual would face the certain wealth $W_1^0 - pL$, implying a total wealth of $2W_1^0 - 2pL$. It is easy to check from the table that in social state 1 this would be less than actual total wealth, in social states 2 and 3 it could be greater or less depending on whether p is less or greater than 0.5, and in social state 4 it would exceed total wealth.

In this economy, therefore, the kind of equilibrium we examined in the previous section, involving full insurance at the fair premium, would not be feasible for every individual, because of the existence of social risk.

What kind of equilibrium *is* possible in the presence of social risk? To analyse this question in two-dimensional terms we change the model of the economy somewhat. Take now a two-person economy in which the risks faced by individuals are perfectly negatively correlated. Suppose that in state 1, individual 1's wealth will be W_1^0, and 2's will be $W_1^0 - L_2$: and in state 2, 1's wealth will be $W_1^0 - L_1$ and 2's will be W_1^0, and assume that $L_1 > L_2$. Then total wealth in the two states is $W_1 = 2W_1^0 - L_2$ and $W_2 = 2W_1^0 - L_1$. Let $(1-p)$ and p be as usual the probabilities of states 1 and 2 respectively. We can represent the situation in the Edgeworth box diagram of Figure 3.3, where the horizontal side measures W_1 and the vertical side measures W_2. 1's wealth is measured from origin O_1, and 2's from O_2. The 45° certainty lines, O_1C_1 and O_2C_2 cannot coincide since the box is rectangular.

The Edgeworth box invites us to consider the question of trade between the two individuals. Note that the box can only represent the situation before the state of the world is known. Once the state is known the economy is at a point on a side of the box and so no

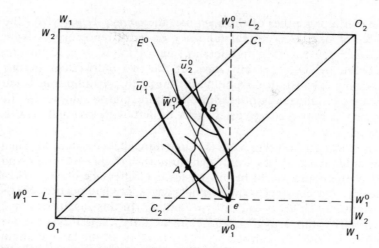

FIGURE 3.3 Social risk, exchange and insurance

exchange would be possible. Clearly, exchange would have to involve one individual promising to give the other some wealth in one state of the world in return for the promise that he will be given some wealth in the other. That is, there would be exchange of *state-contingent claims to wealth*: a claim to wealth in an individual's 'no-loss-state' is exchanged for a claim to wealth in his 'loss-state', where these claims are enforceable if and only if the state to which they refer comes about. This implies that by the process of exchange the two individuals are mutually insuring each other against their respective low-wealth states. We shall now show that the usual kind of exchange equilibrium, which corresponds to equilibrium of insurance in this economy, cannot involve full insurance for either individual, unless at least one of them is risk-neutral.

In the figure, indifference curves $\bar{u}_1^0$ and $\bar{u}_2^0$ represent expected utilities of the respective individuals at the initial endowment point e. The line E^0 through e is an expected value line with slope $-(1-p)/p$. Since the individuals face the same probabilities, the points at which E^0 cuts each of the certainty lines is a point of tangency with an indifference curve. Thus, since the certainty lines are separate, the two sets of indifference curves cannot be mutually tangent along either of them: in fact the *contract curve* AB – the locus of points of mutual tangency of indifference curves lying between the no-trade indifference curves $\bar{u}_1^0$, $\bar{u}_2^0$ – can only lie between the two certainty lines. If the two individuals, in this economy exhaust all possibilities of mutually advantageous trade of state-contingent wealth claims, therefore, and so achieve a point on the contract curve, each must be left with residual wealth uncertainty.

Suppose on the other hand that individual 2 is risk-neutral. Then his indifference curves are straight lines with slope $-(1-p)/p$, and E^0 in the figure would be his 'no-trade indifference curve'.[5] Then clearly, the contract curve would consist of that portion of 1's certainty line OC_1 bounded by $\bar{u}_1^0$ and E^0. In this case therefore 2 *will* fully insure 1 against wealth uncertainty, himself bearing the full social risk, though this will only be done at the fair premium pL_1 if 2 obtains no gains from trade, i.e., if the equilibrium is at point $\bar{W}_1^0$ in the figure.

Finally, we can reinforce the point that the existence of social risk precludes full insurance for all by considering a two-person economy in which individual risks exist and are perfectly correlated but social risk is absent. Thus suppose that in the above example $L_1 = L_2$, i.e. in state 1 individual 1 will have wealth W_1^0 and 2 will have $W_1^0 - L$, while in state 2 the converse occurs, so that total wealth is fixed at $2W_1^0 - L$. The implied Edgeworth box is shown in Figure 3.4. Because of the absence of social risk, the box is square. Then, the two individuals' certainty lines coincide with the diagonal of the box, and the contract curve is that portion of the diagonal bounded by the no-trade indifference curves $\bar{u}_1^0$ and $\bar{u}_2^0$. Thus, if bargaining exhausts all possible gains from trade the equilibrium must involve full insurance for both individuals, though, in this two-person economy,[6] it need not occur at the fair premium point e^0 on the expected value line E^0.

The discussion so far suggests that if we want any insurance market equilibrium with full insurance at a fair premium at least to be feasible *a priori*, and do not want to assume risk-neutrality of at least some individuals, we must somehow exclude social risk. We shall do this in a way which fits best with the idea of a *competitive insurance market*. We assume that there is a very large number of individuals facing identical risks, and then use the 'law of large numbers' to show that if these risks are statistically independent

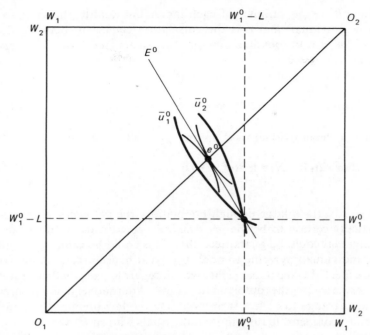

FIGURE 3.4 No social risk implies full insurance

then *per capita* wealth can be treated as certain, and full insurance at the fair premium becomes feasible.

Thus suppose there are N individuals, each with wealth W_1^0 if some unlucky event does not occur, and wealth $W_1^0 - L$ if it does. The probability of the event occurring is p for each individual. Total wealth W^0 in any social state is simply the sum of individual wealths in that state, and so the expected value of total wealth is just

$$\overline{W}^0 = N(W_1^0 - pL) \tag{3.11}$$

i.e. the sum of the individual expected values, all of which equal $W_1^0 - pL$. The standard formula for the variance of a sum of random variables tell us that

$$\text{var}(W^0) = N\sigma^2 + N(N-1)\rho\sigma^2 \tag{3.12}$$

where σ^2 is the variance of each individual wealth (the same for each individual) and ρ is the correlation coefficient between the wealths of each possible pair of individuals (the same for every pair).[7]

The variance of *per capita* wealth is

$$\text{var}(W^0/N) = \text{var}(W^0)/N^2 = (1/N + (1 - 1/N)\rho)\sigma^2 \qquad (3.13)$$

Then if the individual risks are independent, $\rho = 0$, and so

$$\lim_{N \to \infty} \text{var}(W^0/N) = \lim_{N \to \infty} (\sigma^2/N) = 0 \qquad (3.14)$$

In words, for a large enough population, the *per capita* wealth is virtually certain to be the *per capita* expected value, and so each individual could be guaranteed this. This could be achieved by all the individuals agreeing to pool their wealth, each then taking out the expected value of *per capita* wealth regardless of whether or not he experiences the unfortunate event. Alternatively, an insurer could arrange to collect from everyone the fair premium pL, and then to compensate fully those individuals who suffer the loss. His premium income will be $\$NpL$ and his compensation payment will be $\$cL$, where c is the number of people who suffer the loss. For large enough N, $c = Np$, the insurer will just break even, which is another way of expressing the idea that everyone is able to enjoy the expected value of *per capita* wealth.

Two provisos have to be attached to this conclusion. First, if $\rho > 0$ whatever the value of N,[8] i.e. individual risks are correlated, even in the limit, then the variance of *per capita* wealth would tend to $\rho\sigma^2$ as N goes to infinity. Thus full insurance for all would not be feasible. Second, we have implicitly assumed that the activity of organising risk-pooling, or insurance, is perfectly costless. We now make this explicit: in all that follows we assume transactions costs in the insurance market − defined as the costs of drawing up and executing insurance contracts − are zero. Though not realistic, this is to allow us to concentrate on some problems whose consequences for insurance markets are not so immediately obvious as those stemming from the existence of transactions costs.[9]

On the demand side, then, the idea of a 'competitive insurance market' can be taken to imply the existence of a large enough number of buyers for the 'law of large numbers' to apply: individual risks 'average out', and so each individual can enjoy the expected value of *per capita* wealth.

The assumption of a competitive insurance market further means not only that sellers of insurance act as price-takers, but also that there is completely free entry of new insurers into the market. This has two implications which will play an important role in what follows.

First, it implies that in a market equilibrium there can be neither profits nor losses, so every insurer must just break even. Otherwise entry, in search of profit, or exit, in response to loss, would be taking place. Given that each insurer sells to enough buyers for the law of large numbers to operate, this means that in equilibrium *insurance is always sold at a fair premium*, whatever the level of compensation to be paid, so that premium income will just equal the value of claims. Thus in what follows we can, in looking for equilibrium outcomes, restrict our attention to points on expected value lines.

Second, it implies that if the market is supplying a particular insurance contract, and there is another contract which at least some buyers prefer to the existing one, and which will break-even when bought by them, then the existing contract cannot represent an equilibrium. This is because a new entrant would find it profitable to offer this alternative contract, bidding away the buyers who prefer it, whatever the consequences for the viability of the existing contract. As we shall see in the next section, this implication of free entry has important implications for the possibility of equilibrium in the insurance market.

To summarise: we assume that the insurance market is competitive, in the sense that a large number of buyers with identical, independent risks face price-taking insurers, with completely free entry into the market. The implication of this, together with the assumption of zero transactions costs, is that in an equilibrium, insurers must break even, insurance must be sold at the fair premium, and there cannot exist an alternative insurance contract which some buyers would prefer and which would break-even when sold to them. In a competitive market in which insurers possess full information about the buyers of insurance, they act essentially as organisers of social risk-pooling: the insurance market is the means by which, in the absence of social risk, each individual is able to ensure for himself certain wealth equal to the expected value of *per capita* wealth.

3.4   ASYMMETRIC INFORMATION: THE CASE OF ADVERSE SELECTION

Realistically, potential buyers of insurance against some event may face different probabilities of experiencing that event. This may be due to something at least partly under their own control. For example, in health insurance an individual's lifestyle, smoking habits and frequency of exercise are important determinants of the likelihood of suffering various types of illness, and different individuals choose different profiles of these determinants. We shall postpone further discussion of this kind of case to the next section. Here, we consider only differences which are in some sense intrinsic to the individual and outside his or her control. For example genetic factors may predispose a person to particular health problems regardless of that person's choices.

To fix ideas, we suppose that there are two types of individual: low-risk types, for whom the probability of the insured event occurring is p_L, and high-risk types for whom that probability is $p_H > p_L$. In all other respects the individuals are identical. The proportion of low-risk types in the population is λ. It follows that the average probability that a claim will be made on an insurance contract is

$$\bar{p} = \lambda p_L + (1 - \lambda) p_H \tag{3.15}$$

If an insurer is able to observe accurately, before an insurance contract is made, that an individual belongs to one type or the other, and if an insurance market is competitive in the sense of the previous section, then nothing new is involved. We call this the case of *full information*, and Figure 3.5 illustrates the nature of the equilibrium, which can be called a *separating equilibrium*, since the two groups are treated separately. The lines E^L and E^H have slopes $-(1 - p_L)/p_L$ and $-(1 - p_H)/p_H$ respectively, and are expected value lines for the two types. In equilibrium, each individual is offered and accepts a full and fair insurance contract appropriate only to his type. Note that a high-risk type would clearly prefer to buy a

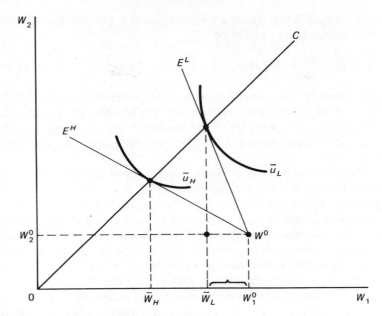

FIGURE 3.5   **Full information equilibrium**

low-risk type's insurance contract, since it offers a lower premium, $p_L L$, but under the full information assumption he would never be offered this. Each type of course receives the same amount of compensation, $C = L$.

Suppose now however that there exists an *asymmetry of information*, in the sense that an insurer cannot observe, before a contract is concluded, whether the individual buying insurance is a high-risk or low-risk type, whereas the buyer himself does know his own type. The first prediction we would make is that the situation illustrated in Figure 3.5 could not be sustained, i.e. it could not be an equilibrium. The reason is obviously that high-risk types would all claim that they were low-risk types in order to take advantage of the lower insurance premium. If the insurer, unable to tell the difference between types, accepts this and sells insurance at the low-risk premium $p_L L$, then he will on average make a loss, since the expected value of compensation payments will be $\bar{p} L$ per buyer, and $\bar{p} > p_L$ if $\lambda < 1$. Since $\bar{p} = \lambda p_L + (1 - \lambda)p_H$, the average loss *per* insurance contract would be

$$(\bar{p} - p_L)L = (1 - \lambda)(p_H - p_L)L \qquad (3.16)$$

The average loss would therefore be greater, the smaller the proportion of low-risk types in the population, the greater the difference in probabilities of the insured event occurring, and the greater the compensation for loss payable under the insurance contract.

The problem here is that if the insurer cannot identify the buyer's type, he cannot afford to go on offering full insurance at a fair premium to the low-risk buyers – the existence of high-risk buyers with an incentive to pass themselves off as low-risk in effect drives out the full-insurance contract for low-risk types. This is an example of the *adverse selection problem* – the 'selection' of buyers made by the insurer is adverse to himself.

There is of course a contract insurers can offer that would enable them to break-even on average. If everyone is offered full insurance at the *pooled fair premium* $\bar{p}L$, then premium income will again equal average claims. Figure 3.6 illustrates the market situation if this contract were the only one made available, with $\bar{E}$ the expected value line with slope $-(1 - \bar{p})/\bar{p}$. The central point is that neither type of insurance buyer is actually obtaining his *preferred* amount of insurance at this pooled premium $\bar{p}L$, or, in the figure, $\bar{e}$ is not a point of tangency with an indifference curve of either type. Because $\bar{p} > p_L$, low-risk individuals would prefer to buy less than full insurance, while $p_H > \bar{p}$ implies that high-risk individuals would prefer to buy more. If this were allowed, however, insurers would again make losses on average. To see this, let $C_H > L$ denote the amount of compensation high-risk individuals would choose at the fair premium $\bar{p}C_H$, and $C_L < L$ the amount the low-risk individuals would choose, at the fair premium $\bar{p}C_L$. The premium income per insurance contract would be:[10]

$$\lambda \bar{p}C_L + (1 - \lambda)\bar{p}C_H \qquad (3.17)$$

while the average claim per insurance contract would be:[11]

$$\lambda p_L C_L + (1 - \lambda)p_H C_H \qquad (3.18)$$

Hence, subtracting (3.17) from (3.18) the average loss per contract would be:

$$\lambda(1-\lambda)(p_H - p_L)[C_H - C_L] \qquad (3.19)$$

Intuitively, the problem arises because those individuals requiring greater compensation $(C_H > C_L)$ are more likely to make a claim $(p_H > p_L)$.

The implication of this is that if insurers wished to go on offering pooled insurance and a fair premium $\bar{p}C$, they would have to specify not only the premium but also the amount of compensation in the contract. As (3.19) shows, break-even requires $C_L = C_H$, and so the natural restriction would be to offer everyone the same compensation, $C = L$, at the pooled fair premium pL. The question then arises, whether this can really be an equilibrium, given that individuals of neither type, and in particular low-risk individuals, are not actually buying their preferred insurance contract in this situation.

Returning to Figure 3.6, we can quickly see that the situation shown there can not in fact be an equilibrium. We note that at point $\bar{e}$, the line $\bar{E}$ intersects the indifference curves of both high- and low-risk types, with the low-risk type's indifference curve $\bar{u}_L$ necessarily steeper at that point.[12] Suppose the market were initially at point $\bar{e}$ with everyone buying the implied contract. An insurer would then find it feasible to offer a new insurance contract which would have the following properties:

(i) it would not make a loss
(ii) it would be preferred by low-risk types to the contract at $\bar{e}$;
(iii) it would *not* be preferred by the high-risk types to the contract at $\bar{e}$.

and so the new contract could be sold to low-risk types alone. An example of such a contract would be any that offered a point between a and b on the line E^L in Figure 3.6. Such a point is above $\bar{u}_L$, and so would be preferred by low-risk types; is below $\bar{u}_H$, and so would not be preferred by high-risk types; and, since it involves less than full compensation $C < L$ at a fair premium $p_L C$, it would break-even when bought only by low-risk types. Clearly, a contract which would allow a low-risk individual to reach any point in the shaded area *ebac* in Figure 3.6 would possess properties (ii) and

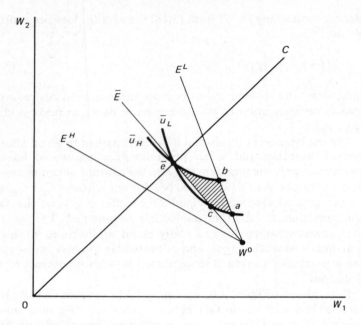

FIGURE 3.6 Pooled insurance

(iii), and contracts giving a point below E^L would yield positive expected profit as well. In a competitive insurance market therefore the situation in which all buyers are offered full compensation $C = L$ at the pooled fair premium pL could not be sustained as an equilibrium, since insurers would find it profitable to offer contracts paying less than full compensation that would be bought if and only if the buyer were a low-risk type. Intuitively, a low-risk buyer would find it worthwhile to accept less than full coverage in exchange for a sufficiently lower premium. Again, note that the insurance contract would have to specify both the premium and the amount of compensation to be paid.

Of course, if low-risk buyers were induced to switch to the contract that is more attractive to them, the contract offering full compensation at a premium $\overline{p}L$ would no longer break-even – it would be bought only by high-risk types and so the expected claim per contract would be $p_H L$. The question then becomes one of whether an equilibrium is possible in which different types buy different contracts, since we have just seen that a situation in which both types are offered the same contract cannot be sustained as an equilibrium – *no pooling equilibrium exists*. We shall now see that the existence of a separating equilibrium depends critically on the value of λ.

For a separating equilibrium to exist we require that three conditions be satisfied:

(i) *The self-selection condition*: high-risk types must prefer their contract to that offered to low-risk types, and conversely, i.e. individuals must 'self-select' the contract appropriate to their type. Of course once the contract has been made the insurer cannot do anything further with this information – anything contingent on buyer's type must be built into the contract before it is offered on the market.

(i) *The break-even condition*: since we continue to assume a competitive insurance market, in equilibrium insurance contracts should make neither a profit nor a loss. In a separating equilibrium this must imply that each type is being offered a fair premium.

(iii) *The no entry condition*: it must not be possible for an insurer to devise a new contract which is profitable and which causes a change in buyers' behaviour. Recall that it was the possibility of entry in this sense that allowed us to show that a pooling equilibrium could not exist.

We saw earlier that when there is asymmetric information the situation in which full compensation at a fair premium is offered for each type violates the self-selection condition – this is the 'adverse selection' problem. Consider however the contracts illustrated by points e_H and e_L in Figure 3.7. High-risk types are offered full insurance at their fair premium $p_H L$. Low-risk types are offered only partial compensation, sufficient for them to reach point e_L on E^L, at their fair premium. It is easy to see that these contracts satisfy the self-selection and break-even conditions: high-risk types are indifferent between points e_H and e_L and so, we assume,[13] choose e_H; low-risk types certainly prefer e_L to e_H; and both contracts break-even since they are on the appropriate expected value lines. However, these contracts may or may not be an equilibrium.

Suppose first that the value of λ is such that the line E' in the

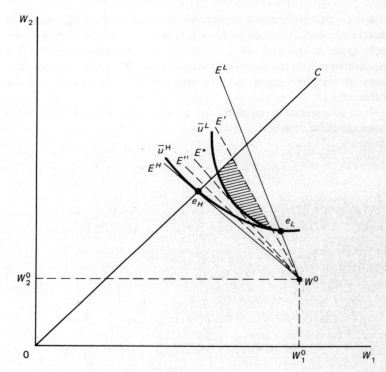

FIGURE 3.7   **Separating equilibrium**

figure corresponds to the pooled probability $\bar{p} = \lambda p_L + (1-\lambda)p_H$, i.e. it has slope $-(1-\bar{p})/\bar{p}$.[14] Then e_H and e_L are not an equilibrium because they do not satisfy the no-entry condition. To see this, note that any point in the shaded area would be preferred by both high- and low-risk types, and would at least break even: thus it would be possible for an insurer to offer such a pooled contract, which would then displace the separate contracts at e_H and e_L. Thus no separating equilibrium would exist. We saw earlier, however, that no pooling equilibrium can exist either, and so we would have to conclude that in this case there is no equilibrium.

On the other hand, suppose that the value of λ was low enough to give the expected value line E'' as that corresponding to the pooled probability $\bar{p}$. Then no point exists which at least breaks even (lies on or below E''') and at the same time is preferred by low-risk types to e_L. Hence in this case the no-entry condition is satisfied and a separating equilibrium exists. The line E^* in the figure can be thought of as defining the critical value of λ: for higher λ equilibrium does not exist, for lower λ equilibrium does exist.

An explanation of this result can be put as follows. In a sense, the low-risk types, with contracts e_H and e_L, are bearing the costs of the adverse-selection problem. In order to make the low-risk contract unattractive to high-risk types, despite the lower premium, a restriction must be placed on the degree of coverage – low-risk types are forced to under-insure by just enough to deter high-risk types. The low-risk types would gladly pay more than their fair premium to obtain extra coverage, and in the case in which equilibrium does not exist this is in fact what happens. Because there is a sufficiently large proportion of low-risk types, the pooled fair premium is not much above the fair premium for low-risk types alone, and so low-risk types can be offered more coverage at a price they are prepared to pay. Thus the separating contracts cannot be sustained. On the other hand, if the proportion of low-risk types is not very large, the pooled fair premium is too much above the low-risk fair premium and so low-risk types do not find it worthwhile to buy extra coverage. Hence a separating equilibrium exists. Everything therefore depends on the value of λ, an exogenous parameter of the model.

If λ is so high that equilibrium does not exist, we would presumably observe the market in a constant state of flux. If existing contracts offer everyone the same compensation at a pooled fair premium, some insurer will find it profitable to introduce a contract with lower premium and more restricted coverage which will be attractive only to low-risk types. This will make the existing pooled contracts unprofitable and presumably we will see a period when separate contracts are offered. But then someone will find it profitable to offer a pooled contract. And so on. On the other hand if λ is sufficiently low for a separating equilibrium to exist, we will observe a stable set of differentiated contracts being offered. In practice, this will often take the following form: a 'standard' contract will be offered giving full coverage at a particular premium. It will however be possible to obtain a reduced premium by accepting an 'excess', i.e. a reduction in the degree of coverage. For example, one may agree to pay the first $500 of the cost of an automobile accident in return for a more than proportionate discount on the standard premium. Thus individuals who perceive themselves as lower risk are being offered a separate contract, and the analysis of this section provides a rationale for this frequently observed feature of insurance contracts.

3.5 ASYMMETRIC INFORMATION: THE CASE OF MORAL HAZARD

It is often the case that an individual could carry out some (costly) action which reduces the probability that the event being insured against will occur. For example, the likelihood that a house will be burgled may be reduced by installing sophisticated locks and an alarm system; the probability that the house will be destroyed by fire can be reduced by installing smoke detectors and a sprinkler system; a smoker's probability of death can be reduced by giving up smoking; and so on. Let us make the simplifying assumption that the individual can choose to make a single expenditure which changes the probability of the insured event from p_0 to $p_a < p_0$.[15] The situation is illustrated in Figure 3.8. The initial distribution is as usual $W^0 = (W_1^0, W_2^0)$. Now if the individual incurs the expenditure a, his wealth distribution will change to point g, with coordinates $(W_1^0 - a, W_2^0 - a)$. If he does not incur this expenditure, then he will face the expected value line E^0, with slope $-(1 - p_0)/p_0$. If he does incur the expenditure he will face the expected value line A^a with slope $-(1 - p_a)/o_a$, which is steeper than E^0 but must originate at point g.

Suppose first that it is possible for the insurer costlessly to observe whether or not the individual does in fact incur the expenditure a.[16] Then two insurance contracts could be offered. One would offer the individual full insurance at the fair premium p_0L, conditional on his not incurring expenditure a, implying an equilibrium at point b in the figure; the other would offer full insurance at the lower premium if and only if the expenditure a is incurred, implying equilibrium at point c in the figure. Clearly, because c is to the right of b on OC, the individual would prefer to spend a and insure fully at the lower premium.[17]

However, now suppose that there is an information asymmetry, in the sense that the insurer cannot observe at any cost whether or not

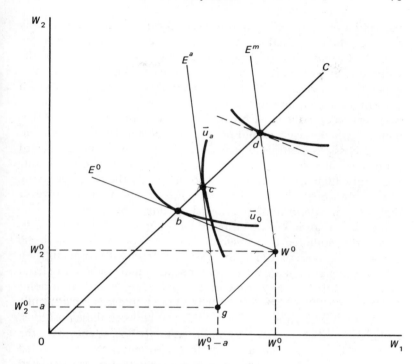

FIGURE 3.8   The moral hazard problem

the individual incurs the expenditure. Then the situation in which insurers offer full insurance at the premium $p_a L$ cannot be an equilibrium, since buyers will find it optimal to take out such insurance but *not* incur the expenditure, thus achieving point d in Figure 3.8.[18] Since the true probability of the event is $p_0 > p_a$ when $a = 0$, insurers will suffer losses on this contract.

We therefore see that the existence of asymmetry of information – in this case the insurer's inability to observe the true value of a – implies that offering a particular contract may give the individual an incentive to choose an expenditure level such that the probability of the insured event will differ from that upon which the contract was based. This is the *moral hazard problem*.[19] Note that the problem is not that the insurer must somehow detect what value of a the individual chooses: this value is perfectly predictable. Under any contract, the individual will choose that level of a which is best for himself. Rather, the problem is to design a contract in which the value of the probability assumed is consistent with the value of a which the individual will choose under that contract, and which constitutes an equilibrium contract in the sense defined in the previous sections: it must break even and there must be no other contract which buyers would prefer and which at least breaks even.

One possible contract which does not present a moral hazard problem is illustrated in Figure 3.8. Insurers could simply assume that individuals will set $a = 0$, and so offer only the contract giving full insurance at the fair premium $p_0 L$. Does point b however represent an equilibrium? We now show that it may not.

Consider Figure 3.9, which reproduces Figure 3.8 with the addition of the indifference curves $\bar{u}_a^*$, $\bar{u}_0^*$ and the line ee', parallel to the line gW^0. Suppose that insurers offer a contract with compensation $C^* < L$ and premium $p_a C^*$ such that the individual would move from point g to point e if he *has* incurred expenditure a, and from point W^0 to point e' if he has not. At e he is on indifference curve $\bar{u}_a^*$, while at e' he is on $\bar{u}_0^*$. Moreover, he is indifferent between these positions, because $\bar{u}_0^*$ and $\bar{u}_a^*$ intersect at f on the certainty line, so they have the same certainty equivalent and therefore represent the same expected utility, i.e. $\bar{u}_a^* = \bar{u}_0^*$. The difference of course is that $\bar{u}_a^*$ is calculated with the probability p_a (*a has* been spent) while u_0^* involves p_0 (*a* has *not* been spent). Finally, note that since f is to the right of b on OC, the individual would prefer this contract to that offering full compensation at premium $p_0 L$. The reduction in coverage is more than compensated by the reduction in premium.

We can see that the contract $(p_a C^*, C^*)$ solves the moral hazard problem, since the individual does not prefer e' to e.[20] It does this by offering less than full insurance at a fair premium. The individual is induced to spend a by the desire to reduce the chance that he will incur the loss $L - C^*$: the fact that he will bear some part of the loss himself provides an incentive to reduce the probability of loss. Note that when the buyer chooses point e the contract $(p_a C^*, C^*)$ breaks even. In this case therefore point b cannot be an equilibrium.

However, Figure 3.9 was rather pulled out of a hat. How do we know that a contract $(p_a C^*, C^*)$ with the properties shown there will always exist, and if it does, that it will represent an equilibrium? To answer this question we need to look more explicitly at the expected

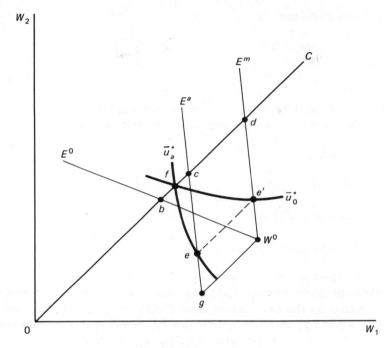

FIGURE 3.9 Solution to the moral hazard problem

utilities involved at the various points – e, e' and b – shown in Figure 3.9.

First, at point b, the individual's wealth is $W_1^0 - p_0 L$ in each state, and so expected utility is

$$\bar{u}_b = u(W_1^0 - p_0 L) \tag{3.20}$$

At a point such as e, where the individual buys the contract $(p_a C^*,$ $C^*)$, with $C^* < L$, *and* spends a, wealth in each state is respectively

$$W_1 = W_1^0 - p_a C^* - a \tag{3.21}$$

$$W_2 = W_2^0 + C^* - p_0 C^* - a = W_2^0 + (1 - p_a)C^* - a \tag{3.22}$$

and expected utility is

$$\bar{u}_a^* = (1-p_a)u(W_1^0 - p_a C^* - a) + p_a u(W_2^0 +$$

$$(1-p_a)C^* - a) \tag{3.23}$$

Finally, at a point such as e', where the contract $(p_a C^*, C^*)$ is bought but a is not spent, wealth in each state is

$$W_1 = W_1^0 - p_a C^* \tag{3.24}$$

$$W_2 = W_2^0 + (1-p_a)C^* \tag{3.25}$$

and expected utility is

$$\bar{u}_0^* = (1-p_0)u(W_1^0 - p_a C^*) + p_0 u(W_2^0 + (1-p_a)C^*) \tag{3.26}$$

Now think of C^* as variable over the range $0 \leqslant C^* \leqslant L$. Note first that $\bar{u}_b$ in (3.20) is unaffected by the value of C^*: it is essentially a constant. On the other hand, from (3.23) and (3.26) we see that both $\bar{u}_a^*$ and $\bar{u}_0^*$ must increase with C^*,[21] and that this is the only variable in these expressions (p_a, p_0, a and L are all fixed). Moreover, (3.23) and (3.26) show that at $C^* = L$ we must have $\bar{u}_0^* > \bar{u}_a^*$.[22]

Consider now what happens if $C^* = 0$. Two cases are possible. Either

$$\bar{u}_a^* > \bar{u}_0^* \tag{i}$$

or

$$\bar{u}_a^* \leqslant \bar{u}_0^* \tag{ii}$$

Figure 3.10 illustrates what will happen in the first of these cases. On the right-hand vertical line, we show the values of $\bar{u}_0^*$ and $\bar{u}_a^*$ at $C = L$. The curves show the two expected utility values as C^* varies from 0 to L. Now if, at $C = 0$, we have $\bar{u}_a^* > \bar{u}_0^*$ (case (i)), then *must* be at least one intersection point,[23] since we have to end up with $\bar{u}_a^* < \bar{u}_0^*$. Suppose for simplicity that this point is unique at C^*, as the figure shows. Then this value is the largest value of C^* which

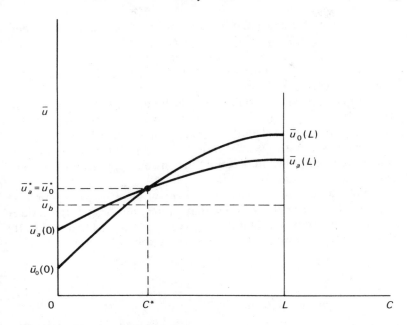

FIGURE 3.10 Optimal partial coverage

solves the moral hazard problem, since in order to induce the buyer
to spend a we require that the condition

$$\bar{u}_0^* \leqslant \bar{u}_a^* \tag{3.27}$$

be satisfied at the chosen C^*.

However, in order for this to be an equilibrium we also require
that this contract be preferred to contract $(p_0 L, L)$, since, if it
were not, a competitive insurance market would offer this latter
contract and drive out the contract $(p_a C^*, C^*)$. But since $\bar{u}_b$ is
independent of C^* this cannot be guaranteed. It may happen that
$\bar{u}_b < \bar{u}_a = \bar{u}_0$ at C^*, as shown in Figure 3.10 (and also in Figure 3.9).
In that case we can say that the contract $(p_a C^*, C^*)$ *is* an
equilibrium: it solves the moral hazard problem because it satisfies
condition (3.27), i.e. it ensures consistency between the premium
charged and the true value of p that will result from the buyer's

chosen value of a under the contract; it breaks even; and no other contract exists which yields a higher expected utility subject to condition (3.27) and the break-even condition.

However, it would also be possible for $\bar{u}_b$ to be high enough to exceed the values of $\bar{u}_a^*$ and $\bar{u}_0^*$ at the intersection point in Figure 3.10. In such a case the point f would lie to the left of point b on OC in Figure 3.9. This is more likely to happen the greater the value of a relative to the difference $p_0 - p_a$. In this case although a contract exists that solves the moral hazard problem, it would not represent an equilibrium because the contract $(p_0 L, L)$ breaks even and yields a higher expected utility.

Finally, let us consider case (ii), where, at $C^* = 0$, $\bar{u}_a^* \leqslant \bar{u}_0^*$. In this case, as Figure 3.11 shows, there may or may not be an intersection between the two expected utility curves as C^* varies from 0 to L. If there is not, then no contract exists that solves the moral hazard

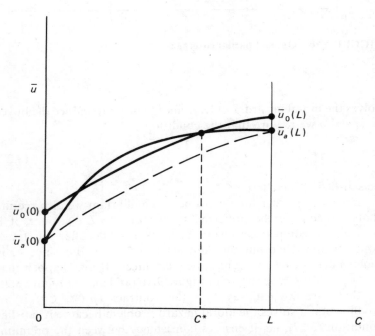

FIGURE 3.11   Optimal partial coverage may or may not exist

problem. If the curves do intersect then we should take the largest value of C^* at which this occurs,[24] and the corresponding contract $(p_a C^*, C)$ *does* solve the moral hazard problem. However, the previous remarks still apply: this contract may or may not represent an equilibrium, depending on whether it yields an expected utility greater than that corresponding to the contract $(p_0 L, L)$.

To summarise the analysis of this section: when an insurer cannot observe whether an individual has in fact incurred the expenditure a, then the contract $(p_a L, L)$ is not an equilibrium. It will not break-even because buyers will not spend a and so the true probability of the insured event is p_0 not p_a. This is (in this context) the moral hazard problem. It may then be possible to define a contract offering partial compensation $C^* < L$, at a fair premium $p_a C^*$, which solves the moral hazard problem in the sense that it provides the buyer with the incentive to spend a. He does this to reduce the probability that he will incur the residual uninsured loss $L - C^*$. For such a contract to exist, a *sufficient* condition is that at $C = 0$, the expected utility of spending a be greater than that of not spending a, i.e.

$$(1 - p_a)u(W_1^0 - a) + p_a u(W_2^0 - a) >$$

$$(1 - p_0)u(W_1^0) + p_0 u(W_2^0) \tag{3.28}$$

implying that in the complete absence of insurance the individual would in fact spend a. However, even if this condition is satisfied, the values of a, p_0 and p_a could be such that the contract $(p_0 L, L)$ would yield higher expected utility and thus the partial insurance contract $(p_a C^*, C^*)$ would not be an equilibrium. If the sufficient condition is not satisfied then there may or may not exist a partial insurance contract which solves the moral hazard problem and, if there does, it may not be an equilibrium for the reason just given.

3.6 CONCLUSIONS

In this chapter we have considered an economy in which everyone could have for certain the expected value of their uncertain wealth endowment. This could be achieved by a competitive insurance market making available full insurance at a fair premium, in the absence of transactions costs. If different (though still very large) groups of individuals face different probabilities of the insured event, they would simply pay different (fair) premiums. If, by undertaking some costly action, individuals could reduce the probability of the insured event and increase the expected value of their wealth, then they would be encouraged to do so by being offered an appropriately lower (fair) premium.

The main concern of the chapter was to show how imperfect information in the form of an information asymmetry between buyer and seller causes the market to fail to achieve these efficient outcomes. We saw that the response to problems both of adverse selection and of moral hazard was to restrict the degree of coverage of some, or all, insurance contracts.[25] In the case of adverse selection, low-risk individuals are offered only partial coverage – and so are left with wealth uncertainty – in order to make their contract unattractive to high-risk individuals. In the case of moral hazard, all individuals are offered only partial coverage to provide them with an incentive to carry out the costly action and so reduce the probability of the insured event. In each case other outcomes are possible: under adverse selection, no equilibrium contract may exist; under moral hazard, a contract may be offered which assumes the costly action is not chosen, and provides no incentive to do so, so that a socially beneficial activity is not undertaken.

We saw in the second section that insurance can essentially be viewed as exchange of state-contingent claims to wealth. Apart from the insights it gives us into the working of insurance markets, therefore, the analysis of this chapter suggests the general nature of the outcome whenever market exchange under uncertainty is associated with asymmetries of information between the parties to the exchange. This covers a wide class of cases indeed, encompassing, for example, markets in second-hand cars (the 'lemons' problem), labour markets and the problem of shareholders' control of companies.

4 Game Theory, Oligopoly and Bargaining

BRUCE LYONS and YANIS VAROUFAKIS

4.1 INTRODUCTION

Game theory is currently having as much impact on certain topics in microeconomics as rational expectations has had on macroeconomics.[1] Yet whilst the modern undergraduate typically has a reasonable grasp of rational expectations macroeconomics, his or her understanding of game theory is likely to be both rudimentary and, even worse, faulty. Most microeconomic texts have a section on the 'prisoners' dilemma' to highlight the problem of establishing cooperation; and somewhere else there will be an exposition of Cournot duopoly which suggests it could only apply to short-sighted firms which cannot predict a rival's reactions; and that is about it. It is one of the purposes of this chapter to point out the richness of the prisoners' dilemma game and another to correct the misperceptions surrounding Cournot. But our hope is that we can take the reader much further. Game theory provides a unifying framework with which to analyse properly any question involving the interaction of rational agents. This includes topics as apparently diverse as oligopoly, externality, public goods, tariff-setting, bequests by parents to their children, wage-bargaining, Mrs Thatcher's macroeconomics, and much more besides. Clearly, there is insufficient space to treat each of these adequately here. Instead, we emphasise the underlying theory of games and give fairly detailed, but intuitive, expositions of just a few topics chosen from two of the best developed areas of research, those of oligopoly theory and wage-bargaining. The reader should then be adequately prepared to tackle other areas of particular interest.

The chapter is divided into three parts. Section 4.2 introduces the basic theory of non-cooperative games and includes a game theorist's view of the familiar prisoners' dilemma and Cournot models. Section 4.3 includes three sections on various topics in non-cooperative game theory. Oligopoly theory used to be a hotch-potch of unrelated models, but recent developments have begun to tie the various insights together within the unifying discipline of game theory. Section 4.4 introduces bargaining theory and emphasises the problem of understanding the emergence of conflict. This uses much the same game theoretic concepts as the two first parts, but a key difference is that individuals or groups are allowed to make binding agreements prior to taking any action. Interest surrounds the way such contracts come about and what division of the benefits is agreed. Finally, Section 4.5 offers some concluding comment.

4.2   THE THEORY OF NON-COOPERATIVE GAMES

Some basic definitions

A game is defined by a number of players each facing a set of possible actions and consequent pay-offs (or utilities). The structure of the game also specifies when each player may make a move. The pay-offs need not be precisely known and may depend on the state of nature. In that case, the players must place (possibly subjective) probability values on the various possible states of nature actually occurring. The motivating force behind game theory is that the pay-offs to one player depend on the actions of others.

Games are normally classified according to:

(1) the degree of inherent antagonism embodied in the pay-offs;
(ii) whether or not binding agreements can be signed;
(iii) the extent to which information is common to all players;
(iv) the sequence in which players take decisions;
(v) the number of times a game is played.

Each of these can have an important influence on the analysis of the game.

(1) *Zero-sum games.* If the game essentially boils down to dividing a cake of pre-determined size then there is pure antagonism and we are in the realm of *zero-sum games.* These were the first games to be formally studied and the remarkable 'minimax theorem' formulated by von Neumann (roughly speaking, that there is always a rational solution to zero-sum games) mesmerised a generation of game theorists. Most games of interest to economists, however, are not zero-sum but involve some mutuality of interests. For instance, oligopolists prefer a high price to a low price even though there remains a conflict of interests. It is the solution of *non-zero-sum games* that concerns us in this section and the next.

(ii) *Cooperative and non-cooperative games.* In a cooperative game, players are free to communicate, before any actions are taken, and come to binding agreements on mutually beneficial courses of action, or strategies. The early effort of game theorists concerned economies with large numbers of players and resulted in the rigorous proof of Edgeworth's famous limit theorem: that as the number of players in an exchange economy becomes very large, then no coalition of players can guarantee themselves a better pay-off than arises from perfect competition. More recent work has concentrated on two-person cooperative games, which are known as bargaining games, (discussed in Section 4.4). One characteristic that might reasonably be expected of the solution to a cooperative game is that it will be Pareto-optimal: if both players can be made better off by adopting a different strategy, then they should agree to do so.

In a *non-cooperative game*, in which binding agreements are not feasible, this is not always possible as will be seen in the examination of the prisoners' dilemma in Figure 4.1. The idea is that two criminals are caught and interrogated in separate rooms. If both confess (i.e. (b_1, b_2) is played) the police will be able to prosecute a major charge successfully, but will recommend lenient sentences. If neither confesses (a_1, a_2), it is likely that only a minor charge can be made to stick. If only one confesses and implicates the other who is denying involvement – i.e. (a_1, b_2) or (b_1, a_2) – the one who confesses

Prisoner 2

		'deny' a_2	'confess' b_2
Prisoner 1	'deny' a_1	5, 5	0, 8
	'confess' b_1	8, 0	3, 3

FIGURE 4.1   Prisoners' dilemma

gets an extremely light sentence, while the other gets 'the book thrown at him'. The set of actions implied by either denying or confessing is known as a *strategy*. Figure 4.1 gives the utility pay-offs to each choice with player 1's pay-off to his strategies a_1 and b_1 coming first in each pair. Notice that regardless of what player 2 does, player 1 does better by confessing than by denying the crime. In such cases, b_1 is called a *dominant strategy*. Similarly, confessing is also dominant for 2. Since b is dominant for each player, in the absence of binding contracts we must expect both to confess. Would it make any difference if the criminals could communicate prior to deciding whether to confess? Suppose they realise the police have found their hideout but they have à few moments for rational debate before being caught. 1 may begin by pointing out that although each has a dominant strategy, to confess would lead to a Pareto-inferior outcome, so why not agree to deny the crime? 2 likes the idea, agrees to it and they shake hands. Two hours later they are being interrogated. Despite their verbal agreement nothing in the pay-offs has changed, and to confess remains dominant. We must therefore expect rational players to confess. Pre-play communication without binding agreements cannot help to resolve the prisoners' dilemma.

(iii)   *Common knowledge.*   If each player in the game has the same information – for instance, on the probability distributions assigned to various outcomes by each other – and each knows that the others have this information, then the game is one of *common knowledge*. A critical piece of common knowledge is that all players are rational in the sense that when presented with the same information they will come to the same conclusion: in particular, they can duplicate each others' thought processes. As will be seen later this idea that players can think through how others are working through the problem is the key to understanding equilibrium in game theory. A modification of this sort of reasoning can also be applied to games where either a rival's pay-offs, or his full rationality, is in doubt. If some players have private information, or even if they think that others might, then we have an *asymmetric information game*.[2] Such games are much more complex to analyse, but they have been the focus of considerable interest in the past few years, and they are introduced in section 4.3.

(iv) *Simultaneous and sequential games.* In a *simultaneous game*, each player chooses his strategy before he knows the choice made by his rival. All decisions must be made on the basis of how one expects rivals to behave. In a *sequential game*, the initial actions of the first player are made known before the second player makes a move (the first player may then get a chance to move again and so on). This gives the first mover the opportunity to influence a rival's choice of strategy. Deliberate actions of this sort are known as *strategic behaviour* and this is discussed at the end of this section. Strategic behaviour can only be effective if the first mover's actions are irreversible. An action of this sort is known as a *commitment* (or credible threat), whereas an action which is reversible at a later stage in the game is known as an *empty threat*.

(v) *One-shot and super-games.* A *one-shot* game is played once only. If the game is played several times by different players then nothing material changes. However, if at least one of the players plays the same game repeatedly, and any new players can observe the results of previous plays, then history is introduced and the possibilities of implicit cooperation and learning arise. Such *repeated games* are sometimes known as *super-games*, though the latter term is more general and includes games which vary over time. The outcome of repeated games can depend crucially on whether the repetition is finite or infinite, and these cases are investigated in section 4.2.

Equilibrium in non-cooperative games

Suppose we have defined an n-person, non-zero-sum, non-cooperative, common knowledge, one-shot game. Despite a long series of careful assumptions, we still need something else if we are to predict how rational players will play the game. What is needed is a solution concept that enables us to establish what assumptions one player will make about the behaviour of others so she can then act accordingly. It turns out that there is currently considerable, though not unanimous, agreement among economists about this. The *Nash equilibrium* (NE) concept is so widely accepted that it is often simply called the equilibrium point.

Let $U_i(s_1, s_2, \ldots, s_i, \ldots, s_n)$ be the pay-off to player i as a function of the strategies played by herself and all others. A Nash equilibrium is a vector of strategies $(s_1, \ldots s_n)$ *such that for each* $i = 1, \ldots, n,$ i selects the strategy s_i^* out of his set of feasible strategies such that

$$U_i(s_1^*, s_2^*, \ldots, s_i^*, \ldots s_n^*) \geqslant U_i(s_1, s_2, \ldots, s_i, \ldots s_n)$$

Thus, given the strategies played by rivals, s_i^* is *i's best reply.* At least one, and sometimes more than one, Nash equilibrium exists for all games in a very wide category. Sometimes, however, the NE may involve *mixed strategies* by which players do not definitely choose to play just one *pure strategy*, but a probability mix of various actions. In the prisoners' dilemma game, since b_1 and b_2 are both dominant, they are clearly best replies and so constitute the NE. In Figure 4.2: for player 1, c_1 is the best reply to a_2, a_1 is the best reply to b_2, and c_1 is the best reply to c_2; for player 2, b_2 is the best reply to a_1, a_2 is the best reply to b_1, and b_2 is the best reply to c_1. The pay-offs to these best replies are marked with a dot. To obtain the pure strategy NE, player 2 reasons as follows: I know my best replies and my rival's best replies. If these coincide then neither of us has any incentive to change what we are doing so (a_1, b_2) is the equilibrium. Any other strategy combination would leave one of us not optimising and so could not be expected to arise from play between rational players. Each of us is able to appreciate this so we will each play our NE strategies.[3] Some game theorists claim that this is how rational players should behave; that is they argue that the equilibrium is *prescriptive*. Others go further to argue that

Player 2

	a_2	b_2	c_2
a_1	5, 5	3, 6*	0, 4
b_1	4, 3*	2, 2	2, 0
c_1	7, 0	1, 1*	4, 0

Player 1

FIGURE 4.2 Best replies and Nash equilibrium

this is how people actually do behave, that is to say, game theory is *descriptive*. The latter view can be justified either on the grounds that decision-makers are very clever or because there are evolutionary forces at work.

The oldest and most familiar example of a Nash equilibrium in microeconomics is the Cournot duopoly model. Two players each know both the demand curve for mineral water and each other's costs (common knowledge). Players must simultaneously choose quantities to supply to the market; so the set of feasible strategies is defined as rates of output between zero and some suitably high maximum (say, that which if supplied would reduce the demand price to zero). For any strategy chosen (output produced) by firm 2 it is straightforward to calculate firm 1's best reply from his costs and the residual demand curve (i.e. industry demand less 2's supply). For the linear-demand curve, $p = a - b[s_1 + s_2]$ where s_1 and s_2 are supplies by each firm, and constant costs, c, equal for both firms, firm 1's profits are $U_1 = [p - c]s_1 = [a - c - bs_1 - bs_2]s_1$. For any given s_2, profit-maximising firm 1's best reply is given by $\partial U_1 / \partial s_1 = a - c - 2bs_1 - bs_2 = 0$, or $s_1^* = [a - c]/2b = [s_2/2]$. Now firm 2 faces a similar problem so her best reply is $s_2^* = [a - c]/2b - [s_1/2]$. Appreciating this, firm 1 can substitute $s_2 = s_2^*$ into his own best-reply function to get the NE which is $s_1^* = s_2^* = [a - c]/3b$. Note that in this linear example each firm supplies exactly one-third of the competitive output (found by setting $p = x = a - b[s_1 + s_2]$). Figure 4.3 plots firm 1's best-reply function as B_1R_1. B_2R_2 is firm 2's best reply to firm 1, and $C = (s_1^*,$

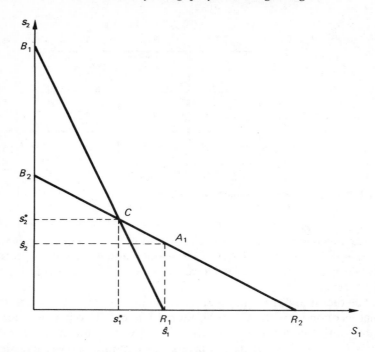

FIGURE 4.3   Cournot–Nash equilibrium

s_2^*) is the Cournot–Nash equilibrium. Had we defined price as the strategic variable, we would have arrived at the Bertrand–Nash equilibrium which is quite different. The fact that changing the set of feasible strategies changes the equilibrium outcome should be no surprise, but recent research discussed below has shown that under certain interesting circumstances the difference is less than is conventionally appreciated.

In deriving the Nash equilibrium, nothing has been said about how equilibrium is attained or how stable it is. Some otherwise very good undergraduate texts motivate the Cournot model by suggesting that firm 1 starts as a monopoly at R_1, whereupon firm 2 enters and produces vertically above R_1 on her best-reply curve, to which firm 1 responds until equilibrium is reached. The criticism that the duopolists are myopic and constantly being surprised by rivals' reactions inevitably follows. But this is the same as criticising standard supply and demand equilibrium on the grounds that you do not like the cobweb model! Yes, dynamics are important: but no, we need not rely on one particular version to motivate our equilibrium. It is far better to view the NE as the only logical result of careful analysis by the duopolists. Bearing in mind that they cannot come to a binding agreement, the attraction of the NE is that each is making the best reply to the other's strategy. With any other pair of strategies, at least one of them would have a unilateral incentive to change strategy.

Alternatives to the NE are not plausible for fully rational players. For instance, consider the case against the Stackelberg point for firm 1 as leader at A_1 in Figure 4.3. By choosing an output $\hat{s}_1 > s_1^*$, it might be argued that firm 1 could force firm 2 to a less advantageous position on her best reply curve at $\hat{s}_2$. Were this to be an equilibrium, firm 1 would be better off than at C. However, since each duopolist must choose output *before* the other's is known, this will never be tried by rational players because firm 1 must expect firm 2 to choose s_2^* (after all, firm 1's choice cannot influence firm 2) and the best reply to that is s_1^*.[4] It is the fact that rational players can duplicate each other's reasoning, and not some unspecified dynamics, that gives power to the NE concept. This is most definitely not to say that dynamics are unimportant, or that a satisfactory dynamic process is not desirable to give the NE credence when players are not trained game theorists, but it is to claim a special position for NE in our analysis of game situations. Binmore and Dasgupta (1986) go as far as to argue it is the *only* rational solution for a non-cooperative game, though Bernheim (1985) and Pearce (1985) suggest that some alternative strategies are 'rationalisable' and so cannot be ignored.

What if firm 1 is able to announce his strategy before firm 2 decides what to do? Does this enable him to attain equilibrium at A_1? The answer depends, as with pre-play communication, on whether or not he can *commit* to $\hat{s}_1$ before 2 can make her decision. A simple announcement will be dismissed as a bluff by firm 2, and knowing this firm 1 will rationally react by reneging on his own announcement and going straight to the Cournot–Nash equilibrium. However, if firm 1 can somehow commit to $\hat{s}_1$, perhaps by signing contracts to supply $\hat{s}_1$ whatever the market price, then firm 2 is left with no option but to comply and produce her best reply of only $\hat{s}_2$. Note that we have not deviated from the Nash equilibrium concept. The rules of the game have changed so that we have sequential decision-making and credible commitment. The outcome in such circumstances is obviously different from the situation where the rules do not give one player an advantage, but the principle that each player adopts her best-reply strategy is maintained. Under the revised rules, A_1 is a NE; in fact, it is an example of a subgame perfect Nash equilibrium, a concept to which we now turn. But note well here that one of game theory's greatest virtues is that it imposes a considerable discipline on the economist to specify *exactly* the nature of the environment and other rules of the game before going on to say how individuals /firms /unions /governments /etc. should be expected to behave.

We earlier noted that there may exist multiple Nash equilibria. Some of these may be more 'reasonable' than others, and recently there has been much intellectual effort in trying to define the term 'reasonable' more explicitly. Consider Figure 4.4 which sets out a game in *normal (or strategic) form*. The normal form game often economises on the presentation of detailed strategies, and simply presents the ultimate pay-offs to all feasible strategy combinations without explicitly showing how actions lead to pay-offs. This particular game is called the entry game because it can be interpreted as player 1 contemplating entry into a monopolist's (player 2's) market. 1's set of feasible strategies is simply either to enter or else stay out. The monopolist can either fight entry with an expensive price war, or else acquiesce to a passive duopoly. The pay-offs, or profits, are given in the boxes. Note that as long as 1 stays out, 2's pricing competitiveness remains hypothetical so the pay-offs are not affected. To search for Nash equilibria, consider each strategy pair in turn: (enter, acquiesce) is a NE because if 1 enters, 2's best reply is

		Firm 2	
		acquiesce	fight
Firm 1	enter	3, 3	−5, −5
	stay out	0, 13	0, 13

FIGURE 4.4 Entry game in normal form

to acquiesce and if 2 acquiesces, 1's best reply is to enter; (enter, fight) is not a NE because fighting is not 2's best reply to entry, and a similar argument applies to (out, acquiesce); however, (out, fight) is another NE because staying out is the best reply to fighting and (threatened) fighting is a best reply to no entry.[5]

Closer examination of the entry game, however, suggests that the two Nash equilibria may not be equally plausible. This is brought out by studying a different presentation of the game, this time in *extensive form* such that the sequence of moves and the information available to each at the time of decision-making, are made explicit in the form of a *game tree*. Importantly, the extensive form explicitly introduces time into the model by specifying what information becomes available as the game progresses. *Decision nodes* are defined as points on the game tree at which one player or the other is able to make a move. Thus, in Figure 4.5 it is clear that 1 has the first move in deciding whether to enter or not (at node 1*a*), and only with this information available to him does 2 have to respond (from node 2*a* or node 2*b*). More formally, 2 is playing a proper *subgame* because he knows exactly where he is on the game tree (i.e. at 2*a* or 2*b*), and there are no subsequent decision nodes that might be confused with some other subgame. He must therefore choose his strategy on this basis. This is often called a *two-stage game* because it can be divided into two separate parts.

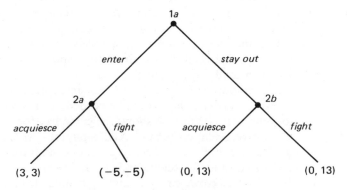

FIGURE 4.5   Entry game in extensive form

A *subgame perfect Nash equilibrium* (SPNE) rules out all potential equilibria that are not Nash equilibria in each subgame (Selten, 1965). All SPNE are NE, but not necessarily vice versa. In the present case, once 1 has entered, 2's best reply is acquiescence so 1 can predict 2's rational response and (enter, acquiesce) is a SPNE. However, (out, fight) is not a SPNE because player 1 would never choose to accept a pay-off of zero when she can earn three in the knowledge that it is not rational for the monopolist to fight once entry has actually occurred. Put another way, the threat to fight is not a *credible threat* in this game because it is never sensible to carry it out.

The reader should be able to convince herself that reversing the order of moves, with 2 able to commit before 1, leads to (threatened) fighting and entry deterrence being the sole SPNE. However, although in the abstract this is a logical possibility, the economist is often able to impose a plausible structure on the sequence of moves such that one model is more appropriate than another. In the present case, for instance, it seems unlikely that incumbents are able to commit to fighting before entry takes place; while a commitment to entry prior to the choice of price seems quite plausible.

Sometimes, the economist may wish to add more features to the model to make it a little more realistic. For instance, even though the incumbent is unable credibly to threaten a fight on the basis of the game shown in Figure 4.5, he may have the opportunity to take some prior action (e.g. investing in excess capacity) that *would* make the threat credible. This is known as *strategic behaviour* which Schelling (1960) defines as an action 'that influences the other person's choice [e.g. entry/stay out] in a manner favourable to one's self, by affecting the other person's expectations of how one's self will behave [e.g. acquiesce/fight]'. As Dixit (1980) shows, this notion can be captured formally by introducing a third, prior stage to the entry game and looking for a new SPNE. For instance, suppose 2 can invest in excess capacity that would be needed in the event of a fight, but not otherwise. Figure 4.6 shows the game tree for the case where the extra investment costs nine. All 2's pay-offs, except that to actual fighting, are thus reduced by nine. At first sight this might seem a pretty stupid thing for the incumbent to do since most pay-offs fall and none rise. However, the cunning behind this strategic behaviour is that 2's pay-off to fighting in the event of entry is now greater than his pay-off to acquiescence ($-5 > -6$). 1 now faces a

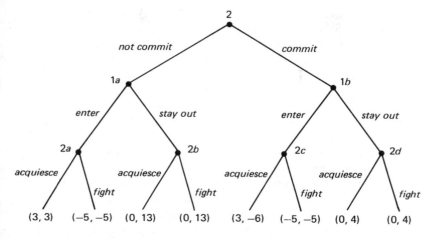

FIGURE 4.6   Pre-commitment in the entry game

credible threat and must expect a fight if she enters. She will therefore stay out (since $0 > -5$). Finally, moving back to the first stage of the game, 1 prefers to commit to the costly excess capacity because the pay-off to committed monopoly still exceeds that of duopoly which results from non-commitment ($4 > 3$). Thus (commit, stay out, threaten fight) is a SPNE for the three-stage game. Note the welfare costs of strategic behaviour in this context: monopoly pricing remains but social welfare is worse than in the absence of the entry threat because of the unproductive investment. (A simple, but deeper, treatment of a strategic behaviour by firms is given in Lyons, 1987a, and the welfare theme is picked up by Fudenberg and Tirole, 1987. An introduction to strategic behaviour by governments in the international arena of subsidies and tariff-setting can be found in Lyons, 1987b).

4.3   MICROECONOMIC APPLICATIONS OF NON-COOPERATIVE GAME THEORY

Simultaneous and sequential moves: the game theory of price competition

It is sometimes argued that in practice firms set prices not quantities as their strategic variables, and that this should be incorporated in oligopoly models. Although this presumption is far from empirically certain, we take it as true throughout this section.[6]

Suppose two duopolists can bottle any amount of homogeneous spring water at the same constant cost, c. Let the monopoly price be p_m. Suppose firm 2 charges a price $p_2 > p_m$, then firm 1's best reply is $p_1 = p_m$. Next suppose $c < p_2 \leqslant p_m$, then firm 1's best reply is to charge $p_1 = p_2 - e$ where e is very small but positive. In slightly undercutting firm 2, the entire market can be supplied whereas price-matching would necessitate less profitable market-sharing and any higher price would give zero market-share. If $p_2 \leqslant c$, then $p_1 = c$ is the best reply because any lower price would give negative returns. A similar analysis can be carried out for firm 2 and it is clear that $p_1 = p_2 = c$ is the unique (Bertrand–) Nash equilibrium. Notice that even with just two firms the market is fully competitive and no profits are earned. The best-reply curves are drawn in Figure 4.7, with the upward sloping parts being e away from the $p_1 = p_2$ line. Next suppose that costs differ such that $c_1 < c_2$. Similar reasoning gives the NE as $p_1 = c_2 - e$ and $p_2 = c_2$. Clearly firm 1 takes the whole market and makes positive profits. In terms of Figure 4.7, 2's best-reply curve becomes horizontal before 1's becomes vertical.

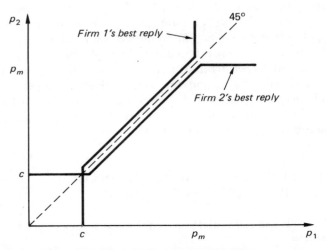

FIGURE 4.7   Bertrand–Nash duopoly with identical firms

Now, return to the case of equal and constant marginal costs, but assume that there is some small cost of entry, *f*. The competitive process can be modelled as a three-stage game with first firm 1 deciding whether or not to enter, then firm 2, and finally the Bertrand–Nash pricing game is played. With extensive form, non-cooperative, full information games, we have already argued that a reasonable NE should also be a NE in all its subgames. The pricing decision constitutes a proper subgame, as does this plus firm 2's entry decision, so we look for a SPNE. The game is set out in Figure 4.8.

Working backwards, which is the appropriate way to solve all such games, we first calculate the pay-offs to the pricing game conditional on there being either one, two or no firms that choose to enter. Let V_m be the profit due to monopoly pricing, and for duopoly we have already shown that price equals marginal cost so net profits are $-f$ each. It should be straightforward to see that a SPNE involves firm 1 entering and firm 2 staying out.[7] In such potentially hyper-competitive markets the explicit modelling of entry plus the addition of even a tiny overhead cost completely changes the simple model of price competition to give monopoly profits instead of none at all! This is a clear example of what is known as a *first mover advantage* because firm 1 earns high profits

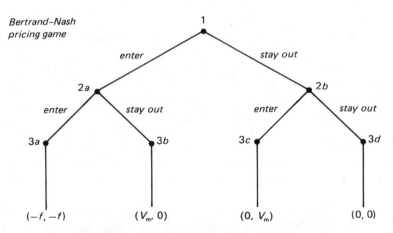

FIGURE 4.8   Bertrand competition with entry and fixed costs

simply because of the historical accident that he was given the first opportunity to enter the industry.

The public policy implications of this are discussed in Williamson (1987) and Dasgupta and Stiglitz (1988). Suppose the pricing game were changed such that the first firm to enter had by law to set a price that could not be altered, particularly *downwards*. If firm 2 decides to enter, then firm 1 would be forced to price competitively (at firm 2's potential average cost) in the first place. Failure to do so would induce entry at price $p_2 = p_1 - e$, so firm 1 would lose f. Paradoxically, then, a legal restraint on price cutting results in a more competitive market. This is an interesting and, on reflection, potentially important policy theme which also arises in a number of related game-theoretic models. For instance, an increasingly frequent strategy in retailing is to promise to match the price of any rival in the same town and this may discourage new entry.

Nevertheless, the hypersensitivity of the Bertrand model to the introduction of even a tiny fixed cost (the outcome switches from perfect competition to pure monopoly) contrasts with intuition and points to some fundamental misspecification of the pricing game. The implicit assumption so far has been that production follows the realisation of the pricing game. Once price has been determined, firms can produce however much they like. It turns out that if production takes place *before* the realisation of the pricing game, then the outcome is very different. Indeed, under certain quite strict but reasonable conditions, Cournot production levels will be chosen even when price competition is expected.

Before pursuing this line, however, it is necessary to investigate capacity-constrained Bertrand equilibria, a topic first tackled by Edgeworth, but which has only recently received rigorous treatment by game theorists. This example will also serve to introduce the idea of a *mixed strategy* equilibrium. For simplicity, assume a linear demand curve, DD' as in Figure 4.9. Furthermore, because a full analysis soon becomes very complex, we shall look only at symmetric situations with identical duopolists, each with capacity k. If $k \geqslant q_c$, where q_c is the competitive output, then there is no capacity constraint and the competitive Bertrand result goes through.

Next suppose $q_c > k > (1/3)q_c$. We assume throughout that if $p_1 = p_2$, then demand is shared equally between the two firms. If $p_1 > p_2$, then either firm 2 will be able to sell its entire capacity, leaving firm 1 with a residual demand, or if p_2 is too high firm 2 will be able to sell only part of her output and firm 1 will sell none. Assume the former case. It turns out to be very important exactly which units of demand firm 2 has satisfied. Two examples illustrate why. If 2 sells to the k units of demand that value the product most highly, then this leaves firm 1 with the residual demand curve dd' in Figure 4.9. In order to sell this entire capacity, it must be true that $p_2 \leqslant d$. Because the highest surplus units of demand have been satisfied, $p_1 > d$ would result in zero sales so for 1 to have positive sales we require $p_1 < d$. Alternatively, if firm 2 has sold its entire capacity to only the most marginal units of demand, this leaves firm 1 with the top of the DD' curve and some customers willing to pay as much as D. Thus the second allocation of customers, or rationing system, gives 2 higher expected sales at any chosen price. Having noted this range of possibilities, however, we proceed by analysing only the first rationing scheme (see Levitan and Shubik, 1972, for more detail on the alternatives).

Now consider 1's best reply to p_2 when $q_c > k > (1/3)q_c$. If $p_m \geqslant p_2 > d$ (i.e. 2 will not have sold her entire capacity), then for

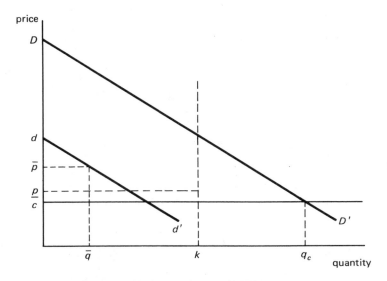

FIGURE 4.9 **Capacity-constrained price competition with $q_c > k > \frac{1}{3}q_c$**

familiar Bertrand reasons undercutting is the profit-maximising response, so the best reply is $p_1 = p_2 - e$. If $p_2 \leqslant d$, then undercutting may still be appropriate, but there will come a point, when $p_2 \leqslant \underline{p}$, where firm 1 can do better by raising price to $\bar{p}$, which is the 'monopoly' price for the residual demand curve. Although 1 will not then be producing to capacity, the profit earned from this strategy will be greater. $\bar{p}$ and the consequent demand $\bar{q}$ are given in the usual way by setting marginal residual revenue equal to marginal production cost, and $\underline{p}$ is defined by $(\underline{p} - c)k = (\bar{p} - c)\bar{q}$. Firm 1's best reply curve is drawn in Figure 4.10, as is that for firm 2 (drawn thinner) which is constructed in an identical manner.

A problem should be immediately apparent. Because of the discontinuities in the best-reply functions, they never actually cross. More formally, a Nash equilibrium in pure strategies does not exist because there is no pair of strategies (prices) for which 1's best reply to 2 is also 2's best reply to 1. For instance, suppose 2 chooses $\underline{p}$ and 1 chooses $\bar{p}$. 1 is making his best reply, but 2 could do better by choosing $\bar{p} - e$, in which case 1 should undercut, to which

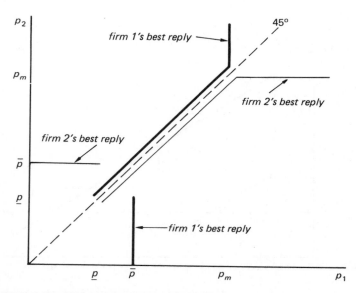

FIGURE 4.10   Discontinuous best-reply curves

2's best reply is to undercut and so on. No pure strategy equilibrium exists. The game theorist's answer to this problem of discontinuous games is to suggest a mixed strategy whereby each firm chooses prices according to a probabilistic formula; in this example it turns out that non-zero probabilities should be chosen to price over the range $[\underline{p}, \bar{p}]$. The essential idea is that if firm 2 is following the appropriate formula, it will leave firm 1 indifferent between choosing any price in the range. This constitutes an equilibrium from 1's point of view because it can do no better by taking unilateral action in choosing one particular price or mixture of prices. Note, however, that firm 1 must also adopt a mixed strategy so as to leave 2 indifferent, otherwise 2 could unilaterally improve her prospects by adjusting her probability formula. In terms of Figure 4.10, the effect of the mixed strategy is to bridge the discontinuity between the two parts of each firm's best-reply curve so that the two curves 'intersect'. Note that in a probabilistic sense, both firms will be operating with excess capacity because neither can expect to sell k *all* the time (even if the sum of capacities is less than q_c). Furthermore, even when the industry has capacity greater than the competitive level, price exceeds marginal cost (as long as $k < q_c$).

Mixed strategies can nearly always provide a Nash equilibrium in discontinuous games (see Dasgupta and Maskin, 1986, for a definitive treatment of the existence problem). Their use remains controversial to many economists, though others see mixed strategies as a natural extension of pure strategies and justify them in exactly the same ways as for any other NE.

If price competition is of the form just described, and if this constitutes the second stage of a game with a first stage in simultaneous output (or capacity) choice, then the outputs (or capacities) chosen will be exactly the same as in the simple case of Cournot quantity competition.

To see this, first suppose that all of marginal cost, c, is associated with capacity. In this case, although the *ex post* profits from the second stage will be different, the *ex ante* profits from the point of view of first stage decisions will be identical to those just described.[8] The first stage problem is to find the equilibrium in capacities in the light of the resulting price game. Again assume symmetric capacity choices. Suppose firm 2's capacity, $k_2 < (1/3)q_c$, then firm 1's best reply must be $k_1 > k_2$ because 1's residual demand curve leaves an expected marginal revenue greater than the marginal cost of capacity. Next suppose that $k_2 > (1/3)q_c$, then if $k_1 = k_2$ firm 1 will choose $p_1 > \underline{p}$ with positive probability and would generally have preferred a smaller capacity. So $k_1 = k_2 > (1/3)q_c$ cannot be a SPNE. Only if firm 2 chooses $k_2 = (1/3)q_c$, is 1's best reply to choose the same capacity. This is, therefore, the only symmetric equilibrium. It is also true to say that a different rationing mechanism or modified cost assumptions can substantially alter the neatness of this result (see Dixon, 1988). Nevertheless, the careful specification of the sequence of output and price decisions does serve to capture the notion that although firms do, in practice, tend to set prices and not auction off predetermined quantities (as is suggested implicitly by the Cournot model) the Cournot model does give intuitively plausible results (e.g. duopoly generates a price somewhere between monopoly and competition).

The purpose of this extensive treatment of price competition in homogeneous goods markets has been more than simply to provide a thorough exposition of one area to which game theory has contributed. It has also been to illustrate the complications which the theorist must confront once real time is introduced into a model. The extensive form of a game forces the theorist to specify exactly what players know at which point in the decision-making process and how it is reasonable for them to anticipate the actions of rivals. Technological considerations must also enter the model explicitly, for instance through capacity constraints. In the remainder of this section, the importance of explicitly modelling demand is similarly brought out. It is *because* game-theoretic reasoning complicates the problem by forcing us to be so explicit that it contributes so much to our understanding of real-world phenomena. The simple textbook model of optimisation in a single-period world ignoring sequential decision-making hides a wealth of important detail, as the distance we have travelled from simple Bertrand duopoly shows. (For further thoughts along these lines, see Fudenberg and Tirole, 1987.)

So far we have considered only homogeneous products. What difference does product differentiation make? At a general level, a price cut by one firm is no longer able to entice all a rival's customers away so the firm's perceived demand curve is no longer perfectly elastic at equal prices. This blunts the edge of price competition and duopolists can expect to earn positive profits even in the simplest Bertrand model. However, the same effect also blunts the prospective competition faced by entrants, so a larger number of firms may enter the market even when there are economies of scale. Chamberlin (1933) christened this sort of market monopolistically competitive as long as it was large so that it could support numerous firms. Game theorists have recently challenged the basis for this conclusion, proving that not all 'large' differentiated markets can support numerous firms even when scale economies are slight. One consequence is that it is dangerous to *assume* that zero profits will be earned in equilibrium (see for instance Shaked and Sutton 1982, 1983, 1984, 1987).

Infinitely repeated games: non-cooperative collusion

Consider again the prisoners' dilemma game. In Figure 4.1 substitute 'collude' for 'deny' and 'cheat' for 'confess'. The only Nash equilibrium in this one-shot game (i.e. played only once) is if both play b. However, note that each could be better off if they could somehow agree to both play a. More formally, the strategy pair (a_1, a_2) Pareto-dominates the Nash equilibrium (b_1, b_2). One way to reach the Pareto-optimal solution would be if binding agreements could be signed. However, here we assume that this option is not possible, perhaps because it is illegal. Instead, we investigate simple intertemporal strategies that can sustain the cooperative outcome in infinitely repeated games without resort to binding agreements.

The essential idea is captured by a *trigger strategy* whereby player 1 chooses a_1 until player 2 chooses b_2, after which a_1 is played for ever (Friedman, 1977). If there is no discounting, this strategy clearly pays because the one-period gain to 'cheating' on the a strategy is $8 - 5 = 3$, which must be compared with the loss thereafter of $5 - 3 = 2$ in each subsequent period when collusion has collapsed. That the trigger strategy is a subgame perfect Nash equilibrium is confirmed as usual by examining best replies. Consider player 1. If 2 chooses a_2 and this is expected to be part of her trigger strategy, then a_1 is the best reply because an infinite stream of pay-offs of 5 is better than a stream of pay-offs of 30. If 2 chooses b_2, then the best 1 can do from then on is to trigger the threat and play b_1. Identical arguments give player 2's best replies. The same proof can be applied at any point in time because infinitely repeated games always look the same, whatever the period. The threat implied by the trigger is credible (i.e. subgame perfect) because it is in each player's own best interests actually to trigger the 'punishment' b; and each player can implicitly collude by always choosing a, because this pays more than triggering the punishment.[9] Note that although verbal pre-play communication to agree on the trigger strategy is not necessary in the strict theoretical sense for non-cooperative collusion to exist, such discussions make the result much more plausible.

Three strong assumptions have been made to get this result. First, the time horizon is infinite; second, players can observe each other's actions with certainty (possibly by their effect on own payoffs); and third, there is no discounting of future pay-offs. Let us consider these in reverse order.

Suppose future returns in period t are discounted by a factor $d^t < 1$. The conventional interpretation is $d = 1/(1 + r)$, where r is the interest rate. However, the effect is identical if there is no time discounting but it is expected that the infinitely repeated game will not, in fact, be definitely infinite and may end in any period with constant probability $(1 - d)$. Either way, with discounting the gains from 'cheating' on implicit collusion now are weighted more highly than the gains from continued collusion in the future. Abiding by 'collude' forever pays $5 + d5 + d^2 5 + \ldots = 5/(1 - d)$, while 'cheating' pays at best $8 + d3 + d^2 3 + d^3 3 + \ldots = 8 - 3 + 3/(1 - d)$; so cheating will not pay as long as $5/(1 - d) > 5 + 3/(1 - d)$, which simplifies to $d > 0.6$.[10]

Recently, Abreu (1986) has argued that trigger strategies are unnecessarily restrictive in that they rely on perpetual reversion to the single-period NE. It will often be the case that a worse punishment can be invoked and this can be used to sustain a greater degree of cooperation. For instance, suppose an option c is introduced as in Figure 4.11. Abreu is able to prove the virtues of a 'stick and carrot' strategy which, for player 1, is as follows: choose a_1 until 2 plays b_2, then play c_1 until 2 plays c_2, after which 2 is rewarded for cooperating in her punishment by playing a_1. We show that this can lead to the cooperative outcome for a wider range of discount factors than does simple trigger, and that it is a SPNE even though (c_1, c_2) is not a NE in the one-shot game. Indeed, c is a dominated strategy for both players. First, the threat of c_1 means that the cooperative pay-off exceeds the return to cheating and cooperating in one's own punishment as long as:

		Player 2		
		'carrot'		'stick'
		a_2	b_2	c_2
'carrot'	a_1	5, 5	0, 8	0, 0
Player 1	b_1	8, 0	3, 3	2, 0
'stick'	c_1	0, 0	0, 2	−1, −1

FIGURE 4.11 Stick and carrot

$$5 + d5 + d^25 + d^35 + \ldots > 8 - d1 + d^25 + d^35 \ldots$$

which implies the gain from cheating now is less than the discounted value of the punishment if, $d(5 + 1) > 8 - 5$ or $d > 0.5$. Second, it is worth cooperating in one's own punishment rather than cheating for two periods before cooperating as long as:

$$8 - d1 + d^25 + d^35 \ldots > 8 + d2 + d^21 + d^35 + \ldots$$

which implies that the gain from immediate remorse exceeds that of one-period recalcitrance if, $d(5 + 1) > 2 + 1$ or $d > 0.5$.[11] Thus, in the repeated game where the carrot can follow the stick, it is credible to threaten to wield the stick, and compliance is the best reply to the stick being used. It is straightforward to further compare the costs and benefits of postponing the end of the punishment period even longer and show that this does not alter the constraints on d. Thus, more sophisticated two-phase punishments which combine a harsher present with a rosier future, are more effective at sustaining non-cooperative collusion than is the single-phase trigger strategy. In a game which permits a wider choice of Pareto-superior strategies which are not single-period NE – for instance, output choice in Cournot duopoly – the 'stick and carrot' permits a higher pay-off (i.e. combined output nearer the monopoly level) to be sustained for any given d. Furthermore, Abreau is able to demonstrate that in many cases not only is the 'stick and carrot' very effective, it is also the best that can ever be done in a non-cooperative environment.[12]

Finitely repeated games: multiple equilibria, bounded rationality and reputation

It might be thought that games which are repeated a very large but finite number of times should exhibit equilibrium characteristics very similar to those just studied with infinite repetition. However, this turns out not to be true. We begin by introducing the 'backward induction paradox' for finitely repeated games.

Suppose the prisoners' dilemma game in Figure 4.1 is to be played 100 times by the same two players. Could something like a trigger strategy sustain collusion? The answer is no. A finitely repeated game is a special type of extensive form, so as before we search for a subgame perfect Nash equilibrium by first considering the final play of the game. Clearly neither player has any incentive to play a because there is no future gain to inducing further collusion; so they will each play the one-shot Nash strategies (b_1, b_2). Next consider period 99. Each player knows that non-collusive choices will be made in period 100, so once more there is nothing to be gained from collusion in period 99. One-shot Nash actions in period 99 similarly mean that they will be optimal in period 98 and so in 97 and so on until period 1. Consequently, trigger strategies are not best replies to each other and they are not sub-game perfect in finitely repeated games. Notice that this backward induction argument is independent of the discount rate, and it can be applied to all conceivable punishment strategies (e.g. 'stick and carrot', or 'tit for tat' which is discussed below). It can also be applied whenever there is some finite date, however large, by which time the game will *certainly* have finished. For instance, if we and our descendants know for certain that the world will end in a trillion years, then unless we anticipate living on another planet, all games must be logically finite. However, if we believe that there is a small chance that the world will go on for ever, even though with probability $(1 - d)$ it will self-destruct in any one year, we can apply our earlier arguments for infinite supergames.[13] The critical point to grasp is that backward induction cannot be applied if the game always looks the same at each point in time, as it does with inifinite repetition or a constant probability of ending; but it must take hold if an end-date is certain. This can be deemed a paradox for two main reasons. First, because the discontinuity in the logic behind very large numbers of repetitions and infinite repeats goes against intuition. Second, because experimental evidence suggests that collusion does emerge in the repeated prisoners' dilemma even when participants are sure that the experiment will not keep them playing for ever! We investigate three ways in which the *backward induction paradox* can be eliminated.

One way to break out of the paradox for finitely repeated games, and reinstate the possibility of non-cooperative collusion, is if there are multiple Nash equilibria in the one-shot game (Friedman, 1985). Consider the example in Figure 4.12 where both (b_1, b_2) and (d_1, d_2) are NE. Suppose the trigger strategy is to play a until the other ceases to play a, whereafter play d. The threat to play d is credible because with multiple NE, there is no reason to expect one to transpire rather than another. Even if the game is repeated only twice (and bearing in mind that no one will collude in the last period), it is better for player 1 to play a_1 in the first period and b_1 in the second, rather than 'cheat' straight away by playing b_1 then have to play d_1 in the last period as long as $5 + d_3 > 8 - d_1$ or $d > 0.75$. With more than one repetition, of course, collusion becomes even more sustainable. Benoit and Krishna (1987) extend this line of reasoning to the application of optimal 'stick and carrot' disciplines to demonstrate that as long as there are multiple

Player 2

		a_2	b_2	d_2
	a_1	5, 5	0, 8	−2, −2
Player 1	b_1	8, 0	3, 3	−2, −2
	d_1	−2, −2	−2, −2	−1, −1

FIGURE 4.12   Multiple Nash equilibria in the one-shot (stage) game

Nash equilibria, finitely repeated games generate results almost identical to the infinite supergame as long as the number of repetitions is large.

The second way around the backward induction paradox is to appeal to 'bounded rationality'. Radner (1986) defines an (epsilon) ε-best reply to be any strategy that pays within $\varepsilon \geqslant 0$ of the true best reply. An ε-equilibrium is then such that each player is making an ε-best reply. Suppose, for simplicity, that there is no discounting in the game in Figure 4.1 which is repeated T times. The pay-off to abiding by the trigger strategy when there are still t periods to go is $0 + 3(t - 1)$ if your rival cheats. The pay-off to cheating is at best $8 + 3(t - 1)$. Thus, cheating gains 8 or, in per period average terms, the gain is $8/t$. Now if players are interested in making ε-best replies of average pay-offs, collusion is sustainable as long as $\varepsilon > 8/t$. For instance, if $T = 100$ and $\varepsilon = 1$, collusion can be sustained for the first 92 periods but will collapse in the last eight. Although it is clearly very interesting to try to introduce bounded rationality into game theory, it is questionable that this is the best way to go about it. First, as Friedman (1986) points out, it might be just as reasonable to assume that players with bounded rationality can only calculate for a small number of periods ahead. In that case, games become even more finite and the backward induction becomes even more forceful. Second, we can question why players do not fully optimise. If this is because of calculation costs then these should be explicitly modelled. Although this might be rather complex, developments along such lines could lead to a better idea of whether ε-best replies or truncated time-horizons or some other approximation is the most appropriate stylisation of bounded rationality in any particular situation.

The third way of attacking the backward induction paradox is the one which has received most attention in recent years. It involves changing one of the most fundamental cornerstones of the game theory discussed so far (and arguably this makes it one of the most exciting developments in game theory since the war), namely the common knowledge assumption. Even a very small amount of *asymmetric information* can significantly alter the equilibrium in repeated games (and, more generally, in extensive form games).

Consider the repetition of the game in Figure 4.1 T times. Player 1 is perfectly rational, but suppose player 2 *might* be 'irrational' in the sense that she fails to appreciate the backward induction argument and insists on playing trigger. Player 2 knows her own true character, but player 1 can only guess, at the beginning of the game, that 2 is rational with probability $(1 - p)$ and trigger with probability p. One might think that this asymmetric information game could be analysed fairly simply by calculating expected profits and proceeding as before. However, two interesting twists are immediately introduced. First, if player 1 is able to observe 2's play as the game unravels, he will pick up new information with which to revise his prior assessment of 2's true nature. Second, if player 2 is in fact rational, she will appreciate 1's ability to learn and may find it pays to bluff and act as if she were indeed a trigger strategist. Of course, 1 will appreciate 2's incentive to dissemble and build this into his expectations, etc. Straightforward application of NE or SPNE is unable to cope adequately with these possibilities, but a variant of subgame perfection known as *sequential equilibrium* (Kreps and Wilson, 1982b) has been developed as an appropriate and natural extension of games in which information is held asymmetrically. The essential insight gained from the formal game theory of asymmetric information games is that even a very small probability, p, is rapidly magnified by repeating the game, such that the incentives to cheat change and, at least for early plays of the game, the backward induction paradox disappears.

Unfortunately, asymmetric information models are very difficult to solve. One way to look at the asymmetric information model is to see it as a way in which reputation can be built. In the prisoners' dilemma game, the reputation is for irrational behaviour (or low pay-offs to cheating). The idea of reputation building can be seen even more clearly in a game known as the 'chain-store paradox', which is a finite repetition of the extensive-form game illustrated in Figure 4.5. Recall that an entrant must decide whether to enter before the incumbent can commit to fighting. The only SPNE is for entry and no fighting because once entry has taken place the incumbent's best reply is to acquiesce. Fighting is an empty threat. Selten (1978) considers the finite repetition of this game and calls it the *chain-store paradox* because he uses the example of a chain-store which has a monopoly in N different towns and entry is threatened in each sequentially, one after the other. The threat to fight early entrants with a view to building a reputation for aggression cannot be part of an equilibrium strategy because of the familiar backward induction argument. In the last town to be threatened, the chain-store will always concede as in the one-off game. Thus, in the town before that it will have no reason to build a reputation and so must acquiesce, and so on. Once again, we encounter the paradox that no matter how many shops are owned by the chain-store, it cannot logically fight early entry in order to build a reputation for aggression and so deter later entrants. Milgrom and Roberts (1982) show that as long as there is a slight possibility that the incumbent is following a simple ('irrational') behavioural rule of 'fight all entry', then entry can be dissuaded. Initially, there may be entry to test the incumbent's mentality. If he concedes, then entry will continue in all markets. But if there is a fight, further entry can be dissuaded at least until the number of towns into which there may be entry becomes small, when entrants may further test the resolve of the monopolist (who will eventually concede if rational).

4.4   BARGAINING AND CONFLICT

Introduction to bargaining theory

Two important questions in games where binding contracts are feasible are:

(i) Assuming we know the characteristics of each bargainer, is there a way of predicting the outcome?
(ii) Moreover, have we anything to say about the occurrence of conflict?

At this point we must define our terms. Antagonism does not automatically lead to open conflict. From now on, the term conflict will be reserved for the 'deadweight' loss, active-fight (e.g. wars, strikes, etc.) type of confrontation while conflict of interest will be referred to as antithesis.

Our two fundamental questions cannot be answered in isolation from each other. A complete theory of bargaining must predict both outcome *and* the peaceful or conflictual means by which it is achieved. A lot depends on the analyst's perception of what is rational.

Consider a simple game called the 'race to twenty'. A fair coin is tossed to decide who plays first. The first player says either '1' or '1, 2'. The second responds with either one or two consecutive integers (e.g. '3' or '3, 4'); then the first player continues the same way. The player who says '20' first, wins £2. If you were invited to pay a fee in order to play 'race to twenty' against an unknown opponent, how much should you be prepared to pay? The answer depends on your probability assessment of winning (p) as well as your risk-aversion. The expected pay-off from the game being $2p - x$ where x is the entry fee, it is not surprising that the more optimistic you are about your chances, the higher your valuation of the right to play. A game theorist would however quickly point out that $p = \frac{1}{2}$ and, therefore, the maximum fee consistent with non-negative returns – as well as risk-neutrality – is £1. The logic is straightforward: if you start first, there is no way you will lose. By saying '1,2' you can get to 5,8,11,14,17 and 20 first whatever strategy your opponent chooses to follow. So provided that both players are aware of this strategy, the game is decided by the initial tossing of the coin: whoever starts will win. Game-theoretic analyses of human interaction begin by assuming that agents are capable of inferring from 'perfect information' environments the dominant strategies for a win. In exactly the same way that 'rational' players can in the 'race to twenty' foresee the outcome and choose to end the game after the tossing of the coin, any two individuals with conflicting interests and perfect information can predict the future of any possible strategy. It would thus make very little sense for such well-informed and intelligent beings to allow confrontation to evolve into costly conflict since they can foresee the outcome of any 'fight' and would prefer to reach it without having to suffer the costs associated with conflict. Models along these lines assuming peaceful resolutions, and thus strict Pareto-efficiency, have dominated early game theory. In this section we discuss these as well as sequential games with and without perfect information while retaining neoclassical rationality postulates. The built-in hyper-rationality of such models inevitably leads to the conclusion that antithesis will invariably lead to a non-conflict outcome. The frequent emergence of conflict in the real world can then only be explained, within the game-theoretic paradigm, by unpredictable mistakes. But conflict often does seem to be predictable, for instance industrial disputes do not appear to be random, and this has led to discontent with the assumption of hyperrationality. We will also therefore illustrate two simple models of bargaining where disagreement leads to conflict as a result of bounded rationality, and outline an alternative approach suggesting that even with full rationality, costly confrontation can result if information is held asymmetrically and the game is finitely repeated. Finally we will discuss the normative implications of game theory and attempt to link it with a more general debate on the nature of human interaction.

The division game

Two relatives inherit a sum of money S although the Will does not specify how it should be divided. What it does specify is that, unless agreement on a division is reached, each gets nothing. Nash (1950) proposed a devastatingly simple distribution theory which predicts that the two sides will agree to the division which maximises the products of their utility gains. The solution follows from certain axioms that Nash regards as 'fair' and 'reasonable' conditions to be fulfilled when bargainers are rational. He first adopts von Neumann and Morgenstern's utility theory as an illustration of his conception of rationality. Briefly, this asserts that a person's preference between a certain pay-off and a given lottery is always consistent with the assumption of expected utility maximisation. In particular, a person has a neutral attitude towards risk if she is indifferent between a gift of value g with probability p and a gift of value $p.g$ with certainty. The second axiom on which the Nash solution depends is that of Pareto-efficiency. A distribution is said to be Pareto-optimal if it places the parties at some point on their utility frontier, which is defined as the locus where, for any given utility of one person, the other's utility is a maximum. In other words, Nash requires that the heirs avoid the 'threat point' (i.e. zero pay-offs to both) by agreeing on a settlement consisting of two shares whose sum equals S. Having assumed that an optimal division will be reached, Nash proposes three critical axioms which uniquely lead to the Nash solution:

(a) *Symmetry axiom.*   Utilities are set equal to zero at the threat point and are positive on the frontier [see Figure 4.13a]. If the frontier is symmetric with respect to the line $u_1 = u_2$, the solution will lie on that line (i.e. it will be given by point N);

(b) *Transformation invariance.* Suppose that we decide to alter the dimensions of Figure 4.13a without changing the underlying pay-offs, e.g. by doubling the magnitude of u_2 while we retain the same magnitude for u_1. Nash's second axiom is meant to preserve the original solution when transformations of this sort take place. It implies that if the midpoint of a linear utility frontier with slope -1 is the solution (Figure 4.13a) so is the midpoint of any other linear frontier (Figure 4.13b);

(c) *Independence of irrelevant alternatives.* While the previous axiom deals with linear transformations of the frontier, an additional axiom is needed to cover transitions from linear to non-linear frontiers. Consider the concave frontier in Figure 4.13c which is dominated by the original linear one everywhere except at the latter's solution point. The new frontier denies bargainers choices that they would not have made even if they were available. Nash suggests that their removal is not going to affect the outcome.

The appeal of Nash's solution stems from the incompatibility of any other solution with the above axioms/conditions. They are sufficient to establish that the Nash point N always occurs at a division maximising $u_1.u_2$.

Is the nature of Nash's solution descriptive, and thus positive, or prescriptive? Should we expect the inheritance to be split according to the utility–product maximisation rule, or should such a solution be forced upon the two relatives if they fail to agree? Luce and Raiffa (1957) argue that since any distribution theory depends on both sides behaving in accordance with it, and in view of possible rationality bounds, bargainers would seldom converge to the theoretical solution unaided; the theory should instead be utilised as a means of setting up guidelines for 'fair' arbitration.[14] The debate on the normative implications of Nash's theory, and indeed of game theory as a whole, is interlinked with issues of rationality and its dependence on the social-physical environment in which 'games' evolve. For the purposes of the present discussion it suffices to point out that whatever the normative implications of Nash's solution, it is only 'fair' and 'reasonable' in the context of relative advantage considerations, with no place for considerations of 'right' and 'wrong'.

Returning to our two relatives, suppose that one of them is suffering from decreasing marginal utility – i.e. she is in such great

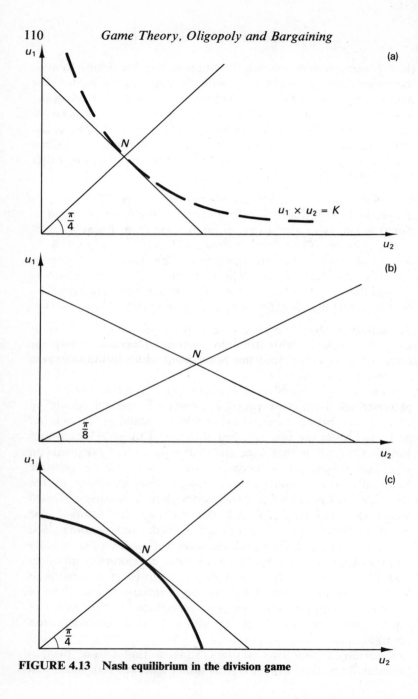

FIGURE 4.13   Nash equilibrium in the division game

need of money that failure to make a small gain is terribly painful as compared with a failure to make an even greater gain. If the second relative is reasonably affluent with constant marginal utility – or even a gambler with increasing marginal utility – the abitrator who follows the Nash script will award most of the inheritance to the one who needs it less. Nash's theorem is essentially an intuitive result based on the idea that the more risk-loving a player, the higher the pay-off. As such, it is vulnerable to the criticism that imposing penalties on risk-aversion is not compatible with the assumption of perfect rationality since it would pay an intelligent player to pretend to be risk-loving. Nash's solution partially overcomes this criticism thanks to the assumption of perfect information about each other's utility functions. It does, however, point to possible benefits from self-persuasion: since the most desirable attribute seems to be a love for risk, it would be wise to take courses in throwing caution to the wind or, alternatively, to practise self-deception prior to the bargaining session. Objections to Nash's theory are not confined to the importance of exogenously given patterns of risk-taking. In particular there is widespread scepticism about the relevance of the proposed solution in view of the restrictiveness of axioms on which it relies.

Axiomatic approaches attempt to sidestep the issue of how bargains are actually reached by examining the properties of outcomes with only passing reference to the process which leads to them (see Nash (1950), Luce and Raiffa (1957) and Braithwaite (1956). In doing so, they fail to describe the important process by which players move from disagreement to concession and, finally, agreement. Two decades before Nash, Zeuthen (1930) had presented a solution to the division game which was geared towards explaining exactly this process. In an attempt to model convergence by considering the realistic uncertainties involved in bargaining, Zeuthen claimed that the one overriding characteristic of the final outcome is that, at the point of agreement, both sides are equally fearful of disagreement.[15] Having received an offer from player *B*, Zeuthen argues that *A* will deliberate between accepting it and holding out by making a counter-offer which may be accepted, or rejected, by *B*.[16] Zeuthen then asks 'What is the maximum subjective probability of conflict that *A* will consider as reasonable and reject *B*'s offer?' The answer is 'the level of probability that will make *A* indifferent between capitulating or persisting'. The motivation that forces bargainers to concede is the fear that if they are too persistant the other side will choose the threat point – i.e. conflict in the form of a strike in the collective bargaining example or no agreement in the inheritance game. Zeuthen then postulates that the party whose 'acceptable' subjective probability of conflict is lower will be forced to concede first that it will be just sufficient to motivate her opponent to concede. Hence, the process of convergence. An obvious disadvantage of Zeuthen's bargaining process is that in computing their subjective probabilities of conflict, bargainers irrationally assume that at every stage of the game they are faced with an all-or-nothing situation when clearly this is not the case. The implicit assumption here is that, during every stage, bargainers behave as if their opponents are either going to agree or head for the threat point. Bargainers are thus assumed to be myopic since their expectations are incompatible with the reality of disagreement often giving way, not to conflict, but to concessions. Despite this problem, however, it is interesting to compare the spirit of Zeuthen's solution with that of Nash. Intuitively they both seem to be telling the same story: the side which is more risk-averse will concede first (Zeuthen), or more (Nash), and there will be no actual conflict. Such coincidence of form and content is not accidental. In a notable proof, Harsanyi (1961) shows that, once von Neumann – Morgenstern utility functions are adopted, the two models generate the same solution: that which maximises the product of the parties' utility gains. The non-existence of conflict in the Nash–Zeuthen–Harsanyi (N–Z–H) solution is due to the ex-ante strict Pareto-optimality assumption rather than ex-post deduction. By defining rationality to be incompatible with conflict, cooperation emerges as the only optimal outcome of confrontation. If, however, one seeks a theory of conflict one should not attempt to read more into N–Z–H than it contains. Hicks (1932) had come to the same conclusion: if bargainers are well-informed about each other's preferences, then rationality is incompatible with conflict. The logic behind this argument is indestructible: perfect information coupled with hyperrationality should make agents capable of predicting the course of the dispute–strike–war. So when conflict does emerge it is 'doubtless the result of faulty negotiation' (Hicks, 1932, p. 146). Hicks's own theoretical contribution was the well-known 'scissors diagram' depicting the two sides' concession schedules as a function of the duration of the dispute.

Sequential bargaining

Although Harsanyi's restatement of Zeuthen's sequential model confirms the Nash prediction about the final division, it is not clear whether agreement is going to be instantaneous or delayed. The reason behind this vagueness is that in the N–Z–H model there is only one type of waste: conflict. As long as conflict is averted, it does not matter whether convergence takes time. In an influential paper, Rubinstein (1982) explicitly introduced costs to the process of bargaining. The derivation of Rubinstein's SPNE requires a slight amendment of the Will. The heirs are told that a series of meetings has been arranged for them in which they are expected to reach a compromise if unable to agree a division immediately. However, the Will specifies that for every meeting that is broken off without a settlement a portion of the inheritance is donated to a charity – i.e. the final share of each is multiplied by a 'discount rate' $\delta < 1$ and n indicates the number of meetings needed for an agreement. To enhance the generality of the analysis, it is useful to allow for different discount rates for the two parties (δ_1, δ_2) (by, for example, assuming that each heir's donation on the aftermath of an unsuccessful meeting should be proportional to her income). Rubinstein's SPNE requires that strategies within every bargaining round are also Nash equilibria (i.e. bargainers do not suffer from Zeuthenian myopia) and predicts immediate agreement with shares

$$\frac{1 - \delta_2}{1 - \delta_1 \delta_2}, \quad \frac{\delta_2(1 - \delta_1)}{1 - \delta_1 \delta_2}$$

for A and B respectively (see Shaked and Sutton, 1984, for a proof).

The evolution of the game cannot be simpler: A demands an amount corresponding to the PE and B accepts any demand which does not exceed this amount. Predictably, the more impatient a player the smaller her share. Notice, however, that there is an unambiguous first-mover advantage (e.g. when $\delta_1 = \delta_2 = \delta$ A receives $(1 - \delta)^2 / 1 - \delta^2$ more than B). This imbalance disappears in the ex-ante sense if a coin is tossed to determine who starts first (see Binmore, 1987). The first-mover advantage also fades to zero, ex-post, as time delay between the two rounds vanishes. Letting the length of time between rounds tend to zero leads, in the limit, to equal shares for both sides (see Sutton, 1986, p. 710). The powerful implications of the SPNE can be illustrated by means of the so-called 'outside option' (see Sutton, Shaked and Binmore, 1986).

Suppose that when B rejects A's offer, a random event may take place which would give B the option of receiving a fixed sum and leaving, thus ending A's hopes of a share of the inheritance. Nash's theory would predict that the effect of the availability of this option would be to shift the 'threat point' in B's favour (i.e. the threat point would no longer mean a zero pay-off for B). An application of Rubinstein's SPNE, however, reveals that there are two possibilities: either B's outside option exceeds the expected pay-off from the original game or it does not. In the first case A's position is indeed worsened, whereas in the second, B's threat of taking the outside option is an empty one. It is thus clear that the 'threat point' will not always shift.[17]

The sequential nature of Rubinstein's analysis is rather academic as far as a theory of conflict is concerned because his framework is incompatible with disagreement. Indeed, although an infinite number of potential stages is allowed, no dynamics ever develop as rational agreement is immediate and the potential costs of delay between stages only affect the size of the respective shares.

In spite of the analytical contribution of perfect equilibria, we are still left without a rationalisation of conflict. Could it be, however, that relaxing the assumption of common knowledge will generate 'optimal' levels of conflict serving the purpose of information-gathering? Suppose, for example, that the size of the inheritance (S) to be divided is only known with certainty by A. B will then formulate a first-period offer that A should accept only if S is large. B's strategy is optimal since she would like as large a share as possible. A, however, can only credibly inform B of the real value of S by either accepting B's offer – in which case it is revealed that S is large – or rejecting it and thus persuading B that S is small by incurring the cost of disagreement (i.e. the price of conflict). Hence conflict may be optimal for at least some of the time.[18] The prospect of a rationalisation of conflict along these lines has naturally

generated a lot of interest and the asymmetric information literature has recently proliferated.

The basic story is as follows. There are a buyer and a seller of a
commodity whose value to the seller is known to be zero; the
buyer's valuation is private information. In each period the seller
announces a price and the buyer accepts or rejects it. Rejection
leads to one period of costly conflict (such as a strike if the seller is
the union and the buyer the firm) which may come to an end in the
next bargaining round. The seller's assessment of the buyer's true
valuation is updated every time an offer is rejected according to
Bayes's rule. It is shown that if the seller's beliefs are consistent
with Bayes's rule and the strategies of the two players at every stage
of the game's history satisfy the condition of subgame perfection,
the final solution will be a sequential equilibrium (see Kreps and
Wilson, 1982b). Put simply, a sequential equilibrium can be
described as follows: there is limited information on what your
opponent's preferences are and therefore at every stage of the game
you act fully rationally and you base your strategy on what
information can be deduced from the opposition's actions. The
only reason why the sequential equilibrium does not collapse to a
perfect equilibrium without conflict is because there is imperfect
information.

The restrictive requirement of asymmetry – where one side is
well-informed while the other is in the dark – has recently been
addressed by Crampton (1984), Gul, Sonnenschein and Wilson
(1985) and Chatterjee and Samuelson (1987). Two-sided uncertainty is introduced by allowing each side to be one of two possible
types (strong/weak or high/low valuation). However, the problem
here is that equilibrium solutions are susceptible to variations in
what is generally referred to as 'out of equilibrium beliefs'. The
equilibrium price predicted by the analysis as the eventual point of
agreement, will be dependent on how one bargainer interprets
messages that might be received even if they are not the type of
messages that would be in anybody's interest to send. Consequently, there is a plethora of equilibria – multiple equilibria –
each one of them associated with how the analyst expects bargainers to respond to signals (offers) that will never be sent.[19]

Despite such problems, it does appear that the introduction of
imperfect information has at long last produced a theory of

conflict between rational agents. Unfortunately, such hopes are quickly dashed once we perform the following mental exercise: if, in any imperfect information model, we let the time-period between bargaining rounds go to zero then the duration of optimal conflict also goes to zero and our conflict theory disappears (see Gul and Sonnenschein, 1985). So, if bargaining is allowed to be continuous, then once more rationality is shown to be incompatible with conflict.[20]

An alternative possibility of salvaging a theory of impasse from imperfect information models is by adopting Crawford's (1982) adaptation of Schelling's (1960) commitment theory. Suppose that there are two stages to every bargain: during the first, bargainers decide on whether they will attempt commitment, while in the second they find out the cost of backing down. Three possibilities exist: if both parties commit there is conflict; if only one side commits, it receives increased pay-offs; finally, if both choose not to commit there is immediate agreement with a solution resembling that of Nash. This type of imperfect information model preserves a positive probability of conflict by offering a rationale for the delay between periods. However, it does not explain what determines the duration of the commitment stage and therefore is again reduced to a non-theory of conflict once agents are allowed to make such decisions instantaneously (see Admarti and Perry, 1985).

In conclusion, it seems to be impossible to reconcile hyperrationality with wasteful conflict unless we are prepared to introduce exogenous restrictions to the process of bargaining. It would, however, be foolish to be surprised by this finding. Just as the 'race to twenty' will not be played if there is full rationality, hyperrational agents will never 'fight it out' provided that there are only two of them; they have nothing to learn about themselves from fighting and, there is no fixed time-horizon. Under such circumstances, it would be paradoxical if a fully rational theory of conflict were possible. If it were, rational agents would have had access to it and would be in a position to use it in order to predict the final outcome in which case there would be no need for conflict.

Bounded rationality models

The problem with these game-theoretic analyses of conflict then, is that they assume away the phenomenon they are supposed to be examining. One possible way out is to discard neoclassical hyper-rationality, and recognise limitations on our own rationality. Even the smallest step away from hyperrationality, for instance some small uncertainty by rational agents concerning everyone else's rationality, can lead to major deviations from the equilibrium strategies of conventional game theory. Indeed, such uncertainty is synonymous with realistic interaction. Milgrom and Roberts (1982, 1987) argue that 'since one doubts that everyone is always certain that everyone else is super-rational and, more generally, that the model of the world they are using is absolutely accurate ... the study of how reasonable forms of bounded rationality affect the sensitivity of models assuming hyperrationality seems especially important' (Milgrom and Roberts, 1987, p. 190).

Ashenfelter and Johnson (1969) take a step along the path of bounded rationality in the context of a static marginalist model. They present a model of union–firm bargaining where a fully rational employer interacts with a myopic union. The firm max-imises an intertemporal objective function and, in deciding to settle immediately or 'take' a strike, balances the short-term costs of conflict against the long-term benefits of a reduced wage bill (reduced in comparison to what it would have been in the case of immediate settlement). Why is there conflict in this model? The reason is that there is nothing that can deflate labour's demand apart from a strike. Therefore, the decision by the employer to provoke conflict is no more than an investment decision. The model is of a one-sided bounded rationality nature. The union resists mechanically without even observing the firm's strategy while the hyperrational employer chooses the strike duration which maximises the firm's present value. Similar models have been presented by Johnston (1972) and Siebert, Bertrand and Addison (1985) (in which the union maximises an objective func-tion while the firm resists mechanically) and some of them have been empirically tested (for a survey see Sapsford and Tzannatos 1989). Because of their uncomplicated determinism, one-sided optimisation models of conflict have been received sceptically. A cynic would go as far as to argue that they purport to explain conflict by excluding actual bargaining from the analysis. Although it is true that bargaining does take a back seat, marginal-ist models can be shown to be more interesting than is generally recognised.

Consider, for example, the dynamic model of Cross (1969). A seller and a buyer bargain about the price of a commodity. Both incur bargaining costs proportional to the delay in reaching an agreement. Once an opening offer is reciprocated by an initial demand, each bargainer forms estimates of how long she will need to hold out for the other side to pay/accept the initial offer/demand. The formation of these estimates is equivalent to predicting each other's speed of concession. At the outset, each side's view of the rest of the game is identical to that of the employer in the Ashenfelter and Johnson game (i.e. they expect that the other side will be conceding at a given rate as the dispute progresses while *they* will remain unmoved). The significant difference is that in Cross' model *both* sides are capable of forming expectations about their opponent's future behaviour. Maximisation of each side's expected utility function subject to an expected concession pattern by the opposition yields the optimal offer and demand. Cross argues that at every point in time each side decides to prolong negotiations when their marginal return from an increase in their resistance to a lower pay-off is greater than their marginal cost of conflict. Once this kind of 'optimal' disagreement is established, Cross addresses the process that leads to agreement. As the dispute goes on, at least one bargainer – possibly both – realise that their initial expectations concerning the opposition's readiness to concede were over-optimistic. The greater the discrepancy between the expected and the actual speed of concessions of the other side, the more extensively they update those inaccurate projections. These learning schemes – which are no more than adaptive expectations rules – when added to the first order conditions for the maximisation of the two sides' expected utility functions complete a system of four equations in four unknowns: the two predicted speeds of concession, the buyer's offer and the seller's demand. Potentially, this system can be solved for the time-paths of all four variables for every point in time. A plot of the time-paths of the offer and the demand provides a diagrammatic exposition of the solution which will be reached at the point of intersection of the two. Figure 4.14 depicts the history of the process and provides a possible rationalisation of Hicks's concession curves.

There are two interesting observations to be made with regard to this solution. First, if the two bargainers are identical the Cross

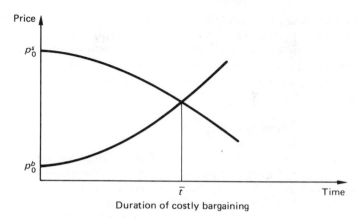

p_0^s : seller's initial demand

p_0^b : buyer's initial offer

$\bar{t}$: length of time before
agreement is 'optimal'

FIGURE 4.14   Duration of costly bargaining

Solution coincides with the Nash distribution. Second, this model provides an intuitively appealing explanation of why bargainers do not attempt to settle immediately without delay or conflict: since offer adjustments do not depend on anything else but the discrepancy between expected and actual concessions, an attempt by one side to speed up the process by conceding more quickly will lead to a greater degree of intransigence by its opponent.

There are two fundamental problems with this type of model: first, it is not a genuine two-sided theory since the implicit assumption is that, when conceding, bargainers are not aware of the fact that by doing so they are reshaping their opponents' behaviour – i.e. although the model allows for interdependence, bargainers behave as if it did not. In that respect, Cross's theory consists of two separate one-sided models stitched together by adaptive learning processes. The second problem is that of 'eternal optimism'. Bargainers never foresee forming erroneous expectations even if they have done so repeatedly in the past.[21] A dynamic rule-of-thumb model such as Cross's can potentially overcome the former problem by resorting to a synthesis of adaptive learning mechanisms and game-theoretic concepts although it is difficult to see how the inbuilt problem of ultra-optimism can be resolved.[22] The only available option is to wish it away by arguing that the best strategy for convincing one's opponent that no concessions should be expected, is first to convince oneself.

A reputation model of conflict

Clearly, if one is both to refrain from ruling out conflict by assumption and to ignore the entanglement of bargainers' webs of belief, then a tricky path between hyperrationality and crude bounded rationality must be trod. Kreps and Wilson (1982a) and Milgrom and Roberts (1982) have attempted just that.

Consider a union–firm bargaining relation where the existing *status quo* is characterised by consensus over a certain division of the producer surplus between capital and labour. The apparent tranquillity is, however, thought to be in jeopardy in view of a recent development which imposes a finite – even if not fixed – horizon on the present circumstances. A recent example of such a development is the effect which plans for a Channel Tunnel had on industrial relations in the British cross-Channel ferry labour market.[23]

Management proposes a 'rationalisation' scheme which would involve employment and/or wage cuts. Figure 4.15 describes the pay-offs that will accrue to the two sides depending on the firm's decision to unilaterally enforce the scheme and also on whether the union chooses to acquiesce or to fight.

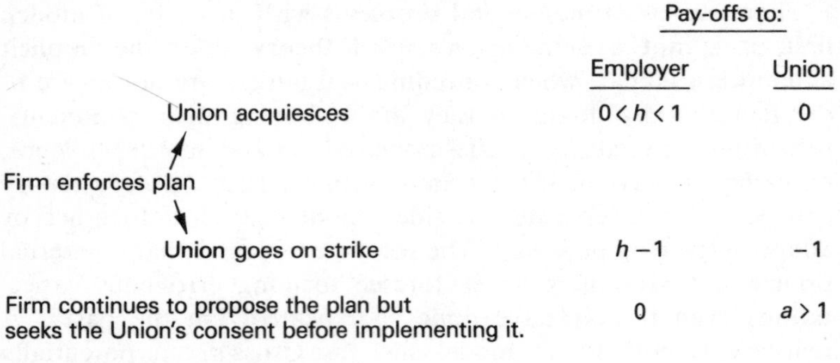

	Pay-offs to:	
	Employer	Union
Union acquiesces	$0 < h < 1$	0
Firm enforces plan		
Union goes on strike	$h - 1$	-1
Firm continues to propose the plan but seeks the Union's consent before implementing it.	0	$a > 1$

FIGURE 4.15   Pay-off matrix

The above game, whether played only once or repeated a finite or an infinite number of times, can only have one outcome: the implementation of the plan followed by union acquiescence (a perfect equilibrium). Against the background of a finite horizon, would it be possible for the union to commit to strike and therefore prevent the firm from challenging? Consider the last time the game is to be played prior to the Chunnel's opening: as the firm is aware that there is no longer any scope for the union to attempt to preserve such commitment, it will choose to enforce the plan. By backward induction, it transpires that at no point in time will the union's threat be credible. That is, until a small amount of uncertainty is introduced concerning its actual pay-offs. When the firm chooses the aggressive strategy, union choice is limited between pay-offs 0 or -1, thus compelling its leaders to acquiesce. These values presumably reflect the fact that the net monetary returns from a strike for labour will be negative. What, however, if the union is known to value, in addition to income, the principle of consultation and thus derive utility from its reputation for being prepared to fight for its principles. In that case, the employer entertains the belief that the union's pay-offs from strike and acquiescence are 0 and -1 respectively with probability p. If $p = 1$, the firm will never challenge since it always expects an industrial dispute to ensue. The interesting twist here is that, not only will a union fight if it is 'ideologically' committed, but it may also wish to do so when it is not, in order to build a belligerent reputation. The game starts at the moment the Channel Tunnel project is announced and is due to end after T periods (T being the length of time before the Tunnel's official opening to the public). Letting δt be the shortest period of time in which a challenge and a strike can materialise (say a day or a week), it will be assumed that when confronted by a massive picket line during period δt, the firm will back down. In the short interval $(t, t - \delta t)$ – remember that time is moving backwards as the countdown to 1993 has commenced – the non-ideological union trying to build a reputation will strike with probability $1 - \Psi_t$ and, therefore, the firm will anticipate a strike with probability $1 - (1 - p_t)\Psi_t$.

In equilibrium, the firm is indifferent between challenging and staying put when the expected returns from the two are equal. So in the interval $(t, t - \delta t)$:

$$[h-1] \qquad + [1-(1-p_t)\Psi_t] + (1-p_t)\Psi] \times h = 0$$

pay-off	probability	probability	benefits to
from strike	of a strike	of union	the firm in
in the	if the firm	acquiescence	this case
interval	challenges		
$(t, t+\delta t)$			

$$(4.1)$$

is the condition for the firm to hesitate. The union must, therefore, strike with probability at least equal to

$$1 - \left(\frac{1-h}{1-p_t} \right) \tag{4.2}$$

if it is to prevent challenges.

Suppose that at time t the union has responded with a strike; how is this going to affect its reputation as measured by the firm's assessment p? Adopting Bayes's rule as a consistent means of updating beliefs we have that in every interval of δt length.[24]

$$p_t - \delta_t \equiv p_\delta(\text{Union is 'ideological'}|\text{it fought at time } t) =$$

$$\frac{p_\delta(\text{fight}|\text{'ideological'}) \times p_\delta(\text{ideological'})}{p_\delta(\text{fight})} =$$

$$\frac{1 \times p_t}{1 - (1-p_t)\Psi_t\delta_t} \tag{4.3}$$

Subtracting p_t from both sides, dividing by δt, and letting δt tend to zero, we derive the rate of increase in the union's reputation as challenges are met by strikes:

$$\dot{p}_t = p_t(1-p_t)\Psi_t \tag{4.4}$$

Substitution of (4.2) in (4.4) leads to the time-path of the union's reputation ($p_t = \exp(h-1)t$) as it responds to challenges aggressively. The following diagram describes the game in its entirety.

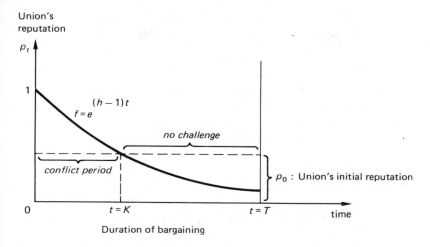

FIGURE 4.16 Duration of bargaining

At time $t = T$, the firm expects the union to prefer a strike if challenged with probability $[p_0]$ which can be thought of as the union's initial reputation for being ideological.[25] The union that is truly so will not hesitate to strike if its only alternative is to acquiesce. However, a union that would prefer to give in, on short-run considerations alone, will also strike if challenged as long as its initial reputation p_0 exceeds the level indicated by f (i.e. up to time-period $t = K$); this strategy is compatible with its goal of keeping managers at bay for as long as possible. The firm, knowing this, will never dare to challenge before $t = K$. At that point it will start thinking about challenging and will do so with a positive probability. When it does, (4.2) provides us with the probability that the 'non-ideological' union will respond with a strike. As we approach the end, the union will eventually give in – unless of course it genuinely prefers a strike. It is interesting to note that the condition for conflict is not that combatants 'prefer' fighting, but rather that given a small probability that they do, they choose to behave as if that were the case (see Kreps and Wilson, 1982a, for a full discussion). (The alert reader will notice that this rationale for conflict is exactly the same as that behind predatory pricing discussed in Section 4.3.) An unfortunate disadvantage of this model is that, given the war-of-attrition nature of the game, there can be no room for compromise: concessions are ruled out by the requirement that a bargainer will be either a winner or a loser.

More recently there have been attempts to refine models similar to the above by allowing for a more realistic outflow of 'signals' in place of the binary responses (e.g. strike or acquiescence) demonstrated here (see Crawford and Sobel, 1985, and Cho and Kreps, 1987) as well as the possibility that bargainers attempt to build multiple reputations (see Hargreaves–Heap and Varoufakis, 1987).

4.5 CONCLUDING COMMENTS

When a bargaining party consists of a group of heterogeneous individuals, uncertainty concerning their collective ability to combine in order to inflict costs on the other side will damage their bargaining strength. Furthermore, if there is a preconception that 'fighting often means fighting well', conflict may emerge as a necessary condition for the creation of a future 'threat point' (Hicks, 1932) – for example, acknowledged that 'Weapons grow rusty if unused ... The most able union will embark on strikes occasionally' (Hicks, 1932, p. 146). The implication here is that if the ability to strike depends on striking experience, conflict has an investment role to play which is largely ignored. Collective participation in threatened conflict is undermined by the fact that the benefits are reaped by participants and non-participants alike. The common interest and the private interest pointing in different directions, free-riding will emerge with a detrimental effect on the group's bargaining power. The logic of collective action (see Olson (1965) for a definition) suggests that conflict may serve the purpose of freeing individuals from the prisoner dilemma preferences which prevent them from being collectively rational. If conflict encourages the adoption of common assurance preferences – i.e. individuals preferring to cooperate rather than defect [see Sen (1967)] – then it may be the appropriate price for the formation of an effective coalition.

Akerlof (1980) offers a simple sociological model that relates the proportion of free-riders to the utility that agents derive from being 'loyal' members of the community. If behaving according to a 'social convention' – for example, not breaking a strike – affects one's preferences in proportion to the community's valuation of that convention, then it is shown that self interested individuals may be driven through the influences of society's values to prefer being selfless rather than egoistic. An alternative reason for not defecting [see Sugden (1987)] is that, if the coalition is fragile, agents choose to cooperate because they think that if they defect everyone will do likewise. However, refraining from being a 'traitor' because you derive utility from being a 'hero' is fundamentally different from doing so simply because you predict a collapse of a coalition whose success is only of pecuniary importance to you. In the former case, individuals are capable of a far-reaching transition from one set of preferences to another due to their experience of conflict, while in the latter, preferences remain unchanged.

The importance of such considerations transcends the study of organisations if it is recognised that, in making hard choices, the individual is presiding over an internal battle between conflicting tendencies. It is the suspicion that the outcome of this internal battle may be intrinsically linked with one's environment which raises doubts about the wisdom of exclusively construing conflict as the by-product of informational asymmetries.

Game theory's preference invariance to conflict is a strong assumption riddled with philosophical, as well as, ideological implications. Whereas it is consistent with – although not apologetic to – Hobbes's pessimistic perception of individuals being engaged in a perpetual war of all against all, it is incompatible with a wide class of alternative perceptions ranging from the Aristotle–Locke conservative consensus view of society which results from a benign view of human nature, to the radical conflict tradition of Plato, Rousseau and Marx who perceive conflict as an inescapable outcome of immature social organisation. The underlying Hobbesian–Humean leanings of game theory can thus be traced to the implicit assumption that individuals are unable to learn from social interaction anything more than the limitation of their bargaining power. This isolation of aspirations from experience is tantamount to a fundamental philosophical bias which prevents game theory from investigating the interdependence of personal development and social evolution.

In conclusion, game theory offers a fascinating insight into interdependent behaviour. However, if it is to constitute the basis for a comprehensive and relevant theory of conflict, it must mature and thus allow its subject matter to retain human nature's ability to undergo fundamental changes as a result of contact with the evolution in social relations.

5 Contract Theory and Incentive Compatibility

MELVYN COLES and JAMES M. MALCOMSON

5.1 INTRODUCTION

What is a contract? In essence, it is a mutual agreement between people to act in some specified way. A common example is an agreement to pay a sum of money on the occurrence of some event that may or may not be controlled by one of the parties. You may place a bet with a bookmaker to receive a specified pay-off if a particular horse wins a race. Whether or not that horse wins is not (or, at least, is not supposed to be) controlled by either of you. An insurance company may agree to pay you a specified sum if your house burns down. Whether or not it does is at least partly under your control. An employer may offer you a job at a specified salary provided that you graduate. Whether or not you do depends not only on how hard you work but also on how clever you are and you may know that better than your prospective employer. All these are examples of contracts.

Contracts are important when agreements and the events to which they refer are separated by time or space. Without a legally enforceable agreement, the fear that one of the parties might later cheat on the deal could prevent that deal taking place even though, were it carried out, all parties would gain by it. This is not a problem in textbook models of markets because there each transaction takes place at a single point in time. One party hands over the goods and the other, simultaneously, hands over the money. But situations in which there are advantages to be had from transactions that are not simultaneous in this way are widespread in economics. To get fire insurance you have to buy it *before* you know whether your house has burned down but the insurance company cannot reimburse a loss until *after* that loss has occurred. You want to be offered a job before you know for sure that you have graduated so that you can make appropriate plans. Owners of firms hire managers but can only find out how good those managers are, or how hard they have worked, when the results come in. So do central planners. Entrepreneurs want to borrow money to put ideas into practice but lenders do not know how good these ideas are until afterwards. Suppliers have to make investments in order to provide goods to retailers before the retailers know how well those goods will sell. These are just a few examples. When the parts of a transaction are not all simultaneous, contracts can help to ensure that people stick to a deal.

The potential gains from contracts are transparent in what is known as the prisoners' dilemma game discussed in the last chapter. In this game, both are better off if neither confesses. Without a contract, however, no matter what A does it is in B's interest to confess to reduce his fine. Similarly for A, so they both confess. But both gain if they make an enforceable agreement not to confess. It is crucial, however, that the agreement be enforceable. If it were not, each would individually gain from confessing. This basic structure, in which there are gains from cooperation but also gains from cheating on a cooperating partner, has applications to many issues in social science. For examples, see Axelrod (1984).

One way of enforcing contracts is to make use of the courts. But it is important to recognise that there are some contracts which courts will not enforce – a contract not to confess to a crime is an obvious example. Other contracts can be enforced only in part. A court cannot enforce terms of a contract that are conditional on some event happening unless it is in a position to assess whether that event has occurred. In practice, what is verifiable in court may not be clear-cut and the outcome of a trial is thus uncertain. That can be of great importance, especially when legal costs are substantial. But the issue with which we are concerned here are highlighted more clearly when everybody knows from the start exactly what is verifiable in court, so that is what we shall assume. When all relevant events are verifiable, there is said to be *full information*.

What courts can verify is clearly important for two types of contracts that are enforceable. It is also important what the parties to the contract can observe. When all parties know what all the others know, information is *symmetric*. In many contexts, however, that is not the situation. A worker may know how much care and effort he has put into a job but the foreman sees only the rate at which the work progresses. You may know if you are a good or a bad driver but your insurance company may not find out until it has to pay for your accidents. In these cases, information is *asymmetric*. Often information that is unverifiable will also be asymmetric, but this need not be the case. A worker and a foreman may both know how hard the worker has worked but proving it in court may be a different matter.

When there is full information, no party can hide the facts and there is at least the possibility of having the terms of a contract enforced in court. In that case, it is usually a straightforward technical problem to specify the requirements for an efficient contract as a maximisation problem, though the contracts that result from that maximisation may be too complex to imagine them actually being written down. When information is unverifiable or asymmetric, however, one party may have an incentive to conceal it. The worker might slack on the job but explain his slow progress to the foreman by claiming that the job is more difficult than expected. You might want to conceal your previous accidents from an insurance company to get a lower premium. Just because the terms of a contract are not enforceable in court does not necessarily mean that the contract is valueless. The Mafia has acted as a very efficient enforcement agency for some prisoners' dilemma games. But it does mean that, if the contract is actually to be carried out, it must be designed so that each party chooses to carry out those terms that are not legally enforceable. When that is the case, those terms are said to be *self-enforcing*. The restrictions this imposes on contracts are called *incentive compatibility constraints*. To determine these constraints in any particular context, it is crucial to specify who observes, or can verify, what information.

An important part of contract theory is analysing the nature and the implications of incentive compatibility constraints. We shall be concerned with two ways in which there may not be full information, *moral hazard* and *adverse selection*. These terms are borrowed from the literature on insurance. Briefly, moral hazard arises when one party to a contract can, after the contract is agreed, take an action that affects the outcome but what action was taken is not verifiable. A classic example is not being careful about your house catching fire after you have taken out fire insurance. Once the house has burnt down, there is unlikely to be evidence of the care you have taken. Adverse selection occurs when one party has information relevant to the outcome that is not known to the other parties before a contract is agreed and not verifiable after the outcome has happened. A classic example is not revealing that you are a bad driver before taking out car insurance. Although borrowed from the insurance literature, these terms have much wider applicability. The worker who slacks when the foreman is not looking generates moral hazard. The doctor who continues to practise despite failing to keep up with advances in medicine generates adverse selection.

In this chapter, we first consider contracts for one-off events when there is no question of the contract continuing or being renewed for subsequent periods. We use the examples of fire insurance and car insurance to illustrate how moral hazard and adverse selection give rise to incentive compatibility constraints in this case. We then show how the structure of these examples can be used to represent incentive compatibility constraints in a general way that can be applied to other situations involving moral hazard or adverse selection. In the final part of the chapter, we consider contracts that can be continued or renewed on terms that depend on what has happened after they have come into force.

5.2 MORAL HAZARD: AN INSURANCE EXAMPLE

Consider a risk-averse house-owner who wants to buy insurance against his house catching fire. Obviously, if the house-owner agrees to take precautions against fire by, for example, not smoking in bed, there is less risk of a fire occurring and one would expect the premium to be lower. But, what if the insurance company cannot prove that the fire started because the owner had been smoking in bed? If the house is insured for its full value, there is no risk for the owner in lighting up if he feels like a cigarette. If the house burns down, the insurance company will bear the cost and will never know that he had actually been smoking.

This is a classic example of moral hazard. The house-owner can take an action (smoking in bed) that affects the chances of the house burning down but whether or not he took that action is not verifiable. It can be analysed in the following way. Let p_c denote the probability of the house burning down if the owner is careful, p_{nc} that if he is not careful. Naturally, one would expect $p_{nc} > p_c$. Let c denote the cost of being careful (the money value of the utility foregone by not smoking in bed). If H is the value of the house, the expected return to being careful, denoted Π_c, is

$$\Pi_c = (1 - p_c)H - c$$

that is, the value of the house multiplied by the probability that it does not burn down, less the cost of being careful. The expected return to not being careful, Π_{nc}, is

$$\Pi_{nc} = (1 - p_{nc})H$$

The potential for moral hazard arises when it is efficient that the houseowner should be careful, that is, $\Pi_c > \Pi_{nc}$, which implies

$$c < (p_{nc} - p_c)H$$

It is then efficient for the owner to be careful because the cost of doing so, c, is less than the increased risk of the house burning down, $p_{nc} - p_c$, multiplied by the cost of replacing it if it does so, H. If there were no insurance, he would certainly be careful because the expected return is greater.

If the insurance company can always tell, and verify in court, whether the owner has been careful, it will be prepared to offer full insurance at a lower premium to an owner who agrees to be careful as a condition of the contract. The 'fair' premium, at which it expects to make neither a profit nor a loss (see Chapter 3 for further discussion of this concept), will be $p_c H$ if the owner agrees to be careful, $p_{nc} H$ if he does not. With full insurance, provided the owner acts as agreed in the contract, the insurance company pays him H if the house burns down. If it does not burn down, he has the house, worth H. Thus, whichever happens, his return from the policy that requires him to be careful is $H - p_c H - c$, that is Π_c. His return from the policy that does not require him to be careful is $H - p_{nc} H$, that is Π_{nc}. Since these returns are both certain and since

$\Pi_c > \Pi_{nc}$, he will choose the former. This is called the *first-best outcome* – the risk-averse owner bears no risk and acts to maximise the expected return.

Things are different when the owner's action is not verifiable in court. Suppose he buys full insurance H at premium P. His private return to being careful is then $H - P - c$. But, if he is not careful, no one can prove it, he avoids the cost c, and his return is $H - P$. So, whatever the premium, it is not in his interest to be careful. Because the insurance company bears all the risk, the action that minimises his private costs is not the efficient action. Risk-sharing has distorted the incentive to take care. And, if home-owners are not careful, houses burn down with probability p_{nc}, the fair insurance premium rises to $p_{nc}H$ and the householder has return Π_{nc}. Because the house-owner cannot credibly commit himself to taking care, he is worse off. The first-best outcome is unattainable.

Can one design a contract which ensures that the house-owner is careful but still gives him insurance? For this, the house-owner must get at least as much expected utility from being careful as from not being careful. That will make the contract incentive compatible. To see what contracts are incentive compatible, we need to be specific about the house-owner's utility function. Suppose he gets utility $u(W)$ from wealth W and the house is his only asset. Suppose also that the cost of not being careful is $u° > 0$ when measured in utility. Then, if the insurance company agreed to insure the house for the amount I (not necessarily equal to its full value H) at a premium P, the house-owner's utility would be $u(H - P) - u^0$ if he took the insurance, was careful, and the house did not burn down. It would be $u(I - P) - u^0$ if the house did burn down. Hence his expected utility from taking the insurance and being careful would be

$$(1 - p_c)[u(H - P) - u^0] + p_c[u(I - P) - u^0] =$$
$$u(H - P) - p_c[u(H - P) - u(I - P)] - u^0 \tag{5.1}$$

Similarly, his expected utility from taking the insurance and not being careful is

$$(1 - p_{nc})u(H - P) + p_{nc}u(I - P) =$$
$$u(H - P) - p_{nc}[u(H - P) - u(I - P)] \tag{5.2}$$

The contract will be incentive compatible if I and P are chosen so that the expression in (5.1) is at least as great as that in (5.2), that is, if

$$(p_{nc} - p_c)[u(H - P) - u(I - P)] \geqslant u^0 \tag{5.3}$$

This is the incentive compatibility constraint for which we are looking.

Since utility is an increasing function of wealth and $p_{nc} > p_c$, (5.3) can hold only if $H > I$, so the house-owner cannot have full insurance. To give him an incentive to be careful, he must be made to carry some of the cost of the house burning down. If the insurance is 'fair', the premium P will be $p_c I$ and then, for a specific utility function and values of the parameters, the equality in (5.3) can be solved to find the maximum sum insured, call it I^*, that is incentive compatible. At a fair premium, the risk-averse house-owner would like full insurance but must be restricted to I^* to ensure that he is careful. But he might then prefer a policy offering full insurance H at the 'fair' premium p_{nc} to one offering I^* at p_c.

Limitations on the maximum sum insurable are a common feature of insurance contracts. They serve to mitigate the effects of moral hazard. But they mean that risk-averse purchasers do not get full insurance so that risk is not efficiently shared between the purchaser and the insurer. This illustrates a central message to be learnt from moral hazard models. Incentive compatibility requirements typically impose a trade-off between providing efficient risk-sharing and providing incentives for efficient choice of action.

5.3 ADVERSE SELECTION: AN INSURANCE EXAMPLE

To use an insurance example again, suppose the population consists of good drivers, who crash with probability p_g, and bad drivers who crash with probability p_b, where $p_b > p_g$. Without a past history of their driving records, an insurance company cannot tell which type an applicant is. Clearly, there is no point in trying to distinguish between types by offering full insurance at low premiums to those who declare themselves to be good drivers because bad drivers can declare themselves to be good to get the lower premiums. Unless some way can be found to induce applicants to separate themselves into their true types, good drivers will have to pay higher premiums for insurance because the insurance company also has to cover the bad risks. Incentive compatibility is concerned with designing contracts that induce such separation.

A useful tool in analysing incentive compatibility is the *revelation principle*. The essence of this principle is that, in looking for efficient contracts, we need be concerned only with contracts that induce people to reveal their type truthfully. This may at first sight seem surprising but the underlying reason is simple enough. To see this, suppose that the most efficient contract that can be devised results in bad drivers claiming to be good. For the revelation principle to hold, there must be an equally efficient contract which results in their claiming to be bad. Is there such a contract? Obviously there is. We simply ask drivers to be honest about their type but guarantee to offer the same contract to those who say they are bad as to those who say they are good. Nothing real has changed. Outcomes are the same, except that we now have truthful revelation of information.

This is trivial if nothing hinges on whether a driver claims to be good or bad. If good drivers separate themselves from bad by their choice of policy, however, then either all drivers tell the truth or all lie. For all to lie, good drivers must be choosing a policy intended for bad drivers and vice versa. But then we can just change the labels on the policies so that all tell the truth and the revelation principle still holds.

Obvious as this may seem, it is valuable in enabling us to formulate incentive compatibility constraints for adverse selection in a way similar to that for moral hazard. We just require the contracts on offer to ensure that every type gets as much utility from revealing their type truthfully as from deception. We can then look for the most efficient contracts that satisfy these constraints knowing that contracts in which information is not truthfully revealed are no more efficient.

To see how this is done, suppose the two types of drivers have the same utility of wealth function $u(W)$ and the only damage in the case of an accident is that the car, worth M if undamaged, is a total write-off. Suppose also that the insurance company offers two policies, one with premium P_g and the car insured for I_g that it intends for good drivers, the other with premium P_b and the car insured for I_b that it intends for bad drivers. To achieve truthful revelation of types, we must ensure that the former is at least as good for good drivers as the latter and the latter at least as good for bad drivers as the former. Since a bad driver crashes with probability p_b, his expected utility from taking the policy intended for bad drivers is

$$(1 - p_b)u(M - P_b) + p_b u(I_b - P_b) \tag{5.4}$$

His expected utility if he takes the policy intended for good drivers is

$$(1 - p_b)u(M - P_g) + p_b u(I_g - P_g) \tag{5.5}$$

Incentive compatibility for bad drivers requires that the expression in (5.4) be at least as great as that in (5.5), that is:

$$(1 - p_b)u(M - P_b) + p_b u(I_b - P_b) \geqslant$$
$$(1 - p_b)u(M - P_g) + p_b u(I_g - P_g) \tag{5.6}$$

A good driver crashes with probability p_g, so her expected utility from taking the policy intended for good drivers is

$$(1 - p_g)u(M - P_g) + p_b u(I_g - P_g) \tag{5.7}$$

and her expected utility from taking the policy intended for bad drivers is

$$(1 - p_g)u(M - P_b) + p_b u(I_b - P_b) \tag{5.8}$$

Incentive compatibility for good drivers requires that the expression in (5.7) be at least as great as that in (5.8), that is:

$$(1 - p_g)u(M - P_g) + p_g u(l_g - P_g) \geqslant$$
$$(1 - p_g)u(M - P_b) + p_g u(l_b - P_b) \tag{5.9}$$

Because they ensure that each type selects the policy intended for them of their own volition, these constraints are sometimes known as *self-selection constraints*.

The constraints (5.6) and (5.9) are obviously satisfied if $I_b = I_g$ and $P_b = P_g$. Then both good and bad drivers get the same insurance so there is no incentive for anybody to be dishonest about their type. This is known as a *pooling* outcome. Such an outcome, however, cannot be an equilibrium in this model if there is a competitive insurance market, see Rothschild and Stiglitz (1976). The alternative is a *separating* outcome in which bad drivers choose one contract and good drivers another.

To see what this requires, suppose we try offering good drivers a lower premium $P_g < P_b$. For (5.6) to hold, we must then have $I_g < I_b$ – the policy for good drivers cannot offer more insurance at a lower cost than that for bad drivers because both good and bad will choose it. From (5.6), it is clear that we should choose P_b and I_b to maximise the bad driver's expected utility, that is the left-hand side of (5.6). Doing that makes bad drivers less likely to choose the policy for good drivers and gives more freedom to choose P_g and I_g to make good drivers better off. We should, therefore, sell bad drivers full insurance M at a 'fair' premium $p_b M$. Now consider the contract for good drivers. We know that if we offer a 'fair' premium, we must restrict the insurance cover so that $I_g < I_b = M$. The most cover we can offer at the 'fair' premium $P_g = p_g I_g$ is that satisfying (5.6) with equality when $I_b = M$ and $P_b = p_b M$. Call this I_g^*. Bad drivers do not then buy the policy for good drivers because they have to bear some of the costs of accidents and prefer full insurance at a higher premium. These contracts also satisfy the incentive compatibility constraint (5.9) that requires good drivers to prefer the policy intended for good drivers to the policy intended for bad drivers. To see this, set $I_b = M$, $P_b = p_b M$ and $p_g = p_g I_g$ in (5.6) and note that I_g^* is, by definition, the value of I_g that makes (5.6) hold with equality. From this, we get

$$u(M - P_b) = (1 - p_b)u(M - P_g) + p_b u(I_g^* - P_g) \tag{5.10}$$

since the terms in p_b on the left-hand side of (5.6) then cancel. With the same values inserted in (5.9), that constraint becomes

$$(1 - p_g)u(M - P_g) + p_g u(I_g^* - P_g) \geqslant u(M - P_b) \tag{5.11}$$

since the terms in p_g on the right-hand side cancel. Note that the right-hand side of (5.11) is the same as the left-hand side of (5.10) so, since (5.10) is an equality, (5.11) will certainly be satisfied if the left-hand side of (5.11) is at least as great as the right-hand side of (5.10). But $I_g^* < M$ implies that $u(M - P_g(I_g^* - P_g))$ and so, since $p_g < p_b$, the left-hand side of (5.11) is necessarily strictly greater than the right-hand side of (5.10). Thus (5.11) holds with strict inequality and so does the constraint (5.9).

Only one of the incentive compatibility constraints binds, therefore, the one that requires bad risks to prefer the contract intended for them. This makes intuitive sense since it is bad risks who have an incentive to cheat if everybody is offered full insurance at a fair premium. Good drivers will not claim to be bad because they would face higher premiums, so their incentive compatibility constraint does not bind. This is a common feature of efficient contracts under adverse selection.

This means that the cost of imposing incentive compatibility is borne entirely by the good risks. With adverse selection, bad drivers can have full insurance because good drivers do not want to claim to be bad risks and face higher premiums. But the level of insurance to good drivers has to be constrained to prevent bad risks from claiming that they are good. This works because, by offering only incomplete insurance, drivers who take this policy are forced to bear some of the risk. For good drivers this is worthwhile because the risk they face is low but bad drivers, knowing that they have a higher risk of an accident, prefer to buy full insurance at a higher premium. Good drivers are worse off with asymmetric information because they cannot have full insurance at a 'fair' premium.

5.4 MORAL HAZARD: THE PRINCIPAL–AGENT PROBLEM

Earlier we gave an example of moral hazard from insurance. A similar structure applies to many other examples. Instead of the contract being between an insurance company and a house-owner who wants fire insurance, it could be between a firm and an employee, a central planning board and a factory manager, or a lawyer and a client. The potential for moral hazard arises when the effort put in by the employee, the manager or the lawyer cannot be monitored perfectly so each may be tempted to put in less than he otherwise might.

Because a similar structure applies to many situations, it is useful to formulate the moral hazard problem in a general way in order to see what general conclusions can be drawn about the nature of efficient contracts. To avoid referring to specific examples all the time, it has become conventional to call the person who has the opportunity to exercise moral hazard the *agent* and the other party the *principal*. The general formulation is thus known as the principal–agent problem. In each case it is the agent who has scope for taking some unverifiable action, the principal does not.

In the general formulation the agent chooses an action a from a set of possible actions A. In the insurance example, the possible actions are to be careful and not to be careful. The action taken is either unobserved by the principal or unverifiable in court so that a contract that makes payment depend on the action is unenforceable. What is verifiable is an outcome that depends both on the action and on a random variable. In the insurance example, the possible outcomes are the house burning down and it not burning down. Which happens depends not just on whether the house-owner is careful but also on chance, on whether his fallen cigarette ash happens to set fire to the bed. In that example, there are only two possible outcomes but in general there may be more. The profits of a firm that employs a manager as an agent can take on many different values. In the general formulation, it is convenient to measure the outcome by its monetary value. Thus, in the insurance example, the outcome would be $-H$ if the house burned down and zero if it did not. For the general case, we assume that the outcome takes one of n possible values, denoted $x_1, x_2, \ldots, x_n$ and ordered so that $x_1 < x_2 < \ldots < x_n$. For there to be moral hazard, the probability that a particular outcome occurs depends on the action taken by the agent. We therefore denote the probabilities of the n outcomes when the agent takes action a by $p_1(a)$, $p_2(a), \ldots p_n(a)$.

The principal's aim is to design a contract which maximises his expected utility but in doing this he needs to take account of the action the agent will choose when faced with a particular contract. Because only the outcome is verifiable, the payment to the agent under a contract can depend only on which of the possible outcomes occurs. It is convenient to formulate the problem so that the principal receives the monetary value of the outcome and the only monetary pay-off to the agent is that paid by the principal, which we denote by w_1, w_2, ... w_n for the n different possible outcomes. These form the contract. In the insurance example, this is as if the insurance company owned the house and paid the house-owner its value minus the premium if it did not burn down, or the sum insured minus the premium if it burnt down. This may seem a slightly odd formulation for that application but it is a natural one when, for example, the principal is a firm and the agent its manager. The n possible outcomes x_1, x_2, ... x_n then correspond to the profits of the firm and the payments w_i, $i = 1, \ldots, n$, to the salary paid to the manager if outcome x_i occurs. It should be remembered that this is purely a matter of notation – one can interpret the payments in the appropriate way for each specific application.

The principal, therefore, receives the outcome less the amount paid to the agent. We denote his utility by $V(x_i - w_i)$ if outcome i occurs. The agent's utility depends on what she receives from the principal and the action she takes. We denote her utility by $U(w_i, a)$. The expected utility of the agent if she takes action a for given w_1, w_2, ..., w_n is then

$$\sum_{i=1}^{n} U(w_i, a)p_i(a).$$

In the same way as we constructed the incentive compatibility constraint in the earlier example, we can ensure that the agent takes a particular action a^* by choosing the contract $w_1, \ldots, w_n$ so that a^* gives the highest expected utility of any action. Formally this is ensured by imposing the incentive compatibility constraints

$$\sum_{i=1}^{n} U(w_i, a^*)p_i(a^*) \geqslant \sum_{i=1}^{n} U(w_i, a')p_i(a'), \text{ for all } a' \in A \qquad (5.12)$$

The left-hand side of this is the expected utility of the agent if she chooses action a^*. The right-hand side is the expected utility if she chooses some other action a'. By requiring (5.12) to hold for all possible a', we ensure that a^* is the optimal choice. In using a weak inequality, we assume that an agent who is indifferent between two actions chooses whichever the principal would prefer. (Note that, formally, we allow $a' = a^*$ but clearly (5.12) is always satisfied then.)

An efficient contract maximises the expected utility of the principal for a given expected utility of the agent that we denote by U^0. If the principal is hiring the agent as an employee in a perfectly competitive market, U^0 will be the expected utility the agent can obtain by taking a job elsewhere. But also, by letting U^0 take different values, we can determine which contract is efficient for each expected utility level of the agent, thus tracing out the frontier of efficient contracts. (We could equally well maximise the expected utility of the agent for given expected utility of the principal, as in the earlier insurance example. By picking different values of the principal's expected utility we would trace out the same frontier.)

Suppose the principal decides that a^* is the action he wants the agent to take. He will then choose the contract $w_1, \ldots, w_n$ to maximise his expected utility

$$\max_{w_1, \ldots, w_n} \sum_{i=1}^{n} V(x_i - w_i) p_i(a^*) \tag{5.13}$$

subject to the contract satisfying (5.12) so that the agent chooses a^*, that is,

$$\sum_{i=1}^{n} U(w_i, a^*) p_i(a^*) \geqslant \sum_{i=1}^{n} U(w_i, a') p_i(a'), \text{ for all } a' \in A \tag{5.14}$$

and the contract giving the agent the required expected utility U^0, that is:

$$\sum_{i=1}^{n} U(w_i, a^*) p_i(a^*) \geqslant U^0 \tag{5.15}$$

This tells the principal which contract maximises his expected utility if he wants the agent to choose action a^*. By doing this for each possible action, he can see which of those actions gives him the highest expected utility and choose to offer the best contract that will induce the agent to take that action. In fact, this choice can be included directly in the maximisation problem above by replacing (5.13) by

$$\max_{a^*, w_1, \ldots, w_n} \sum_{i=1}^{n} V(x_i - w_i) p_i(a^*) \tag{5.16}$$

and maximising this subject to (5.14) and (5.15). We can then think of the principal as choosing the combination of contract and action which maximises his expected utility while ensuring that the contract induces the agent to carry out the action.

What can we say in general about efficient contracts under these circumstances? One straightforward result is that, if the agent is risk-neutral, the efficient contract's net profits $x_i - w_i$ are independent of the outcome i, so the principal bears no risk. As we saw in the insurance example, risk-sharing is typically at the expense of distorting the incentives for the agent to choose the efficient action. But, when the agent is risk-neutral, there is no gain in efficiency from sharing risk and, by not doing so, one avoids distorting incentives.

In most applications the agent is risk-averse. One might then imagine that it would be efficient for both risk-sharing and incentives for the agent to receive higher payments when good outcomes occur. In the house insurance example, the agent is better off if the house does not burn down since she then has the value of the house H rather than the compensation $I < H$. But Grossman and Hart (1983) have shown that this is not necessarily true if there are more than two possible outcomes. To see why, consider the case in which the principal is the risk-neutral owner of a firm and the agent its risk-averse manager. The owner, being risk-neutral, wants the manager to undertake risky projects that have a high average return. Undertaking such projects increases the probability of very low profits, as well as of very high ones, relative to a less risky strategy. To persuade the risk-averse manager to undertake them, it may be efficient to reward him well both for very high profits and for very low ones, with lower rewards for the intermediate levels of profits that are more probable under the less risky strategy. Thus, one cannot conclude that, as a general rule, the reward to the agent is greater the better the outcome. For further discussion of these issues, see the survey by Hart and Holmstrom (1985).

Formalising the principal–agent problem in this way does not, therefore, give us much in the way of general results to apply to specific examples. What we get from the general formulation is a framework within which many examples can be analysed. The nature of the efficient contract needs to be worked out for each specific example. The procedure outlined above provides a way of doing that. In both the insurance example and the general formulation we started by considering what action the agent would take for any given contract. This gives the incentive compatibility constraints (5.3) or (5.14), which tell us which contracts make each of these actions incentive compatible. In the general formulation, we then, in maximising (5.13) subject to (5.14) and (5.15), determined the incentive-compatible contract that is efficient for each choice of action. The final step was to determine which of these contracts, and the outcomes they implement, give the principal the highest expected utility. We can combine these last two steps by using (5.16) as the maximand.

In some problems, the choice of action a is continuous rather then discrete. Then a natural way to analyse the agent's optimal choice of action for a given contract is to use the appropriate first-order condition. But with that approach we need to be careful about the second-order condition. Since risk-aversion implies a strictly concave utility function, in many economic problems that is enough to ensure that there is a unique solution to the first-order condition that is always a maximum. In principal–agent problems, however, strict concavity of the utility function is not generally enough because the first-order condition for the agent's maximisation problem depends on the contract offered, so we need restrictions on the form of the contract to ensure that the agent's maximisation problem is concave. But the essence of the principal–agent problem is to *find* the efficient form of contract so it is not appropriate to *assume* from the start that it has the required properties. Rogerson (1985) gives conditions under which it will have those properties. But for more general cases one needs a solution procedure like the one suggested above.

5.5   ADVERSE SELECTION: MORE GENERAL TREATMENTS

With the use of the revelation principle, we can construct incentive-compatibility constraints for the case of adverse selection in much the same way as we constructed those for the case of moral hazard in (5.12). To illustrate the similarity of approach to these two cases, we continue to use the term 'agent' for a party that has information unknown to the other, who is still called the principal. Indeed, we continue to use the symbol a for that information, though this will not be an inherent attribute of the agent rather than an action chosen, and will let A denote the set of all possible attributes.

In view of the revelation principle, we need be concerned only with contracts for which it is in an agent's interest truthfully to reveal her type. As in the moral hazard case, we denote the possible outcomes by the n values $x_1, x_2, \ldots, x_n$ but, because the contract offered can now depend on what type the agent claims to be, we must let the payments under the contract depend on the attribute claimed. We denote by $w_i(a)$, $i = 1, \ldots, n$, the payment if x_i occurs under a contract for those who claim to be type a. Now consider an agent of type a^*. Truthful revelation will be optimal if, given the utility function and the probabilities of the different outcomes for type a^*, the expected utility from taking a contract with payments $w_i(a^*), \ldots, w_n(a^*)$ is at least as great as that from taking a contract $w_i(a'), \ldots, w_n(a')$ for some other type a'. For this to be true for all a^* in A and all a' in A requires

$$\sum_{i=1}^{n} U[w_i(a^*), a^*]p_i(a^*) \geqslant \sum_{i=1}^{n} U[w_i(a'), a^*]p_i(a^*),$$

$$\text{for all } a^*, a' \in A \tag{5.17}$$

Note the difference from the incentive compatibility constraint (5.12) in the case of moral hazard. In that case, the agent is choosing a^* optimally so (5.12) has to hold only for the a^* that the principal wants the agent to choose. In the adverse selection case a^* itself cannot be chosen. It is an inherent attribute of the agent. What can be chosen is the type a' the agent reveals herself to be. But revealing the wrong type affects only the contract, not the utility function or the probabilities.

The incentive-compatibility constraint (5.17) corresponds to the incentive-compatibility constraint (5.12) or (5.14) in the case of moral hazard. To specify the requirements for an efficient contract, we also need to consider the minimum expected utility constraint for the the agent corresponding to (5.15) and the objective function of the principal corresponding to (5.13). There are some minor differences in these. Since the principal is faced with an agent who can be of any type a, his expectation must be taken not only over the different possible outcomes but also over the distribution of a. Moreover, the minimum expected utility constraint corresponding to (5.15) must be satisfied for every a in A that the principal wishes to attract into a contract. We do not give further technical details here.

In this formulation, self-selection is induced because the contracts that are intended for one type of agent are chosen to impose higher costs on other types. This can be done because the differences between types result in their being willing to trade one characteristic of a contract for another at different rates. In the insurance example, the limitation on the sum insured for good risks is more costly for bad risks because they have a higher probability of making a claim. Thus they are induced to opt for full insurance at a higher premium rate. Good risks signal their willingness to bear such costs by choosing the contract with limited cover.

It is also possible for agents to signal their type by incurring costs before agreeing to, but in anticipation of, a contract. Spence (1974) has argued that in labour markets education can be used as such a signal. Suppose the more able potential employees can acquire a given level of educational qualification at lower cost in terms of either money or effort than the less able. Then, if better qualified employees are offered salaries higher, but not too much higher, than less well qualified ones, the more able will be prepared to undertake the cost of acquiring qualifications whereas the less able will not. By using the additional information provided by the signals, firms can reduce the cost of ensuring self-selection. See Stiglitz (1975) and Riley (1979) for further discussion of these ideas.

A similar idea is exploited in the model of labour contracts originated by Grossman and Hart (1981) and developed by Hart (1983), Chari (1983) and Green and Kahn (1983). In that model, the marginal product of employees is a random variable whose realised value is observed only by the firm so this is an adverse-selection model in which, in the terminology we have used above, the firm is the agent and its employees the principals. The firm is risk-averse so it is efficient for it to share some of the risk with its employees. Before it learns the true marginal product, therefore, it wishes to make a contract to pay a low rate if marginal product is low and a high rate if marginal product is high. If that is all the contract says, the firm will always claim that marginal product is low in order to pay a lower wage. But it can be induced to tell the truth if hours of work are restricted when it claims productivity is low. Restricting hours reduces profits more when marginal product is high so, with the contract chosen appropriately, it can be made worthwhile for the firm to reveal that marginal product is high even though it has to pay a higher wage. Again, one goes about constructing incentive-compatibility constraints by requiring that truthful revelation is optimal.

5.6 TOURNAMENTS

The preceding discussion has considered contracts where there is some verifiable outcome on which payments can be based. But there is not always an outcome that is readily verified. A court can check whether a house has burnt down but it is not so easy to check the productivity of a bureaucrat or of a worker in a team. If wages are based on productivity, the manager may lie about productivity to get away with paying less. What sort of contract can deal with this additional problem?

Suppose the principal has more than one agent. He could then, much in the spirit of prizes in a competition, offer a contract in which the agent who had the best outcome received a large reward, the agent who received the second-best outcome a slightly lower reward, and so on. Like the prizes in a competition, the total payment by the principal is then independent of who does best. All the principal has to do *after* observing the outcomes is to announce which agent did best, which second-best, and so on. But since the total payment is fixed from the start, the principal has no incentive to misrepresent the outcome. Moreover, the agents still have an incentive to compete in order to get the higher rewards. Because of the analogy with winning prizes in competitions, such contracts have become known as tournaments.

In some circumstances, a contract of this sort is precisely equivalent to the separate contracts that would be agreed with each agent if the outcome were verifiable. This applies to both moral hazard and adverse selection, see Malcomson (1986). Even when they are not equivalent, however, tournaments provide a means of ensuring that the contract is incentive-compatible for the principal when outcomes are not verifiable. In the employment context, the prizes can take the form of being selected for promotion ahead of others of the same rank, as happens in corporate hierarchies. See

Lazear and Rosen (1981), Malcomson (1984) and Rosenbaum (1984) for further discussion of this.

There is another role for contracts with payments that depend on comparisons between agents. Consider a team of salesmen who each cover their own geographical area. To provide them with an incentive to work hard, their employer may want to reward each on the basis of the sales he achieves. Whether sales are good or bad depends not only on a salesman's own efforts but on other factors too. Some of those other factors may be common to all agents – it may be a good year for car sales so all salesmen achieve high sales without any extra effort on their part. If the employer is risk-neutral and the salesmen risk-averse, it is inefficient for the salesmen to bear more risk than is essential for providing appropriate incentives. But the risk associated with random effects common to all agents can be removed from their rewards, while still providing incentives for effort, by making the payment to each salesman depend on his performance relative to that of others. That way, the employer takes the profits when everybody has a good year and the losses when everybody has a bad one. The precise nature of the efficient contract depends of course on the precise nature of the random components. For details, see Green and Stokey (1983), Holmstrom (1982) and Nalebuff and Stiglitz (1983).

5.7 CONTRACTS FOR LONG-TERM RELATIONSHIPS

So far we have considered only contracts for one-off events where there is no question of their being continued or renewed in the future on terms that depend on what happens after they have come into force. In many situations of interest to economists, however, contractual relationships continue over time. Employers keep on some employees for long periods of time, see Hall (1982), and many insurance contracts are renewed year after year.

When there is a possibility of continuation or renewal, actions taken today are going to be modified if they involve repercussions tomorrow. This has two important consequences. First, people may adopt strategies to punish other parties in the future if they find out that they have not been doing what was agreed. Second, even if they do not know for certain whether the other party has been cheating, the conditions for renewing the contract tomorrow can be based on today's observed outcomes. The latter is well illustrated in practice by car insurance where agents lose all or part of a no-claims discount if they have a crash.

To see the effect that the possibility of punishment can have, consider the prisoners' dilemma game again. We argued earlier that, when this game is played only once, the only equilibrium is for both parties to adopt the strategy of confessing (C), even though, if neither confessed, they could get away with their misdemeanour. Now suppose the game is to be repeated each period for ever. Suppose, moreover, A and B agree beforehand that, if caught, they will both play the strategy of not confessing (NC) as long as the other has played NC in the past but, if one deviates by confessing (C), the other will respond by playing C for ever after. Will they then stick to their agreement? Will it be self-enforcing?

Think about B's best response to the agreed strategy. If he always plays NC and A responds as agreed, then he pays a fine of, say, £10 per period for ever. Let δ denote his discount factor, that is, if r is his discount rate, $\delta = 1/(1 + r)$. Then the present discounted value of the cost of this strategy is

$$10 + 10\delta + 10\delta^2 + 10\delta^3 + \ldots = 10/(1 - \delta)$$

If, on the other hand, he ever cheats on the agreement by playing C even though A has not previously played C, A will play for ever after. Once that has happened, it is always best for B to continue to play C since that way he incurs a fine of only, say, £20 per period, instead of a higher fine of £40 he pays if he plays NC. If he cheats today, of course, he escapes with no fine in the first period since A will still play NC under the agreement. But, since both play C for ever after, he will be faced with a fine of £20 in every subsequent period. The present discounted value of the cost of this strategy is therefore given by

$$0 + 20\delta + 20\delta^2 + 20\delta^3 + \ldots = (20\delta)/(1 - \delta)$$

Hence, provided that A is not going to cheat on the agreement, it will not be worth B cheating if

$$10/(1 - \delta) \leqslant (20\delta)/(1 - \delta)$$

that is, if $\delta \geqslant \frac{1}{2}$. In other words, if he does not discount tomorrow's costs too highly, the threat of lost cooperation in the future is sufficient to prevent cheating today. A precisely symmetric argument applies to A, so A will also find it worth not cheating for $\delta \geqslant \frac{1}{2}$. Moreover, because of the infinite time horizon, the calculation of whether it is worth cheating will be just the same tomorrow as it is today, so for $\delta \geqslant \frac{1}{2}$ neither will ever cheat. Thus, they will both stick to their agreement. Note that we have not required any part of this agreement to be legally enforceable. The entire agreement is self-enforcing without the need for a formal legal contract.

This type of result has a number of economic applications. One example is the case of oligopolistic firms which punish rivals who undercut them with an expensive price war. Then, even though explicit collusion may be illegal, it is in the interests of competitors to collude implicitly and maintain a high price, see Friedman (1971). Similarly, it may be in the interests of workers not to shirk on the job, even when their wage does not depend on performance, if they are better off working than unemployed and might lose their job as a result of shirking. This can lead to involuntary unemployment, see Shapiro and Stiglitz (1984) and MacLeod and Malcomson (forthcoming).

For sustaining such outcomes, it is important that A believes that B will not confess, B knows this, and so on. They do not actually have to have an agreement to this effect as long as they both believe that this is what the other will decide. With or without an agreement, however, if either believes that the other is actually going to confess, it becomes in his interest to confess too. This has two important consequences. First, there is no guarantee that cooperation will ever get off the ground, though it would seem more likely if the two parties had at least communicated beforehand. Second, it is crucial that the repetition goes on for ever. If it ever comes to an end, each party can gain, without risking any future loss, by confessing in the final period. Moreover, knowing that the other party will thus confess in the final period makes it in each party's interest to confess in the second-to-last period, and so on, so that the whole edifice unravels and cooperation never gets started.

In this example, one party knows straightaway if the other has cheated on the contract. Even if this is not the case, however, repetition can be used to make cooperation self-enforcing. To see this, consider the principal–agent problem of a risk-averse employee whose level of effort is unobserved by the foreman. The tasks he is given vary in difficulty and the foreman does not know how difficult any particular task is. If this was a one-off situation with just one task to be done, an efficient contract would require the employee to bear some risk in order to provide an incentive to work hard – if not, the employee would have an incentive to slack and claim that the task was more difficult than average. If, on the other hand, there is a sequence of tasks, the foreman will be somewhat sceptical if the employee claims that all the tasks he is given are more difficult than average. In the long run, if the number of jobs completed does not correspond to the average expected by the foreman, he will infer that the employee is slacking and fire him. As in the case of certainty, if the cost of being fired is sufficiently high, the employee will not slack. Rubinstein and Yaari (1983) have shown how no-claims discount rules can be used to avoid inefficiency arising from repeated moral hazard in insurance – if you are careless and so have a lot of claims, the premium will increase. Green and Porter (1984) have shown how cartels, even though technically illegal, can be sustained (with the occasional price war) by firms colluding as long as price remains high but competing if, as would be the case if some other firm was cheating, price falls below a certain level. A similar argument applies to the Grossman–Hart (1981) model of labour contracts in which only the firm observes the marginal product of its employees. If the firm does not claim that marginal product is high the correct proportion of the time, the employees will know it is cheating and can punish it appropriately, thus inducing truthful revelation in the first place.

One way to formalise this insight is along the lines of Radner (1981, 1985). If an employee slacks, the probability that the outcome will be poor is higher than if he does not. For any given sequence of outcomes, the foreman can thus apply a statistical test for the hypothesis that that sequence would arise by chance if the employee were not slacking. If the hypothesis is rejected, he punishes the employee. By the nature of such tests, the longer the relationship has lasted, the closer must be the average of the actual outcomes to the expected value. Radner (1986) has extended this approach to situations with more than two parties.

When the time-horizon is finite and no contract is legally enforceable, both parties in the prisoners' dilemma game confess from the start, as we have seen. If there is some verifiable outcome, it will then be efficient to make a legally enforceable contract. But would it be better to make a long-term contract rather than a series of short-term ones? A long-term contract is one that commits the parties to behave in the future in a way that they would not choose if making a short-term contract at the time. With just moral hazard, short-term contracts are as efficient as long-term contracts provided there is sufficient scope for penalising an agent in the short term, see Malcomson and Spinnewyn (1988). With adverse selection, however, if an individual's type remains the same over time (or, more generally, is not an independent random variable), the outcome in one period provides information about the distribution of outcomes in future periods. Then a long-term contract can typically offer efficiency gains. To illustrate the kind of commitments involved, consider the central planning model analysed by Freixas, Guesnerie and Tirole (1985) and Laffont and Tirole (1987). Factory managers know more about the productivity of their factories than does the central planning board. Suppose a manager reveals in the first period that his factory is highly productive. It is then optimal for the central planning board to require a higher output from given inputs in the following period. This is the so-called 'ratchet effect'. But if the manager knows this is going to happen, he has an incentive to produce too little output in the first period, so as not to reveal that his factory has high productivity, and enjoy some extra leisure. To induce the manager of a high-productivity factory to produce a high output now, the central planning board must commit itself *not* to demand too high an output in the future. It may not, of course be believed and this has important implications for how effective the contracting arrangements will be.

5.8   CONCLUSION

When information is asymmetric or not verifiable and agents have an incentive to cheat, contracts have to be designed to be incentive compatible. In the case of one-off events, this will normally prevent contracts from achieving the first-best outcome that would be achieved if there were full information. Efficient risk-bearing must then be sacrificed in order to provide incentives for the appropriate choice of action in the case of moral hazard and for self-selection in the case of adverse selection.

With repetition over time, however, one party can punish the other for cheating by refusing to renew the contract, or continuing it on less favourable terms. If the future is not discounted too highly, this can reduce or prevent cheating. Even if, because of random events, it is not possible to tell for certain whether one party has cheated, the other can tell in the long run by checking the statistical distribution of the sequence of outcomes and appealing to some law of large numbers to test how probable it is that such a sequence would arise if no cheating were taking place. By maintaining long-term relationships and making strategies depend on the past in this way, the cost of asymmetric or unverifiable information can be reduced, and may be eliminated altogether. Such long-term relationships enable people to reap the benefits of cooperation which might not otherwise take place.

6 Experimental Economics

GRAHAM LOOMES

6.1 INTRODUCTION

Laboratory experiments are such a firmly established part of teaching and research in the natural sciences that it is hard to imagine how any Department of Physics or Chemistry could function for long without access to a suite of laboratories. In certain behavioural sciences, too, experimentation is regarded as a key part of the discipline: for example, almost every undergraduate student of psychology will be encouraged to learn something about the basic principles and techniques of experimental investigation.

In economics, however, things are very different. At the time of writing, only a handful of North American universities, and very few anywhere else in the world, can claim to have an economics laboratory worthy of the name. Students may come across occasional references to experimental studies in their reading lists, and from time to time a lecture or seminar may draw their attention to some experimental evidence. But even in the USA there are very few accredited courses devoted to this kind of work, and in the whole of the UK at present there is only one: a one-term optional 'module' at the University of York.

However, phrases such as 'at the time of writing' and 'at present' are used advisedly. In recent years the situation has begun to change quite rapidly. In the 1960s, papers reporting the results of economics experiments were few and far between. In the 1980s, such papers are being published sufficiently often in mainstream journals to justify the introduction of a separate new category into the *Journal of Economic Literature's* classification system – No.215: Experimental Economic Methods.

Twenty years ago a chapter about experimental economics would probably not have been commissioned; and if it had been, the author would have struggled to find sufficient material to give it real breadth. Today the problem is deciding what to select and what to leave out when there is so much good material to choose from. The rest of the chapter is divided into three parts. Section 6.2 gives a fairly brief outline of what experiments might be designed to do. The rather longer section, 6.3, indicates, with examples, how experiments have been and are being used. Section 6.4 is a discussion of some of the limitations and possible problems facing experimenters, together with a view of the main tasks and prospects for the future.

6.2 WHAT EXPERIMENTS MIGHT BE DESIGNED TO DO

There are three main categories of uses to which experiments might be put. They are outlined below in a general way. In Section 6.3 we shall look at some specific examples.

To test theories and discriminate between them

If there are two or more theories about a particular area of economic behaviour, which should we choose? Traditionally, economists have relied on some mixture of judgement (e.g. how persuasive are the assumptions? How far is a particular model consistent with economists' general preconceptions about the world?) combined perhaps with some statistical or econometric analysis (if appropriate data is available). However, as we shall see later, there may be important cases where conventional wisdom is called into question and/or the available data are inadequate. In these circumstances (although *not only* in these circumstances) experiments may help to provide valuable evidence and powerful tests.

The principle is relatively straightforward. In the case of a particular theory, apply the theory to some (preferably simple) situation where it generates at least one clear prediction. Then design an experiment which captures the essential features of that situation and, as far as possible, controls for other factors, but which allows the possibility of other outcomes besides those predicted. Finally, observe the results. If observed behaviour runs counter to the predictions to an extent which is unlikely to be due to chance or simple error, the theory is called into question. Of course, even if most observed behaviour is in line with the prediction(s), it does not prove that this theory is *the* correct one: but it may increase our confidence in the model.

In the case of two or more competing theories, the challenge is to design a single experiment where the different models predict measurably different behaviour. Ideally, the results should be capable of providing evidence of the relative strengths or weaknesses of any or all of the theories concerned.

However, even if Theory *A* does consistently better than Theory *B* in one situation, that does not mean it will do better in others. And even if a variety of experiments all suggest that Theory *A* predicts better than Theory *B*, it is rarely the case (in behavioural sciences, at least) that a single simple model will be able to explain all, or nearly all, the behaviour to which it relates.

So a further possible role for experiments may be to investigate the 'sturdiness' of a theory, i.e. see how far the parameters of the situation can be changed before the model begins to fail, how well it captures responses to sudden disturbances or unexpected new developments, and so on. But although the principle may be straightforward enough, it may not be so straightforward in practice to design and conduct such experiments and interpret their results.

Searching for new information and fresh insights

In the course of conducting experiments primarily designed to test theory, researchers may produce some quite unanticipated patterns of behaviour which do not appear to fit in very well with any existing models. Of course, it is always necessary to check that this is not some artifact of the experimental design itself; but when such patterns continue to show up in further experiments using somewhat different designs, they can provide an enormous stimulus to extend existing theories and/or lay the foundations of new ones.

Sometimes too, experiments may be intended purely and simply as voyages of discovery. When we reach the limits of a particular model, introspection alone may not be sufficient to indicate how we should develop it further. One way forward may be to design experiments which set up situations of the kind we might wish to explore, and then just see what happens. This may not be as 'hit and miss' as it sounds: after all, we may often know in which direction we want to go, even though we may not have any very clear idea of what the terrain will be like. Of course, there will undoubtedly be misses; but this may be the price that has to be paid for hits which might not have been achieved (or at least, not so quickly) by any other means.

To try out practical solutions to practical problems

Although the various branches of physics and chemistry have amassed considerable knowledge and theoretical understanding about the properties of various substances, and their responses to being heated, vibrated, compressed, etc., it is quite usual for engineers contemplating some new form of construction to build a scale model – or several alternative scale models – before building begins in earnest. Similarly, psychologists may know a good deal about human perception of colour and shape, and about the associations set up by words and images, but companies will nevertheless often employ market researchers to measure public reactions to alternative brand names and labels before deciding exactly how to package their latest product. In economics too there may be some practical problems where theoretical introspection alone may not be sufficient, but where a well-focused experiment may provide useful guidance. We shall consider some examples in due course.

6.3 WHAT EXPERIMENTS HAVE BEEN AND ARE BEING USED TO INVESTIGATE

In the following two subsections, a selection of studies will be discussed. The idea is to give a taste of (and for) what has been achieved in certain areas where experimental methods have been applied.

Individuals dealing with an uncertain world

In Chapter 2, Mark Machina described developments up to the present time in modelling individual decision-making under risk and uncertainty. He indicated how modern theory may be traced back to a very early 'thought experiment' centring on what is now known as the St Petersburg paradox (see Section 2.2). The power of Bernoulli's example was such that it had the effect of stimulating alternative ideas leading to the formation of an early expected utility rule. During the past forty years, the modern form of expected utility theory – based on sets of axioms or postulates such as those proposed by von Neumann and Morgenstern (1947) and Savage (1954) – has come to dominate economic models involving risk and uncertainty.

In many ways this area of theory is an ideal subject for experimental investigation. The axioms give rise to clear and potentially refutable predictions about relatively simple and well-specified decision problems. The ability to set up such problems and present them to individuals under carefully controlled conditions makes experimental methods eminently suitable as a means of testing expected utility theory and many of its more recent rivals.

Experimental tests of expected utility go back almost as far as the theory itself. Machina (Chapter 2) describes some early examples, including the 'Allais paradox' which initially caused Savage to violate one of his own postulates. But Savage convinced himself – and many others, then and since – that his initial decision had been 'an error', and that on reflection he preferred to behave according to his postulates rather than his instincts. Many economists found the basic axioms so intellectually appealing, and the mathematical properties of the theory so tractable, that for many years they largely ignored the growing body of unfavourable experimental evidence, and concentrated instead on extending and adapting expected utility theory to almost every other area of economic theory which required its models to take some account of risk and uncertainty.

Meanwhile, as Machina's chapter shows, the evidence of systematic departures from expected utility theory continued to accumulate. That chapter summarises the material very effectively, and there is no need to review it all here. However, it may be instructive to take one section from that chapter, and look in more detail at a number of interesting issues it raises. The section in question concerns the 'preference-reversal phenomenon', described and discussed in Section 2.4. What I am about to say next will be best understood if you are familiar with the material covered in those pages. So please (re)read those pages before continuing.

The early preference-reversal experiments illustrate very well how to construct a simple but powerful experimental test. Participants might behave in one of four ways:

(i)   choose the *P*-bet and value it more highly than the $-bet
(ii) choose the $-bet and value it more highly than the *P*-bet
(iii) choose the *P*-bet but place a higher value on the $-bet
(iv) choose the $-bet but place a higher value on the *P*-bet.

Of these, only (i) and (ii) are consistent with expected utility theory. If the experiment had shown that there were many observations which violated conventional theory, but that they were reasonably evenly distributed between (iii) and (iv), the result might have tarnished the theory a little, but would not have represented a fundamental challenge: the reaction would probably have been to treat valuations of risk a little more cautiously, but to assume that on balance these were simple errors that would tend to cancel out.

However, the fact that Lichtenstein and Slovic had an alternative model which predicted that (iii) would be observed relatively more frequently than (iv), and the fact that this asymmetry *was* observed to an extent which could not readily be accounted for simply in terms of 'errors' (see Lichtenstein and Slovic, 1971, pp. 52–3 for an explanation of how they reached this conclusion) presented a much more substantial challenge to conventional assumptions.

Even so, the results took some time to percolate through to economics. Fortunately, two economists with knowledge and experience of experimental work became aware of the results. Their response – see Grether and Plott (1979) – is a fine example of how to conduct a follow-up study to check whether the earlier results might be largely explained by factors not fully controlled for in the original experiments. But although Grether and Plott, and others since, modified the experimental design in various ways, the preference-reversal phenomenon stubbornly persisted. The repeated failures to demonstrate that it was some kind of experimental artifact began to force more and more economists to look for some theoretical explanation.

Of course, one explanation already existed – the information-processing argument proposed by Lichtenstein and Slovic, 1971. Other models have also been suggested since, but for the moment let us focus on the one discussed at some length by Machina, namely 'regret' theory.

If there are two alternative explanations for the preference-reversal phenomenon, can we design an experiment which can discriminate between the two? The essence of Lichtenstein and Slovic's 1971 explanation is that individuals handle choices and valuations differently: they suggest that when making *valuations*, individuals tend to focus attention on the amounts that might be won or lost, and give particular weight to the *pay-offs*; whereas when making *choices*, they believe that people give a greater weight to the relative *probabilities* of winning at least something. By contrast, regret theory makes no distinction between valuation and choice: it explains preference reversals as one manifestation of predictable cycles of non-transitive pair-wise choice. We do not need to go further into the theoretical details here: what has just been said indicates that it should be possible to design an experiment which can distinguish between the two explanations, as follows.

First, we identify some pairs of *P*-bets and $-bets. Then we recruit a large number of participants and allocate them *at random* to one of two groups. Members of one of the two groups are presented with the standard set of three problems: that is, they make a choice between a *P*-bet and a $-bet; they announce a minimum selling price for the *P*-bet; and they announce a minimum selling price for the $-bet. Meanwhile members of the other group are presented with a somewhat different set of three problems. The *P*-bet and $-bet are the same, and the first problem is the same, i.e. they choose between the *P*-bet and the $-bet. But then instead of making two valuations, they make two choices: between the *P*-bet and some certain amount *C*; and between the $-bet and that same certain amount *C*. Then the behaviour of the two groups is compared.

The point of randomising participants between the two groups is to make the two groups as similar as possible. It is desirable to check that the randomisation has achieved its objective, and in the experimental design there is a natural check, because both groups have one problem in common: the choice between the P-bet and the $-bet. If there is no significant difference between groups in the proportions choosing each bet, it does not *prove* that the randomisation has worked, but it may increase our confidence that it has.

Then comparisons can be made between the answers to the other two questions. If, as regret theory assumes, there is no significant difference between the way people handle valuations and the way they handle choices, then we would expect to find that the proportion of the first group who gave the $-bet a value higher than C would not be significantly different from the proportion of the second group who chose the $-bet rather than the certainty of C; and likewise for the P-bet. Alternatively, if Lichtenstein and Slovic (1971) are correct in thinking that valuations are processed differently from choices and that this tends to lead individuals to overvalue the $-bet relative to the P-bet, we would expect this to show up in the comparisons of valuations and choices between the two groups.

When looking for violations of conventional theory, we would *not* expect to see as many non-transitive cycles in the second group as preference reversals in the first group, for the following reason. In the second group, where each individual makes three straight choices, the behaviour which is analogous to preference reversal involves choosing P rather than $, choosing $ rather than C, and choosing C rather than P. However, any individual who values both the $-bet and the P-bet more highly than C, or who values both bets lower than C, cannot be *observed* to commit any violation simply by looking at their choices. Thus even if regret theory is correct in suggesting that preference reversals are a reflection of predictable non-transitive behaviour, fewer 'violations' will be observed in the second group simply because that second group is presented with a fixed value of C chosen by the experimenter, whereas members of the first group are able to express their own valuations of the two bets at whatever levels reflect their individual preferences.

On the other hand, if preference reversals are primarily due to differences in the ways people make valuations and choices, the elimination of all valuation tasks in the second group should not simply reduce the number of observed violations: it should eradicate them altogether. Or, if we allow the possibility that *some* cyclical choices will still occur simply as the result of errors, the effect should be to end the imbalance between the numbers of predicted and unpredicted cycles: the implication of the Lichtenstein and Slovic type of argument is that the cycle where *P* is preferred to $, $ to *C*, and *C* to *P* should be no more common than the opposite cycle where $ is preferred to *P*, *P* to *C*, and *C* to $.

Robert Sugden, Chris Starmer and I have reported an experiment – Loomes, Starmer and Sugden (1989) – where 186 participants were divided into two groups of 93 along the lines described above. Briefly, the experiment found that the proportions of the first group who valued each bet higher than *C* were both slightly larger than the proportions of the second group who chose each bet in preference to *C*, but that these differences were not statistically significant.

As expected, violations of both kinds (i.e. predicted and unpredicted reversals/cycles) were less frequently observed in the second group; *but the imbalance remained, and was statistically significant*. So the elimination of valuations did *not* eliminate the preponderance of preference-reversal-type cycles over cycles in the opposite direction. This suggests that the phenomenon is not just an information-processing effect, but may represent a more fundamental challenge to the transitivity axiom – an axiom which forms a cornerstone of conventional expected utility theory, and which many economists regard as a fundamental requirement for rational choice under uncertainty.

This provides an interesting example of the productive tension between experimental results and theory. By the beginning of the 1980s a growing number of economists working in the area of decision theory had begun to come to terms with the idea that *some* concessions had to be made to the weight of experimental evidence. As Machina shows in Chapter 2, most of that evidence related to the independence axiom, and in the late 1970s and early 1980s several models were developed which 'relaxed' the independence axiom in various ways without completely undermining the theory: Machina's (1982) generalised expected utility theory (expected utility analysis without the independence axiom) is a case in point.

However, many economists who have accepted the modification of the independence axiom have been rather more reluctant to make similar concessions in relation to transitivity. Instead, some have begun to develop alternative explanations for the preference-reversal phenomenon which leaves the transitivity axiom intact.

Two examples of this kind of argument – by Holt (1986) and by Karni and Safra (1987) – are described by Machina (Chapter 2, note 24) as 'a final "twist" on the preference reversal phenomenon'. He says 'How (and whether) experimenters will be able to address this issue remains to be seen.'

In fact, the issues raised by Holt and by Karni and Safra are ones which experimenters simply *must* address, because they have important implications which go far beyond the preference-reversal phenomenon: both papers raise questions about whether or not certain common experimental procedures actually reveal individuals' true underlying preferences, i.e. whether the evidence they generate is really valid.

This is certainly quite a challenge. To provide an acceptable test of whether or not certain experimental procedures have distortionary effects, we need to design an experiment which must itself be free from those effects. There is not enough space here to go into great detail about how this might be done, but it seems safe to say that the story has not yet reached its *final* twist. Attempts to design appropriate experiments will begin by looking for the distinctive refutable predictions of the Holt, and Karni and Safra, arguments, and this in turn may encourage those authors to specify in more detail the behavioural implications of their arguments in a way that can be tested: at present the Holt argument is more of a conjecture than a formal proof; and although Karni and Safra show how preference reversals in the predicted direction *might* result from particular cases, they do not show that *in general* their argument will explain the striking preponderance of 'predicted' over 'unpredicted' reversals.

Clearly there is still a great deal more to come from the interaction between theory and experimentation in this field – and in other areas of individual behaviour. Since this chapter is not intended to be a comprehensive survey, only a couple of examples will be given here. Interested readers might like to look at the work by Knetsch and Sinden (1984) which suggests a disparity between willingness to pay for improvements and willingness to accept compensation for losses which is not easily reconciled with the conventional wisdom of welfare economics. And in an even more recent paper, Loewenstein (1987) revives some earlier notions about individual preferences concerning delayed consumption and presents some preliminary experimental evidence which challenges some of the assumptions (including the intertemporal analogue of the independence principle) which have become widely accepted in post-war models of intertemporal choice.

Since the concept of 'rational economic (wo)man' plays such an important part in economic models, it is clearly important to investigate individual behaviour carefully and comprehensively; and, as already indicated, experimental methods may be able to make a valuable contribution in this respect. However, most economic activity is not conducted by individuals in isolation, but often involves interaction of various kinds and at different levels: sometimes cooperative or collusive, sometimes competitive; sometimes between individuals, sometimes within or between organisations, sometimes in the context of the market-place and sometimes in the sphere of social choice and the political process.

Indeed, there are those who argue that it is precisely the forces of economic interaction which compel individuals to act rationally – or, at least, which punish persistent deviations from rationality. Some experiments have already been conducted to explore the impact of market pressures on individual 'irrationality', or to discover whether individual 'irrationality' translates into market inefficiency. Examples include a study by Berg, Dickhaut and O'Brien (1985) which introduced trading into a preference-reversal experiment, and a study by Knez, Smith and Williams (1985) which examined the impact of repeated market-trading on the disparities between buying prices and selling prices found in 'one-off' elicitations of value. Both papers are accessible, and I will not spoil the reader's pleasure by revealing the results of these studies.

Of course, there is a great deal of experimental work investigating many aspects of interactive behaviour. A substantial body of research, dating back several decades, has been concerned with 'games' between two or more agents. That literature will not be reviewed here, but those readers who were interested in the subject matter of Chapter 4 might begin their exploration of the experimental work in this area with a couple of the references described briefly at the end of this chapter. I shall deal with the experimental work on voting behaviour and social choice in the same way. This should not be regarded as a signal that those experiments are somehow less important or less interesting: on the contrary, they are often very stimulating. But space allows only one other area of experimental economics to be discussed in reasonable detail, and the natural candidate is the area which has to date received most attention from economists (and rather less from non-economists).

The operation of markets and the price mechanism

One of the earliest examples of experimental work in this area can be found in an article by Chamberlin (1948) examining behaviour under monopolistic competition. During the 1950s and 1960s only a handful of researchers – principally in the USA and West Germany – were using experiments to examine market behaviour, particularly in oligopolistic markets. Since then there has been an enormous growth in the range of issues explored in experimental markets.

The essential features of a simple experimental market are as follows. Some participants are given the role of demanders or buyers, while others may act as suppliers or sellers. The commodity being traded has no intrinsic value, but buyers are induced to purchase it because they are each given a 'redemption-value schedule' which shows them how much they will be paid by the experimenter for each unit of the commodity they have purchased during a particular experimental period. The left-hand column in Table 6.1 gives an example of a redemption-value schedule: a buyer who purchases three units during a particular period would be able to cash them in for a total of £17.10 (£6.15 + £5.70 + £5.25), while

TABLE 6.1 Demand and supply schedules

Unit	Redemption value £	Marginal cost £
1st	6.15	1.65
2nd	5.70	2.20
3rd	5.25	2.75
4th	4.80	3.30
5th	4.35	3.85
6th	3.90	4.40
7th	3.45	4.95

a buyer who purchases seven units would get a total redemption value of £33.60. Of course, to obtain those units, buyers must purchase from sellers. Whatever a buyer has paid to his/her suppliers is deducted from the total redemption value; what is left is the buyer's profit (analogous to the consumer's surplus) and his/her payment for taking part in the experiment is usually based directly on this surplus. For example, if the two buyers mentioned above had paid sellers £4.00 per unit, the first buyer would have £12.00 deducted from the £17.10 redemption value leaving a surplus of £5.10, while the second value would have £28.00 deducted from the £33.60, giving a surplus of £5.60. It should be clear from studying the redemption-value schedule that when the market price is £4.00, buyers who want to maximise their earnings should purchase five units, yielding a surplus of £6.25.

The redemption-value schedule is under the control of the experimenter and so demand can be manipulated as required: for example, experimenters can examine the impact of shifting the schedule up or down, or changing its slope, or giving different buyers different schedules, and so on.

Those participants who act as sellers are given similar incentives, except that for them the redemption-value schedule is replaced by a cost schedule, such as the one shown on the right-hand side of Table 6.1. In that example, a supplier who sells three units at £4.00 each would receive a total of £12.00 from buyers, but would then have to deduct total costs of £6.60 (£1.65 + £2.20 + £2.75), leaving a profit of £5.40. Again, it is clear that when the market price is £4.00, the profit-maximising volume of sales per supplier is five units. As with the redemption schedule, the cost schedule can be manipulated by the experimenter as required.

In the example given, demand and supply intersect when the quantity is five units: if the 'law of demand and supply' operates, this quantity should exchange at the price somewhere between £3.90 and £4.35. The first and most basic question to ask is: *does the law of demand and supply operate as economists tend to assume?*

To answer this question experimentally, it is necessary to do more than simply provide some participants with redemption-value schedules and others with cost schedules. Buyers and sellers must be brought together in some form of market. One of the issues which has been the focus of much attention is whether different kinds of market and different rules of conduct have systematic effects on prices and/or the quantities transacted. Do some forms of market tend to achieve equilibrium while others fail to do so? Do some forms of market reach equilibrium faster than others? If demand and supply schedules remain constant, is the equilibrium stable? If demand and/or supply conditions change, how quickly do different kinds of market reach a new equilibrium?

It is hard to imagine how fundamental questions such as these could be satisfactorily answered with non-experimental data. But well-designed experiments can provide many insights because they can create markets where basic demand and supply conditions are the same, and then vary the market institutions in a controlled way and observe the impact of these variations on market behaviour. For example, in some cases both sides of the market (i.e. buyers *and* sellers) are active, while in other cases only one side may be active. In some cases trading takes place openly, with all bids by buyers and/or offers (henceforth called 'asks') by sellers being announced to all traders, while in other cases bids or asks may be submitted separately and secretly (for example, in sealed envelopes) or deals may be negotiated privately between pairs or groups of buyers and sellers.

There are many other variations, but for the purposes of this chapter it will be sufficient to consider just two or three examples which illustrate a number of points of interest.

Let us begin with the case where the seller has just one item to sell and decides to put the item up for sale by auction. But what kind of auction? One well-known kind of auction is the *English auction* where the price starts low and competing potential buyers make successively higher bids until eventually one buyer makes a bid which is not superseded: trade then takes place at that price. However, there are other kinds of auctions. For example, in a *Dutch auction* the asking price starts high and then gradually decreases until someone accepts the price. Another form of auction requires all potential purchasers to submit 'sealed bids' before some specified deadline. Then all the sealed bids are opened and the purchaser who has submitted the highest bid acquires the item at that price. This is known as a *first-price sealed-bid auction*. There is a variant known as the *second-price sealed-bid auction* which operates in the same way except that the highest bidder only has to pay the amount offered by the second-highest bidder.

Coppinger, Smith and Titus (1980) conducted an experiment intended to compare behaviour in these four types of auctions. In the first part of their paper, they focus on English and Dutch auctions, and in the second part they are concerned with first-price and second-price sealed-bid auctions. However, the procedures they use in both parts are sufficiently similar to allow some four-way comparisons to be made.

Experimental sessions involved participants in a series of auctions of one or at most two types. Before each auction, each participant was given a 'resale value' (i.e. a redemption-value schedule for just one unit) with the incentive that if he won the auction, he would keep for himself the difference between the resale value and the price paid in the auction. Each participant knew only his own resale value, but the experimenters knew all the values and could therefore calculate whether the different types of auction tended to produce systematic differences in the means and variances of the prices at which sales occurred.

Before hearing the results of the experiments, you might like to consider how you would have behaved in the various circumstances, and compare that with some of the theoretical predictions. Suppose you were told that in a particular auction your resale value was to be £8.00. You do not know what other participants' resale values are, but in an English auction you can at least observe the bidding after someone else has made a bid of, say, £7.20, it clearly makes sense for you to make a slightly higher bid. Perhaps you bid £7.30. If this is met with a counter-bid of £7.40, it makes sense for you to bid £7.50, and thereafter to reply to further bids up to, but not beyond, a bid of £8.00.

Now if the truth is that you have been assigned the highest resale value, and if the next highest resale value is £7.50, you should win the auction with a bid of either £7.50 or £7.60. Alternatively, if £8.00 is in fact the second highest resale value, you should not win the auction: the person with the highest resale value should win with a bid of £8.00 or £8.10. In other words, under the rules of an English auction, the expectation is that the purchaser who places the highest value on the item should acquire the item and pay a price equal to, or just above, the second-highest valuation.

How does this compare with a Dutch auction? Suppose the asking price starts at £12.00 and, in the absence of takers, is steadily reduced. If no one has accepted by the time the price falls to £8.00, what would you do? You could bid immediately and win the auction – but since your bid would equal your resale value, you would not make any money. Alternatively, you could wait until the price has fallen lower: but how far should you let it fall? The longer you wait, the more money you stand to make; but the longer you wait, the more likely it becomes that someone else will accept the price and win the auction, in which case you earn nothing.

If the truth is that you have the highest resale value and the second highest value is £7.50, you may be able to let the price fall a little below £7.50 and still win the auction so long as the participant with the second highest valuation also decides to wait a while. However, you do not know what the second highest valuation is, or what that bidder's temperament is like. Indeed, the fact that the price has fallen as far as £8.00 does not even tell you that you have the highest resale value – it could be that someone else has a value of, say, £8.30 and has decided to wait a while. So at what price would you make your move?

Clearly there is more room in Dutch auctions than in English auctions for two kinds of misjudgement: some participants with the highest resale values will bid too soon and pay a price substantially above the second highest valuation; while others may wait too long and be beaten by participants with lower resale values. If one measure of the efficiency of an auction is the percentage of times that the item goes to the purchaser with the highest valuation, it seems likely that Dutch auctions will be less efficient than English auctions. But overall, will 'bidding too soon' and 'waiting too long' tend to cancel out? On average will sale prices in Dutch auctions be higher, or lower, or about the same as in English auctions? We shall soon see what happened in the experiment.

Meanwhile consider the two types of sealed-bid auction. What would you do under the rules of the second-price auction? Suppose, as before, that your resale value of £8.00 is truly the highest, with the second highest being £7.50. Assuming that no one bids *more* than their resale value, you will win the auction and pay not more than £7.50 whether you bid £7.60 or £7.80 or £8.00. In other words, there is no advantage in bidding less than your full resale value, because you will only pay the amount of the second-highest bid. On the other hand, there is a *disadvantage* in bidding less than your resale value: you could lose the auction when you should have won it, and end up with nothing when you might have had something.

According to this reasoning, each participant should bid their full resale value, in which case the participant with the highest valuation of the item will always acquire it, and the price paid will be equal to the second highest valuation. Thus this type of auction should produce much the same results as the English auction, so long as everyone acts according to the above reasoning. Of course, if some participants do not reason in that way and enter bids below their resale values, two things might happen:

   (i) participants with the highest valuations may sometimes fail to win the auction;

  (ii) the second highest bid may sometimes be less than the second highest valuation so that average sale prices may be a little lower than in English auction.

The extent of (i) and (ii) will depend on the proportion of participants who do not act according to the reasoning suggested above. How big that proportion is, and whether the proportion changes with experience, are questions on which an experiment can shed light.

Finally, consider the first-price sealed-bid auction. In this case if you win you pay the full amount you have bid. So, as with the Dutch auction, if you have the highest resale value and bid it, you will win the auction but make no money. To make money you must enter a bid below your resale value. But again, as with the Dutch auction, the problem is: how far below? According to Vickrey (1961, p. 20) 'The motivations, strategies and results of (first-price sealed-bid auctions) can be analyzed in exactly the same way as was done above with the Dutch auction.' In other words, behaviour is predicted to be the same in first-price sealed-bid auctions as in Dutch auctions – one of several predictions the experiment set out to test.

On the basis of the data generated by Coppinger, Smith and Titus, the following conclusions can be drawn. The English auction was most efficient, as measured by the percentage of times that the participant with the highest valuation won the auction. Moreover prices tended to be closely grouped around the optimal price (i.e. the second-highest valuation), although on average slightly above the optimal, mainly because bids are stepped up in finite increments. In Dutch auctions prices were liable to deviate much more from the optimal price, sometimes above and sometimes below. In some sessions this appeared to produce rather lower average prices than in comparable English auctions, but in other sessions the difference was not significant.

In the second-price sealed-bid auctions the evidence suggest that quite a large proportion of participants did not bid their full resale values. There appears to have been some learning with experience (although it is not clear exactly how this learning occurred), but the net result is that average prices tended to be a little below the optimal price, although the difference was not statistically significant.

By contrast, prices in the first-price sealed-bid auctions were significantly above the optimal level. This appears to run counter to Vickrey's conjecture. The authors suggest several possible reasons for this, but cannot confidently discriminate between these explanations on the basis of the experimental evidence available to them. This was clearly something that required further investigation.

Of course, we must be careful not to generalise too freely from these results. The experiments were designed to test certain theoretical predictions or conjectures rather than to mimic non-experimental auctions. For example, in every auction each participant knew exactly what his/her resale value was, whereas in many non-experimental auctions, purchasers may not know the value of the item so surely and precisely. Or again, in many sessions participants' resale values were drawn from a rectangular distribution of such values, whereas in reality valuations may not be distributed in this way.

However, these are not objections to the experiments conducted and reported by Coppinger, Smith and Titus. No single experiment can do everything, and they were operating quite properly within specific terms of reference. Other questions – such as the effect of varying the number of bidders under each type of auction or changing the size of the decrements in the Dutch auctions, or the impact of uncertainty about the true value of the item – might reasonably be left to later studies. Indeed, the authors themselves indicated ways in which their experiments might be followed up, and some issues have been examined subsequently – for example, by Cox, Roberson and Smith (1982). More recently, Kagel and

Levin (1986) have investigated the impact of uncertainty about the 'true' value of the item being auctioned and have considered the extent to which such uncertainty may contribute to the 'winner's curse', whereby winning bids overestimate the true value and result in financial losses.

Having looked at some of the work that has been concerned with single-item auctions, let us now move on to other kinds of market that have received considerable attention – markets with a number of both buyers and sellers, each equipped with redemption-value schedules and cost schedules of the sort shown in Table 6.1.

A particular market form which has attracted much attention is the *double auction*. In essence, these markets work as follows. When a trading period opens, any buyer (seller) can announce publicly that he/she is willing to purchase (sell) a unit at a specified price. If that bid (ask) is accepted by any seller (buyer), the unit is traded and it is then up to any buyer (seller) to announce a fresh bid (ask) for another unit. Alternatively, if the initial bid (ask) is not accepted, buyers may make progressively higher bids and/or sellers may announce successively lower asks until someone accepts and the unit is transacted. This procedure is repeated until no further trades occur, or until the pre-specified trading time has elapsed, at which point that period ends. Then a new trading period opens, with buyers and sellers starting the process afresh.

Again, you might like to imagine how you would behave in such a market. Suppose you are a buyer with the redemption-value schedule shown in Table 6.1. There are, let us say, three other buyers each with their own schedules (which may be different from yours) and four sellers each with cost schedules (which may be different from each other). Would you make an opening bid? If so, how much would you offer? Or if a seller made the first move, with an ask of, say, £6.00, would you accept? Your redemption value schedule will pay you £6.15 for the first unit, so you could accept and make 15p. But if you wait – or make a counter-bid – the price might fall. On the other hand, if the price does fall, some other buyer might jump in. What would you do?

Since all buyers and sellers face similar dilemmas, and since initially they all know very little about each other's propensities to buy or sell, the first couple of trading periods typically involve trades taking place over a fairly wide range of prices; but it has frequently been observed that as participants gain experience of the market, the spread of prices tends to reduce, and prices and quantities tend to converge towards competitive equilibrium. Moreover, there is much evidence to suggest that if the equilibrium is disturbed – for example, by a change in some or all of the schedules – double auction markets seem to adjust fairly to the new competitive equilibrium.

Because this has been observed so frequently with many different configurations of demand and supply, a number of experienced experimenters have come to regard double auctions as a kind of standard against which other forms of market might be compared. The study we shall now consider is a comparison between double auctions and the posted-offer type of market.

Although double auctions often perform at high levels of efficiency, most people rarely trade in such markets under non-experimental conditions. Most people make the majority of their purchases in markets where sellers simply 'post' a price, i.e. put price labels on the goods and/or announce the price in advertisements or catalogues. It is then up to consumers to try to buy the quantities they want at the most favourable prices they can find. There is often little opportunity for haggling, and although sellers may adjust prices up or down periodically, they are normally thought to do so in response to *quantity* signals: that is, if goods sell faster than anticipated, fresh stocks may be supplied at a higher price; alternatively if sales are sluggish, prices may be cut. Since this kind of market is such an important part of economic life, it clearly warrants study.

Ketcham, Smith and Williams (1984) mounted such a study. Their paper describes the computerised experimental design clearly. Readers will see how they tried to achieve a high level of comparability between double auctions and posted-offer markets, while also trying to control for factors such as the level of experience of participants and the amount of information sellers have about the prices being posted by other sellers. Although their double auctions were not continued beyond ten trading periods (on the grounds that their convergence and stability properties were already well established), the posted-offer markets lasted for up to twenty-five periods. The authors consider that their experimental data generally support the view (formed on the basis of a number of earlier smaller studies) that prices tend to be higher and efficiency lower in posted-offer markets than in comparable double-auction markets, although they acknowledge that other factors in the experimental design, and the level of experience of the participants, may also play a role. One possible reason why prices may tend to be higher in posted-offer markets is that price-posting gives sellers a means of signalling to each other and establishing some tacit collusion. The authors suggest that the experiments provide considerable evidence of attempts to use price signals to establish tacit collusion, but they conclude that by and large such collusion was unstable in their experimental markets.

Alger (1987) also investigated this question in relation to posted-price markets. He allowed for large numbers of trading periods and incorporated several features favourable to an equilibrium price above the competitive level. Several interesting trends were observed. In some trials, from quite an early stage, the market began to trade at prices near the monopoly level, and tended to stabilise at that level. In a number of other trials, prices initially moved down towards the competitive level, but then there appear to be attempts by traders to raise prices. In some cases these attempts are successful in the sense that prices reach and stabilise at near-monopoly levels; in other cases, prices fall back and are on average closer to the competitive level, although they tend *not* to stabilise.

The suspicion that posted-price mechanisms might facilitate collusion and encourage higher prices lay behind several 'applied' experiments which may be of interest. One of these was concerned with the question of whether owners of inland water-barges should be required to post their prices for carrying freight rather than negotiate prices privately with their various customers, as was currently the practice. The experiment involved building a 'scale model' of a stretch of waterway (a section of the Mississippi river) and comparing the performance of the two forms of market. The results suggested that the introduction of price-posting would raise prices, reduce efficiency and disadvantage owners of small barges. The proposal to require price-posting lapsed. Fuller details of this experiment can be found in Hong and Plott (1982); a short article by Plott (1986) summarises this and some other applications and implications of posted-price experiments.

A variety of other market experiments have covered a range of interesting issues too extensive to be properly dealt with here. However, the examples given may be sufficient to convey a sense of how economics experiments operate. Perhaps they have also caused a number of questions, doubts and criticisms to begin to form in your mind. In section 6.4 some of the most common doubts are raised, and some possible responses are discussed.

6.4 THE POTENTIAL AND THE LIMITATIONS OF EXPERIMENTAL METHODS

One of the most frequently expressed doubts about economics experiments is that they are too *artificial, over-simplified* and *unreal* to be of much genuine value. This kind of criticism has a number of aspects.

The first point to make is that experiments *are* artificial, in the literal sense that they are deliberately (and, one hopes, artfully) constructed. Of course, this is true not only for economics experiments, but for experiments in physics, chemistry, biology, medicine, psychology and so on. Artificial does not necessarily mean shallow or false. The important questions are: what is the purpose of the experiment? how worthwhile is that purpose? and how well does the experiment achieve its purpose?

If the purpose is to test some aspect of theory, then so long as the experiment is appropriately designed for the task, simplicity may be a virtue rather than a vice. To illustrate the point, consider some of the more recent experiments designed to test expected utility theory. Many of these have asked participants to make decisions involving actual sums of money and probabilities which are relatively straightforward. If one or more of the fundamental axioms of expected utility theory fail under such apparently favourable conditions, there are surely grounds for questioning the power of the model as a *general* theory of individual decision-making under risk and uncertainty. If the basic axioms are substantially and *systematically* violated in these simple cases, how confident can we be about their validity in more complex situations? The fact that those axioms underpin many practical policy decisions with very real implications for people's welfare would seem to be good reason for putting them to the test.

Another source of doubts about the 'realism' of experimental tests concerns the validity of the assumptions built into experiments. On this question, a comment by Heiner (1985) and the reply by Smith (1985) are worth reading. One of the points Heiner makes is that many market experiments induce demand and supply by means of schedules which give participants precise, well-ordered preferences. However, 'in reality' many individuals are far from precise and certain about their own preferences. Heiner recognises that some experiments build in an element of uncertainty, but he regards this as only a 'limited step' because it involves *controlled* uncertainty imposed by the experimenter rather than individuals' *intrinsic* uncertainty about their own preferences. In reply, Smith acknowledges the need to examine the fundamental assumptions of conventional theory, but suggests that 'experimental methods are entirely competent to examine these important issues' – and he cites some of the expected utility experiments to illustrate his case.

However, Heiner's point about consumers' imprecision and uncertainty concerning their own preferences might also apply to suppliers' uncertainty about their cost schedules. Even with sophisticated accounting systems, many multiproduct multisite companies might find it difficult to give confident and precise estimates of their marginal cost functions. Moreover, many of the market experiments to date have implicitly encouraged suppliers to act as simple profit-maximisers, and have given less attention to other models of corporate motivation.

In response to this, it might be argued that there is no reason why experiments should not be designed to examine the behaviour of firms modelled in a different way: for example, it is not hard to imagine how a system of incentives and rewards might be organised to encourage participants to maximise market share, or maximise sales revenue subject to a minimum profit constraint.

On the other hand, it may be a great deal more difficult to explore experimentally some of the managerial or behavioural models of the firm. Such models may involve a variety of motives and objectives – status, power, ideological conflicts, job (dis)satisfaction, political influence, and so on – which would be hard to replicate under experimental conditions. Moreover, in order to try to incorporate even some of these factors into experiments in a meaningful way, it would probably be necessary to study them in depth by other methods such as questionnaires or participant observation – in which case, it may be that further experimental replication may not have much to add.

However, no one (as far as I know) is arguing that experimental methods are the only, or always the best, techniques for improving our understanding of economic behaviour. Yet even in cases of considerable complexity they may have something to contribute. For example, in many organisations there is often a good deal of negotiation and bargaining – between employers and unions, perhaps, or between one department and another. This may be represented in terms of game theory, which in turn may be investigated experimentally.

A further doubt about the 'realism' of experiments relates to the fact that participants are frequently recruited from among student populations: how confident can we be that students operating in environments with which they are unfamiliar will give us worthwhile insights into the behaviour of experienced decision-makers familiar with (and perhaps highly trained to deal with) the problems which they repeatedly face?

This kind of question raises several issues. The first is whether different types of participants exhibit significantly different patterns of behaviour. In his survey article, Plott (1982, p. 1522) wrote 'To date, no subject pool differences which bear on the reliability of economic theory have been reported.' However, more recently there have been some studies which suggest that there *are* cases where interesting differences may arise. For instance, Kahneman, Knetsch and Thaler (1986) constructed a number of economic scenarios and elicited judgements from a sample drawn from the telephone-owning population of Vancouver about whether certain kinds of behaviour were fair or unfair. Subsequently Kunreuther (1987) reported that his colleague Colin Camerer had put some of the same questions to a group of graduate business-administration students, and that in some scenarios these students had made rather different judgements about what was or was not fair behaviour.

Does this mean that producers and consumers hold substantially different views about what constitutes fair business practice? Alternatively, is it the case that when students take jobs which bring them into contact with consumers' reactions, they learn to modify their views (or at least their behaviour) accordingly? This prompts a further question about the validity of results generated by inexperienced participants: with greater experience does learning occur – even within a given experimental environment – which significantly alters observed behaviour? (Recall the Coppinger,

Smith and Titus study, which suggested that some learning about the optimal strategy in second-price auctions took place as the experiment progressed.)

More work to investigate the nature and importance of learning and experience in different kinds of experiments will undoubtedly form part of the research agenda during the coming years. Related to this, we may also expect to see more studies of a kind that have already begun, to examine more closely the formation and revision of expectations, and the development and relative performance of various rules and procedures to deal with complex problems within the constraints of 'bounded rationality'. Here, too, comparisons between different subject pools may prove instructive. For example, Burns (1985) ran the same auction experiment with two different types of participants – one group being 'inexperienced' undergraduate students, while the other group consisted of a number of 'experienced' professional wool-traders. Surprisingly (or so it seemed at first) the students did rather better at making profits than the professional traders. This prompted Burns to follow up the study by interviewing the traders about why they had behaved as they did in the experiment, and these interviews revealed that the traders were bringing to the experiment a number of patterns of behaviour which they had developed to meet the circumstances of their professional lives, but which were inappropriate to the rather different conditions in the experimental market. There is something in this example for both critics and proponents of experiments: critics will take it as further evidence of the 'irrelevance' of results generated by student participants in simplified environments; proponents will point to the way in which a comparative experimental study, intelligently followed up, can help to reveal something about the procedures that actual traders may adopt to facilitate long-term survival in a 'real' market.

The debate about such issues will no doubt continue – and so it should, for the signs so far are that it has been productive. On the one hand, close critical scrutiny by sceptics provides a useful check on the reliability and validity of experimental results, and stimulates further improvements in experimental designs. On the other hand, the exposure of a growing number of areas of economic theory and practice to increasingly sophisticated experimental investigation can be expected to yield fresh insights and new ideas of a kind that might not be generated by any other method of research.

Besides their value as research tools, economics experiments may also have considerable potential for training and education. In principle, many existing experimental designs could be adapted for teaching purposes. Involving people in experimental environments can be a good way of generating interest – even enthusiasm – in topics and concepts which may sometimes appear rather abstract. For example, it can be a good deal more stimulating to be a participant in a market interacting with other buyers and sellers (even on a hypothetical basis) than to be a spectator watching demand and supply curves intersect on a blackboard. People may be much better motivated to analyse data which they have themselves helped to generate, and may feel much more committed to understanding their own and others' behaviour in an environment in which they have themselves played a part.

At present, the lack of readily available materials and the fact that few economists have much experience of experimental procedures undoubtedly constitutes a barrier. Yet if, as seems inevitable, the scope and influence of experimental methods continue to grow, it will become increasingly important to make future generations of economists aware of the strengths and weaknesses, the possible uses – and the possible abuses – of this kind of activity. Moreover it will be necessary to take increasing numbers of students beyond the stage of being observers or participants, and introduce them to the issues involved in *conducting* experimental work. Those of us who have undertaken such research have found that the process of designing, piloting, and modifying experiments can itself be a valuable discipline which is at least as challenging as the more traditional forms of research activity.

However, the importance of giving economists more experience and a better understanding of experimental methods goes far beyond the desire to use those methods for research in academic institutions. In the past, a great many experiments have been conducted which were not primarily economics experiments but which have had substantial economic and social welfare implications. For example, every year in the field of health care there are a large number of experimental studies (sometimes known as randomised controlled trials, or RCTs) that may lead to decisions which have considerable implications for the use of scarce social resources and for the quality and length of people's lives. However, with only a few exceptions, there has been little input from economists *at the design stage* of such studies, with the result that the data necessary for a thorough evaluation of costs and benefits has either not been collected or else is incomplete, and a great deal of guesstimating has ensued.

This is partly the result of the trial organisers being unfamiliar with economic analysis; and it is partly because of the lack of economists who are sufficiently familiar with experimental design. However, what it adds up to is the fact that millions of pounds are spent on RCTs and other health-care studies with minimal economic content, and policy decisions involving yet more millions of pounds are taken without the benefit of a proper economic appraisal. In the USA since 1970 more than $500m have been spent on 'social experiments' of various kinds, but a number of researchers familiar with some of those experiments regard them as inadequately designed or conducted. By developing a stronger experimental tradition, and by producing more economists with greater experience and understanding of experimental methods, it is possible that social experiments and health-care studies in the future will generate better economic data and provide a sounder basis for a range of important policy decisions.

7 General Equilibrium and Disequilibrium and the Microeconomic Foundations of Macroeconomics

PAUL MADDEN

7.1 INTRODUCTION

The elementary theory of consumer and producer behaviour under competitive conditions, and the resulting elementary supply/demand model of the partial equilibrium of a single market are the foundations on which the models of general (economy-wide) Walrasian equilibrium are built. By 1960 a rigorous development of such models, in the context of what has become known as the Arrow–Debreu economy, had taken place. As economy-wide models, these can claim to be macroeconomic; and yet their clear specification of the behaviour of individual agents (consumers and firms) which leads to the macroeconomic outcome, gives them a microfoundation. However, at that time they presented a dilemma to economic theory, since most of the central features of interest to macroeconomists (including e.g. money, expectations, involuntary unemployment) are missing from these Walrasian, Arrow–Debreu models. On the other hand, the then popular macroeconomics built on aggregate demand/supply analysis, IS–LM analysis and the Phillips curve trade-off between output and inflation clearly involved money, expectations, etc., and thus did not rest on the

Walrasian, Arrow–Debreu base; the appropriate microeconomic foundation for this macroeconomics was not clear. From then on it is possible to identify a number of themes in the literature aimed at providing a microfoundation for macroeconomics. The objective of this chapter is to introduce the reader to some of the important surviving themes from this literature.

Section 7.2 addresses the initial *Walrasian, Arrow–Debreu model*, in which there are *complete markets* (including all future markets) at the initial date, thus removing any essential role for money, expectations etc. Introducing transactions costs to endogenise an incomplete market structure led to the *money and general equilibrium* literature (also Section 7.2). Mostly, however, the literature has so far taken the short cut of assuming an exogenous incomplete market structure. Models of *short-run Walrasian equilibrium* (Section 7.3) look for market clearing on current (incomplete) markets given expectation formation mechanisms about the missing future markets. Moving beyond the short run allows expectation revision to be modelled and leads to the extreme *perfect foresight* (Section 7.4) and *rational expectations* Walrasian models of the stationary variety. Attempts to uncover business cycle features e.g. Phillips curves, in such Walrasian models led to a relaxation of the Walrasian perfect information assumption (Section 7.5). The entire *search unemployment* literature emerged. Most influential has been Lucas (1972) where an *imperfect information, rational expectations* model produces no usable Phillips curve trade-off – the curve is vertical at the so-called *natural rate* – and yet the stochastic specification would generate evidence in favour of such a trade-off, supporting the emasculation of the real power of economic policy associated with so-called *new classical macroeconomics*. Recently (Section 7.6) Grandmont (1985) has provided a significant new twist to this story by relaxing the stationarity assumption in a perfect foresight Walrasian equilibrium and generating *cyclical* or *periodic* solutions which support a Phillips curve trade-off and a real role for stabilisation policy. All these more or less Walrasian models provide no account of involuntary unemployment. Section 7.7 looks at non-Walrasian approaches, especially the short-run *disequilibrium* or *fixed price* approach which provides a microfoundation for aggregate demand–supply and IS–LM analysis, and the *imperfect competition* approach where partial equilibrium oligopoly (especially) models are transferred to a general equilibrium framework. Omitted here are discussions of *bargaining* and *implicit contracts*, respectively discussed in Chapters 4 and 5.

7.2 GENERAL WALRASIAN EQUILIBRIUM AND THE ARROW–DEBREU ECONOMY

The elementary supply and demand model of the determination of equilibrium price on a competitive market is based on the *ceteris paribus* assumption that incomes and prices on other markets are fixed. Models of general Walrasian equilibrium take this partial equilibrium analysis, relax the *ceteris paribus* assumption and focus on competitive equilibrium throughout the economy. The individual agents in such an economy are perfectly and costlessly informed of current prices; they formulate desired demands and supplies for each good, subject to budget and technology constraints, and on the competitive assumptions that they have no market power over current prices and that they will be able to transact their desired demands and supplies at these prices without any transactions costs. General Walrasian equilibrium occurs at prices which equate total aggregate desired demand to supply on every market. Interest focused initially on general Walrasian equilibrium in what has come to be known as the Arrow–Debreu economy, after Arrow (1953) and Debreu (1959). This economy lasts for a finite number of periods (maybe one). In the first period agents know their lifetime preferences and production possibilities and markets for every commodity, current and future and at every location are open. In addition there is a full set of contingency markets, where future exchange is conditional on some specified state of the world. At the initial date there are then *complete markets*.

Clearly complete markets are empirically implausible. Moreover with complete markets at the initial date, all economic activity, present and future, can be settled at the initial date after which no further markets are necessary. Agents would then never demand worthless paper money at the initial date; nor do they need to form expectations about markets in the future. The value of the Arrow–Debreu story is that it is idealistic, abstracting from a number of complicating factors. Once the Walrasian Arrow–Debreu model is understood extensions towards a more interesting macroeconomic scenario can be addressed. The rest of this section is devoted to a discussion of the central features of Walrasian equilibrium theory in the Arrow–Debreu framework. These ideas will be presented initially in the context of an *exchange economy*, where there are m consumers and n goods and the only economic activities are exchange and consumption; firms will be added later.

Consumer h has an *endowment* $e^h = (e^h_1,...,e^h_n)$ of the n goods; endowments are exogenously given in the model. $U^h(C^h) = U^h(C^h_1,...,C^h_n)$ denotes consumer h's *utility function* representing preferences over final consumption of the n goods. C^h must belong to h's *consumption set* which is the set of feasible consumption vectors for h. Given prices $p = (p_1,...,p_n)$ for the n goods, consumer h would like to exchange the initial holding e^h for a vector C^h which is utility-maximising subject to the budget restrictions:

$$\max_{C^h \geqslant 0} U^h(C^h) \text{ subject to } \sum_{i=1}^{n} p_i C^h_i \leqslant \sum_{i=1}^{n} p_i e^h_i \qquad (7.1)$$

This formulation reflects the competitive nature of the economy; market prices p are given to the consumer who believes he has no control over them (C^h is chosen, not p) and the consumer believes he can supply or demand as much as he wishes given p and subject only to budget constraints.

A crucial assumption in Walrasian models is *convexity*. Here this would require formally that the set $\{C^h | U^h(C^h) \geqslant U^h(\hat{C}^h)\}$ is a convex set for all $\hat{C}^h \geqslant 0$; or, equivalently, the function U^h is quasi-concave. More informally, the requirement is that given two consumption vectors between which the consumer is indifferent, the consumer would prefer (or be indifferent to) any weighted average of these two vectors to either alone.

Another assumption is *monotonicity* which, roughly speaking, requires that more goods are preferred to less; e.g. $C^h > \hat{C}^h$ implies $U^h(C^h) > U^h(\hat{C}^h)$. Under these assumptions and also assuming that for every p there is a unique solution to (7.1), the solutions to (7.1) can be described by functions $C^h_i(p)$, $i = 1,...,n$, known as the consumer's *Walrasian demand functions*; then $z^h_i(p) = C^h_i(p) - e^h_i$, $i = 1,...,n$ are the consumer's *Walrasian excess demand functions*, and they indicate, at prices p, the consumer's desired demand of good i (if $z^h_i(p) > 0$). At solutions to (7.1) the budget constraint will be satisfied with equality (from monotonicity), which implies

$$\sum_{i=1}^{n} p_i z_i^h(p) = 0.$$

Moreover multiplying every price by the same factor $\lambda > 0$ leaves the budget constraint unchanged and hence solutions unchanged; thus $z_i^h(\lambda p) = z_i^h(p)$ for all i, h, p, which is homogeneity of degree zero of the excess-demand functions. Finally, it can be shown that, under convexity, the $z_i^h(p)$ will be continuous functions. The *aggregate excess demand* for good i, denoted $Z_i(p)$ is defined as

$$\sum_{h=1}^{m} z_i^h(p);$$

$Z_i(p)$ measures 'total desired demand = total desired supply' at p. Thus, *Walrasian equilibrium prices* are defined as p such that:

$$Z_i(p) = 0 \qquad i = 1, \ldots, n \qquad (7.2)$$

At such prices all markets in the economy clear, and every agent can then execute his desired trades, giving rise to a post-trade *Walrasian equilibrium allocation*. Walrasian models assume that the economy finds itself in a state of Walrasian equilibrium and analyse properties of such equilibria. The first question to be asked concerns the logical consistency of such models or the existence question: do there exist Walrasian equilibrium prices – is it possible that all markets clear simultaneously?

The answer hinges on the three properties of aggregate excess demands which follow from their analogous individual properties. Adding individual budget constraints gives

$$\sum_{i=1}^{n} p_i Z_i(p) = 0$$

which is *Walras law* and implies that if $n-1$ markets clear at p (e.g. $Z_1(p) = , \ldots, = Z_{n-1}(p) = 0$) then the remaining market clears also. In addition $Z_i(p)$ are *homogeneous of degree zero*, *continuous* functions and satisfy certain *boundary conditions*, not mentioned earlier. Homogeneity implies that

$$Z_i(p_1, p_2, \ldots, p_n) = Z_i \left[\frac{p_1}{p_n}, \frac{p_2}{p_n}, \ldots, 1 \right]$$

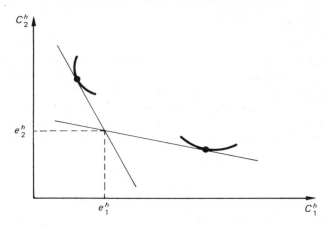

FIGURE 7.1   Individual demands at small and large p_1

for instance, and it means there is no loss of generality in equating or normalising p_n to 1 (good n becomes *numéraire* throughout from now on, letting merely $p_1,\ldots,p_{n-1}$ denote the price of good i in terms of good n). Mathematical proofs of existence can now be found in many texts (e.g. Varian, 1938); for the purposes here, a brief intuitive discussion of the simple 2 good case will be found useful. Indifference curves and two budget lines are shown in Figure 7.1 for a consumer with endowment (e_1^h, e_2^h). When the budget line is very flat p_1 is very small and, as shown, $z_1^h(p_i, 1) > 0$; and when the budget line is very steep, p_1 is very large and $z_1^h(p_2, 1) < 0$. In aggregate, the following boundary properties of $Z_1(p_1, 1)$ follow: as $p_1 \to 0, Z_1(p_1, 1) > 0$ and as $p_1 \to \infty$, $Z_1(p_1, 1) < 0$. Figure 7.2(*a*) illustrates these boundary properties: joining up the segments in Figure 7.2(*a*) *continuously* means that the graph crosses the axes at least once (three times in Figure 7.2(*b*)), where $Z_1(p_1, 1) = 0$ and by Walras law $Z_2(p_1, 1) = 0$ also. Thus at least one (normalised) Walrasian equilibrium price vector exists. Convexity and monotonicity ensure the logical consistency of the Walrasian equilibrium, Arrow–Debreu model.

As Figure 7.2(b) stresses, convexity and monotonicity are not enough to ensure *uniqueness* of Walrasian equilibrium. $\partial Z_1|\partial p_1 < 0$ everywhere would do this but is an extra assumption, since Giffen goods can occur under convexity, monotonicity and can create

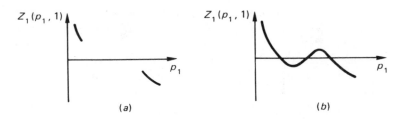

FIGURE 7.2 Aggregate excess demand for good 1: the existence argument

$\partial Z_1 / \partial p_1 > 0$. In the general n good case the best-known extra restriction to ensure uniqueness is *gross substitutes* which requires that all pairs of goods behave in aggregate like gross substitutes at the individual level. Compared with existence, uniqueness is a somewhat problematic property.

The term equilibrium suggests a rest-point of some dynamic process. One model of competitive price adjustment which leads to Walrasian equilibrium would be:

$$dp_i/dt = a_i Z_i(p_1, \ldots, p_{n-1}) \qquad i = 1, \ldots, n-1 \tag{7.3}$$

where a_i are positive and constant price adjustment speeds. Equation (7.3) requires that p_i goes up (down) if $Z_i > 0$ (< 0) or if demand exceeds (is less than) supply, reflecting the familiar partial equilibrium price adjustment. Implicit in (7.3) is the assumption that endowments do not change during convergence, thus assuming *no trading out of equilibrium*. Again implicit, therefore, is the assumption that convergence takes place 'very quickly'. For historical reasons, process (7.3) is known as a *tâtonnement process*. And again the best known condition which ensures global convergence of (7.3) to equilibrium is the problematic gross-substitutes assumption. A variety of local stability and non-*tâtonnement* results (where activity out of equilibrium is allowed) are known. It is particularly worth noting here, however, that there is something of a logical problem with price adjustment in a Walrasian model; simply, who is changing prices, since all agents in the economy take prices as given in formulating demands and supplies? One answer is that this model is an idealisation or limit of how economists believe that an economy with a large number of price-setting or bargaining competitors on each market would behave. Sometimes the logical gap is admitted by speaking of a hypothetical extra individual, *the Walrasian auctioneer*, who changes prices according to (7.3) or some similar rule; in terms of the original answer, this auctioneer becomes the mythical embodiment of the effect of the forces of competition amongst a large number of agents on price adjustment.

Although they impinge less directly on what follows, two final properties of Walrasian equilibria are worthy of brief mention. First, a Walrasian-equilibrium allocation is *Pareto-efficient* (i.e. it is impossible to make somebody better off without making somebody else worse off), which leads to the so-called fundamental theorems of welfare economics (see Varian, 1978). Second, a Walrasian-equilibrium allocation also belongs to the *core* of the economy (i.e. no subset of agents – known as a coalition – can distribute their endowments among themselves so as to make some member of the coalition better off and no member of the coalition worse off than at the equilibrium). Generally the core includes, but is much bigger than, the set of Walrasian equilibrium; however, in 'large' economies where agents are small relative to the market, the core is 'not much bigger than' the Walrasian equilibrium set and coincides with the latter when each agent is truly negligible (e.g. a continuum of agents), thus providing an elegant alternative justification for the belief that perfect competition leads to Walrasian equilibrium (see Hildenbrand and Kirman, 1976).

Turning to *production economies*, we now add a set of ℓ firms and it is technologically feasible for firm j to engage in any production plan $y^j = (y^j_1, \ldots, y^j_n)$ belonging to its *production set* or technology, Y^j. Conventionally $y^j_i < 0$ means good i is an input to the production plan and $y^j_i > 0$ means i is an output. With this sign convention profits are

$$\sum_{i=1}^{n} p_i y^j_i$$

and the firm's profit maximisation is:

$$\max \sum_{i=1}^{n} p_i y^j_i \text{ subject to } y^j \in Y^j \tag{7.4}$$

Convexity again is crucial in the assumption that Y^j is a convex set, requiring that any weighted average of two feasible production plans is also feasible. This rules out increasing returns, requiring constant or decreasing returns.

Let $\pi^j(p)$ be the maximum profits attainable by firm j at prices p. In *private ownership* economies consumers own the firms and since there can never be a role for retained profits in Arrow–Debreu, consumers receive the profits of the firms according to their shareholding. The distribution of share-ownership is a datum of the model: consumer h receives a fraction θ_{hj} of the profits of firm j. The utility maximisation problem of a consumer thus becomes:

$$\max_{C^h \geqslant 0} U^h(C^h) \text{ subject to} \tag{7.5}$$

$$\sum_{i=1}^{n} p_i C_i^h \leqslant \sum_{i=1}^{n} p_i e_i^h + \sum_{j=1}^{\ell} \theta_{hj} \pi^j(p)$$

Solutions to (7.4) and (7.5) then give individual excess-demand functions for firms and consumers, and hence aggregate excess demands by summing over all agents. These aggregates satisfy Walras law, homogeneity and continuity and earlier results on existence, uniqueness, stability, efficiency and (with some difficulties regarding what technology belongs to a coalition) the core continue to hold in the production setting. All these results were more or less known by 1970.

Since about 1970 there have been numerous technical developments in Arrow–Debreu theory refining results discussed above. In addition, and not discussed above, there has been much interest in the relation between the set of Walrasian equilibria of an economy and its data (endowments, preferences, technology). Consider an exchange economy and (for simplicity) let only endowments vary: how does the set – in particular the number – of equilibria vary? We already know that we do not have uniqueness in general under only convexity and monotonicity. Indeed a continuum of equilibria is easily possible in an Edgeworth box world. This literature, however, has shown that 'almost always' under convexity, monotonicity and differentiability assumptions, the set of equilibria is finite: if you pick a point at random in an Edgeworth box there is probability zero that you will hit an endowment from which the number of equilibria is not finite. Such finite equilibria economies are then the norm and are called *regular economies*.

As we have remarked before it is not possible to generate a role for an intrinsically worthless fiat money in the Arrow–Debreu economy, since all transactions in the future course of the economy can be settled at the initial date. One strategy pursued in the literature is to amend the Walrasian Arrow–Debreu assumption that the execution of desired trades is a costless activity, and to introduce *transactions costs*. It is then possible that a future market at the initial date may be too costly to be active, transactions in that commodity taking place on a spot market at the later date: the market structure becomes endogenous, incomplete and a potential role for money is created. In a series of elegant papers Hahn (1971) and (1973) and Starrett (1973) have pursued this enquiry. Generally, however, the strategy of the contributions discussed in the rest of this paper has been less ambitious, assuming instead an *exogenously given* incomplete market structure.

7.3   SHORT-RUN WALRASIAN EQUILIBRIUM

The literature on *short-run* or *temporary Walrasian equilibrium* assumes that the economy has an incomplete set of markets at each date. It is possible to expose the central ideas by concentrating on the special case where there are only spot markets at each date, for current delivery of current goods, although the literature allows more general structures. Furthermore, and again for expositional convenience, assume that goods are non-durable and cannot be stored from date to date, thus immediately creating a role for an intrinsically worthless (but durable) fiat money as the only route by which intertemporal wealth transfers can be made. At the current date agents still know (as in Arrow–Debreu) their preferences, endowments and technological possibilities regarding future goods, but have now to form currently *expectations* about conditions which will prevail in the markets in the future where these goods will be exchanged. All markets continue to be Walrasian. The short-run or temporary equilibrium methodology here is to assume that the expectations-formation-mechanisms of agents are a datum of (exogenous to) the model, and to look for prices which clear only the current markets given such expectations: what happens tomorrow is beyond the remit of this approach (to be addressed in the next section). The primary issue is then existence of short-run Walrasian equilibrium.

The existence issue is the same as in Arrow–Debreu except for the complicating presence of expectations. Historically speaking, some fundamental disputes in macroeconomic theory hinge on the answer. For instance, it was felt in the 1950s and 1960s that Keynesian economics was denying such existence – flexibility of wages and prices in the Walrasian fashion was not enough to ensure clearance of all current markets, especially that for labour. Patinkin's (1965) elegant account of *real balance effects* (more on this below) in the 1960s shifted emphasis in the opposite direction leading to a neoclassical resurgence in which the Keynesian lessons were demoted to the level of theoretical invalidity but possible empirical relevance. A clear resolution of the issue did not come until the 1970s, using and extending the rigorous formal methods of the earlier Arrow–Debreu inquiry (see Grandmont, 1977 for a technical survey). Interestingly it turned out that as well as the convexity and monotonicity needed for existence in Arrow–Debreu, certain expectation assumptions were needed, and these bore a close resemblance to the inelastic expectations of Hicks (1940) some thirty-five years earlier in his seminal discussion of the temporary equilibrium method. Moreover, real balance effects were not, of themselves, enough to ensure existence; some reinforcement was necessary, the most general of which came from the so-called *intertemporal substitution effect*.

Consider again a simple exchange economy setting with m consumers. At date 1 (the current period) and date 2 there are spot markets for the exchange of fiat money and a single non-durable consumption good. Consumer h is endowed with e_1^h of the consumption good at date 1 and also then with $\bar{m}^h$ of fiat money; the consumer knows that an endowment, e_2^h of consumption good will appear at date 2. No consumer plans beyond period 2 and preferences of consumer h are represented by $U^h(C_1^h, C_2^h)$ where C_i^h is final consumption of the good at date i, $i = 1,2$. Fiat money is *numéraire* (price 1) and the money price of consumption good at date 1 is p_1. Expectations by consumer h about the consumption good price at date 2, p_{2h}^e say, depend on current price p_1 (and past prices but these are historical constants by date 1), and the dependence is a datum of the model, written $p_{2h}^e = \Psi^h(p_1)$. Thus expected prices are single-valued functions of current prices. At date 1 the consumer now faces a sequence of budget constraints for date 1 and date 2 and hence, the following utility-maximisation problem, where m^h is the quantity of money held over from period 1 to 2:

$$\max U^h(C_1^h, C_2^h)$$

subject to

$$p_1 C_1^h + m^h \leqslant p_1 \bar{e}_1^h + \bar{m}^h$$

$$\psi^h(p_1) \cdot C_2^h \leqslant m^h + \psi^h(p_1) \cdot e_2^h$$

$$C_1^h, C_2^h, m^h \geqslant 0$$

Combining the two budget constraints by elimination of m^h and division by p_1 gives the equivalent formulation:

$$\max U^h(C_1^h, C_2^h)$$

subject to

$$C_1^h + \frac{\psi^h(p_1)}{p_1} \cdot - C_2^h \leqslant e_1^h + \frac{\psi^h(p_1)}{p_1} \cdot e_2^h + \frac{\bar{m}^h}{p_1}$$

$$C_1^h \leqslant e_1^h + \frac{\bar{m}^h}{p_1}$$

$$C_1^h, C_2^h \geqslant 0$$

The first constraint here is the *intertemporal budget constraint*, whose slope is $dC_2^h/dC_1^h = p_1/\psi^h(p_1)$ and on which lies the point $C_1^h = e_1^h$, $C_2^h = e_2^h + \bar{m}^h/\psi^h(p_1)$. Figure 7.3 illustrates a possible solution. Generally under Arrow–Debreu assumptions on preferences the solution defines a Walrasian demand function for current consumption, $C_1^h(p_1, \psi^h(p_1), \bar{m}^h)$ and a corresponding excess-demand function

$$z_1^h(p_1, \psi^h(p_1), \bar{m}^h) \ (= C_1^h(\cdot) - e_1^h)$$

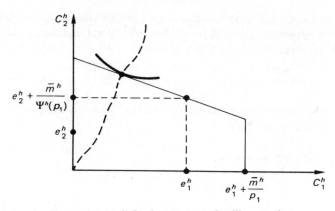

FIGURE 7.3 Expansion path for intertemporal utility maxima

From the first-period budget constraint, excess demand for money $(m^h - \bar{m}^h)$ is written

$$z_m^h(p_1,\psi^h(p_1),\bar{m}^h) = -p_1 z_1^h(p_1,\psi^h(p_1),\bar{m}^h)$$

Short-run Walrasian equilibrium price is then p_1 which clears both the current consumption good and money markets:

$$\sum_{h=1}^{m} z_1^h(p_1,\psi^h(p_1),\bar{m}^h) = 0 \tag{7.6}$$

$$\sum_{h=1}^{m} z_m^h(p_1,\psi^h(p_1),\bar{m}^h) = 0 \tag{7.7}$$

Adding first-period budget constraints gives 'Walras law':

$$p_1 \sum_{h=1}^{m} z_1^h(\cdot) + \sum_{h=1}^{m} z_m^h(\cdot) = 0 \text{ for all } p_1$$

Thus (7.6) implies (7.7) and vice versa, as usual. The existence question reduces to: does there exist p_1 satisfying (7.6)? It is easy now to illustrate the new existence problem emerging in the temporary equilibrium setting by considering in some detail the case of unit elastic expectations: for all h and p_1, $\psi^h(p_1) = tp_1$, where t is some positive constant ($t = 1$ gives 'static expectations').

First a general observation: the second-period budget constraint in the original formulation of the utility-maximisation problem will be satisfied with equality giving

$$C_2^h = m^h/\psi^h(p_1) + e_2^h.$$

Substituting this into the utility function gives the *derived current-period utility function*:

$$U^h(C_1^h, m^h/\psi^h(p_1) + e_2^h)$$

With unit elastic expectations this becomes

$$U^h(C_1^h, m^h/tp_1 + e_2^h)$$

which can be written $V^h(C_1^h, m^h/p_1)$ since t, e_2^h are constant. The Patinkin device for incorporation of money into short-run value theory of 'real balances (m^h/p_1) in the utility function' thus emerges under unit elastic expectations. However, of itself this is not enough to ensure existence of a short-run Walrasian equilibrium. Under unit elastic expectations the slope of the intertemporal budget line in Figure 7.3 is constant ($= 1/t$) for all p_1. Changing p_1 shifts this line parallel to itself through changes in the point on the line $(e_1^h, e_2^h + \bar{m}^h/tp_1)$ which, in turn, changes because of changes in real balances $\bar{m}^h/p_1$: these are pure real-balance effects. However, suppose the expansion path of indifference tangencies to lines of slope $1/t$ follows the dotted curve in Figure 7.3 so that for all p_1, the solution in C_1^h is less than e_1^h. If everyone is similar in this property then

$$\sum_{h=1}^{m} z_1^h(p_1, tp_1, \bar{m}^h) < 0 \text{ for all } p_1:$$

there is persistent excess supply and no short-run equilibrium exists. The problem (cf. Figure 7.1) is that not enough variation is being allowed by unit elastic expectations in the relative price of C_2^h for C_1^h. This is the *expected real interest rate* or, with only spot markets, *the expected rate of inflation*. One way round this problem is to find expectation assumptions which do allow 'sufficient' variation in expected real interest rates, or 'sufficient' changes in slope of the intertemporal budget line in Figure 7.3. Such slope changes induce so-called *intertemporal substitution effects* to reinforce the pure (income) real-balance effects. Hence 'sufficient' reinforcement of real-balance effects with intertemporal substitution effects is one way to ensure the existence of a short-run Walrasian equilibrium. It turns out that the expectational assumptions needed to do this are relatively mild (but exclude everywhere unit elasticity); if just one agent's expected price does not depend 'too much' on current price, this will do.

The reader is again referred to Grandmont (1977, 1983) for a fuller exposition of these matters and the consequences of the model for monetary theory in the short run. A general problem with the short-run approach as defined here is that there are too many expectations assumptions possible – the concentration on current period equilibrium only means there is no way of choosing amongst these possibilities on the grounds of their value as forecasting mechanisms. The model has to be 'run on' to allow this possibility, and we now turn, therefore, to an opposite extreme.

7.4 LONG-RUN PERFECT-FORESIGHT WALRASIAN EQUILIBRIUM IN OVERLAPPING GENERATIONS MODELS

In the short-run scenario of the last section there is no way to verify the correctness of currently held expectations. Running the model on to future periods would reveal the required information and allow agents the opportunity to amend their forecasting procedures if these had produced biased estimates of the future prices. A natural 'equilibrium' assumption is then that agents form unbiased estimates of future prices which lead to (deterministic) *perfect foresight models* and (stochastic) *rational expectation models*. The literature has concentrated on more or less Walrasian models of this genre and important contributions (especially in Sections 7.4 and 7.5) are in the context of *overlapping generations models*. We present now a simple example of such a model and its *stationary* perfect forecast equilibrium. This leads naturally into a discussion of the contributions of Lucas (1972) and Grandmont (1985) in the next two sections.

The economy evolves over an infinite sequence of date or

periods, $t = 1, 2, \ldots,$. At each date a generation of consumers is born who live two periods; for simplicity, assume just one consumer in each generation. Then, in period t there are just two people alive, the 'young' person who was born in period t and the 'old' person born in $t - 1$. Assume that in their youth, and only in their youth, agents can supply labour up to a maximum of $\bar{n}$ hours. Assume also (inessentially) that no consumption is desired during youth and wage proceeds of labour are spent on the single non-durable consumption good in old age. This creates a demand for money by the young to transfer income to old age. Let $U(\bar{n} - n_t, C_{t+1})$ denote the lifetime utility function of every generation, where n_t is labour supply (young) and C_{t+1} is consumption (old). Assume that production of the consumption good from (young) labour is via the constant-returns production function $f(n_t) = n_t$. Walrasian equilibrium in period t, with profit maximisation subject to this function, requires a real wage $w_t/p_t = 1$ (giving zero profits) where w_t is the money wage and p_t is the money price of consumption good (money is *numéraire*). Since $w_t = p_t$ always, p_t is used for both in what follows. The lifetime utility-maximisation problem of the generation born in t is then:

$$\max U(\bar{n} - n_t, C_{t+1})$$

subject to

$$m_t \leqslant p_t n_t$$

$$p_{t+1}^e C_{t+1} \leqslant m_t$$

$$0 \leqslant n_t \leqslant \bar{n}, \quad C_{t+1}, m_t \geqslant 0$$

where m_t denotes money held over to $t + 1$ and p_{t+1}^e is the price expected at $t + 1$. The problem reduces to:

$$\max U(\bar{n} - n_t, C_{t+1}) \quad s.t. \quad C_{t+1} \leqslant n_t p_t / p_{t+1}^e$$

$$0 \leqslant n_t \leqslant \bar{n}, \quad C_{t+1} \geqslant 0$$

Under the usual assumptions on U let $n(p_t/p_{t+1}^e)$ be the solution in n_t which is also output supply in t from the technology assumption.

The only demand for output in t comes from the old in t who will be carrying money $\bar{m}$ over from their youth $(t-1)$ and wish to spend it now in the last period of their lives. Demand equals supply for output in t then requires:

$$\bar{m}/p_t = n(p_t/p^e_{t+1}) \tag{7.8}$$

Labour market clearance in t is then ensured by the real wage equal to one and equilibrium employment is $n_t(p_t/p^e_{t+1})$, and the money market clears. *Perfect foresight* requires that actual price in $t+1$, $p_{t+1} = p^e_{t+1}$. *Stationarity* (to be relaxed in Section 7.6) requires $p_{t+1} = p_t = p$, say, for all t. *A stationary perfect-foresight Walrasian-equilibrium price* is then a value of p such that $p_t = p^e_{t+1} = p$ satisfies (7.8) for all t; this gives $\bar{m}/p = n(1)$ or $p = \bar{m}/n(1)$ as the unique equilibrium price (assuming $n(1) > 0$). Figure 7.4 illustrates the equilibrium $\bar{m}/p$ in terms of the solution to the lifetime utility-maximisation problem at stationary prices. Generally, existence requires agents who wish to transfer income forward at stationary prices (cf. Section 7.3), a role played easily by the young in this simple model; if, for instance, young consumption had also been desirable, an assumption that, at stationary prices, desired young consumption is less than desired labour supply would have been needed to ensure existence.

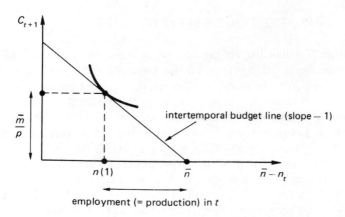

FIGURE 7.4 **Equilibrium real balances in a stationary, perfect foresight equilibrium**

A particular property of the model is worthy of mention now. Suppose the government announced publicly a once-and-for-all change in the money stock, executed by changing the money-holdings of all agents by the same multiplicative factor λ (>0). This money transfer is then free of distribution effects, and its only impact on the above model is to change equilibrium price proportionately to $p = \lambda \bar{m}/n_t(1)$, output and employment remaining unchanged; the monetary change has no real effects, producing only a corresponding change in money prices. This is a classical *neutrality of money* result for a so-called Ricardian scalar change of money-holdings. The classical dichotomy holds whereby real factors (preferences, endowments, technology) determine real variables (output, employment) and monetary factors determine money prices. The implicit emasculation of the power of policy is a very old idea in economics, presented here in a slightly newer format of overlapping generations. The reader is again referred to Grandmont (1983, Chapter 2 *et seq.*) for a fuller discussion. Although the stationary perfect-foresight Walrasian model provides a coherent account of money and expectations, the stationarity clearly precludes any notion of a business cycle in such an economy, however. We now turn to more recent attempts to remedy this latter defect whilst remaining within a more or less Walrasian framework.

7.5   IMPERFECT INFORMATION

Section 7.4 has led to the following question: is it possible to explain observed features of the business cycle in a model of essentially Walrasian origin? Successful answers have come from models which are Walrasian *except* for the removal of the assumption that agents are costlessly informed of all current prices. One theme is found in the search-unemployment literature; if workers are not fully informed of the wages available for their labour, it may be optimal for them to forgo a current employment offer in order to engage in job search, thus generating a level of search-unemployment. Early contributions can be found in the Phelps volume (1970); recently Pissarides (1985) has surveyed the issues in this particular area. A second theme has been the attempts to explain the *Phillips curve* – the observed positive correlation between output and inflation – in such an imperfect information world (see Santomero and Seater, 1978, and also Phelps, 1970, Pissarides, 1985). In particular the notion has emerged that there is no usable trade-off between output and inflation, and the Phillips curve is vertical at the so-called *natural rate* of output. The observed positive slope may then be attributed, for instance, to sluggish adjustment of inflation expectations in the expectations-augmented Phillips curve of Friedman (1968), Phelps (1968). Perhaps most influential here, however, has been the contribution of Lucas (1972) and we devote the rest of this section to a discussion of this particular paper.

Lucas's model has a simple stochastic overlapping-generations structure with rational expectations and imperfect information. There are both real and monetary stochastic variables, so the economy is subject to both real and monetary disturbances. Agents cannot then, in general, ascertain whether a recent local price change, say, has been driven by real or monetary disturbance; they cannot infer whether the price change indicates inflation through-out the economy or merely indicates a change in prices locally relative to the economy as a whole. It then turns out that this creates an equilibrium in the economy in which Ricardian-type monetary changes have no real effect, and yet the stochastic aspects create output and inflation observations which support a positive-sloped Phillips curve; there is no usable output–inflation trade-off, although econometricians would report a positive-sloped Phillips curve.

The model has a number of simplifying features to highlight the Phillips-curve aspect. We simplify a little further and follow Azariadis (1981). Start with an overlapping-generations model, as in the last section, now with N identical agents in each generation, each supplying labour in their youth and consuming only in old age. Add on the facts that there are two physically separated markets in the economy (north and south, say) and that the allocation of new-born agents to these markets is stochastic, a fraction $\theta_t/2$ to the north in t and $1 - \theta_t/2$ to the south; θ_t is a random variable with mean 1 and the θ_ts are independently and identically distributed. θ_t is the real disturbance. At the beginning of period t the old are carrying the pre-existing money stock, denoted Nm_t, of the economy. At that point government policy alters the money stock to $x_t \cdot Nm_t$ where x_t is a random variable with mean 1; the x_is are independently and identically distributed independent from θ_t and are the monetary disturbance. $Nm_{t+1} = Nm_t x_t$ becomes the pre-transfer money stock in $t+1$. A particular simplifying assumption is that the old are allocated so as to equate the money stock held in each market. In the last period of their lives the old supply all their money to demand output, giving money value for output demand in t in each market of $Nm_t x_t/2$.

For simplicity we take the following, specific lifetime von Neumann–Morgenstern utility function for the young in t:

$$U(n_t, c_{t+1}) = c_{t+1} - n_t^2/2.$$

If n_t is supplied in t money earnings are $p_t n_t$ which become augmented by government transfer to $p_t n_t x_{t+1}$ allowing $c_{t+1} = p_t n_t x_{t+1}/p_{t+1}$. The young know the value of p_t and m_t prior to their labour supply decision in t but do not know x_t, θ_t or future disturbance values: hence they solve:

$$\max_{n_t} E[p_t n_t x_{t+1}/p_{t+1}|p_t, m_t] - n_t^2/2$$

whose solution is:

$$n_t = E[p_t x_{t+1}/p_{t+1}|p_t, m_t]$$

Output supply in the *north* in t is then $n_t \cdot N \cdot \theta_t/2$ and output supply equals demand in the northern market requires

$$m_t x_t/p_t = \theta_t E[p_t x_{t+1}/p_{t+1}|p_t, m_t] \tag{7.9}$$

Market clearing in the north requires this equation for all t. The independence of disturbances suggest that a solution will depend only on m_t and the realised value of x_t, θ_t; $p_t = J(m_t, x_t, \theta_t)$ say. Agents know J and use this information in forming their (rational) expectations in (7.9). An equilibrium in the north is then a function J satisfying for all t:

$$\frac{m_t x_t}{\theta_t J(m_t, x_t, \theta_t)} = \tag{7.10}$$

$$= E\left[x_{t+1} \cdot \frac{J(m_t, x_t, \theta_t)}{J(m_t x_t, x_{t+1}, \theta_{t+1})} \Big| J(m_t, x_t, \theta_t) \right]$$

where m_t has been treated as a known parameter on the right-hand side and the conditional expectation there is taken with respect to known distributions of the disturbances.

The south is symmetric except $2 - \theta$ replaces θ: thus equilibrium in the south is again described by (7.10) with this change throughout.

Two extreme cases are informative, although atypical. First suppose that there are only monetary disturbances, so that $\theta_t = 1$ with certainty for all t. Then $J = m_t x_t / \theta_t = m_t x_t$ satisfies (7.10) for north and south with both sides identically equal to one. n_t is then one and output/employment in the economy equal N, independent of m_t and x_t. This is an extreme classical case where monetary disturbances (even unanticipated) affect only the price level (J) and have no real effect. Second, suppose there are only real disturbances so that $x_t = 1$ with certainty for all t. Consider

$$J = \frac{m_t}{E\theta^{\frac{1}{2}}} \cdot \left[\frac{x_t}{\theta_t}\right]^{\frac{1}{2}} = \frac{m_t}{E\theta^{\frac{1}{2}}} \cdot \frac{1}{\theta_t^{\frac{1}{2}}} \qquad (7.11)$$

Substitution into left- and right-hand sides of (7.10) shows that J is an equilibrium, since both are then equal to $E\theta^{\frac{1}{2}}/\theta_t^{\frac{1}{2}}$ which is the equilibrium n_t in the north. Employment in the north is then

$$\frac{\theta_t N}{2} \cdot n_t = \frac{NE\theta^{\frac{1}{2}}}{2} \cdot \theta_t^{\frac{1}{2}} \qquad (7.12)$$

Corresponding formula for the south change θ_t to $2 - \theta_t$ in (7.11) and (7.12). The output level in the economy is then independent of m_t but dependent on θ_t. In the light of these examples the output level in the economy is independent of monetary disturbances but dependent on real disturbances. However, these examples are *atypical* since in both cases the current price $J = p_t$ reveals the value of the unknown disturbance – $x_t = p_t/m_t$ in the first and $\theta_t = (m_t/p_t E\theta^{\frac{1}{2}})^2$ in the second. When both monetary and real disturbances are present the price signal does not so reveal the full nature of the disturbances, causing confusion as to the values of the underlying disturbance term. The main Lucas result (in a very similar model) is that generally there is a unique solution J to (7.10) and its form is

$$J = m_t \cdot \varphi(x_t/\theta_t)$$

where φ has elasticity between (but excluding) 0 and 1. (In the first example this was true with elasticity 1: in the second the elasticity was $\frac{1}{2}$.) Moreover, the corresponding value for n_t is:

$$n_t = \eta(x_t/\theta_c)$$

where η has positive derivative. Aggregate output in the economy is then

$$Y_t = N \left\{ \frac{\theta_t}{2}\eta(x_t/\theta_t) + \frac{2-\theta_t}{2}\eta(x_t/2-\theta_t) \right\}$$

which does depend positively on x_t, but not on m_t. The former means that monetary disturbances do indeed have real effects in general when agents cannot distinguish real and monetary disturbances perfectly. The latter means that if a monetary expansion took place so that money supply in t was $\lambda Nm_t x_t$ instead of $Nm_t x_t$ there would be no real impact of this change – the distribution of output would be unchanged; this is the vertical Phillips curve. These neutrality properties coexist in the model with a dependence of output on monetary disturbances. When x_t is high, Y_t is high and when x_t is low Y_t is low, other things being equal. Moreover, other things being equal, a high x_t creates higher prices and inflation. The actual observations on output and inflation for this economy will indeed look like evidence for a positive-sloped Phillips curve.

These arguments, broadly speaking, provide support for the new classical macroeconomic view: crudely, there is a natural rate of output independent of monetary factors and attempts to influence output by monetary policy will be unsuccessful.

7.6 CYCLICAL PERFECT-FORESIGHT WALRASIAN EQUILIBRIA

Stationary-perfect foresight Walrasian equilibria offer few insights into business cycles. The Lucas model of Section 7.5 shows how introducing stochastic components in the data of the model and imperfect information can lead to a stochastic stationary model where development of output and inflation over time might be interpreted as evidence of a Phillips curve although there is no

usable long-run trade-off between output and inflation in the
economy. In a recent paper Grandmont (1985) has taken this story
in a new and interesting direction. Returning to a perfect-foresight,
Walrasian equilibrium world, he relaxes the *ad hoc* stationarity
assumption of Section 7.4. Roughly speaking, the idea is that while
perfect foresight of price developments over time which have no
'pattern' is perhaps stretched, perfect foresight of regular periodic
price cycles is perhaps plausible. The question then is: do there
exist such periodic cycles (with period >1) in a perfect-foresight
Walrasian equilibrium model? In his OLG model both young and
old work and consume; however, the basic idea can be more or less
conveyed in the simpler world of Section 7.4.

Consider Figure 7.5 which includes Figure 7.4 and adds the *offer
curve* of the consumer. The consumer's lifetime budget-constraint
goes through the point $(0,\bar{n})$ and has slope p_t/p_{t+1} $(=p_t/p_{t+1}^e$ under
perfect foresight). As p_t/p_{t+1} varies, the budget line swivels around
$(0,\bar{n})$ and the offer curve is the locus of resulting indifference curve/
budget-line tangencies. The solid budget-line in Figure 7.5 corresponds to $p_t/p_{t+1}=1$ or stationary prices; the flatter dotted budget
line has slope p_2/p_1 (<1) and the steeper has slope p_1/p_2 (>1). The
offer curve has been drawn backward bending or 'humped'. As the
expected real rate of interest (p_t/p_{t+1}) increases, income effects

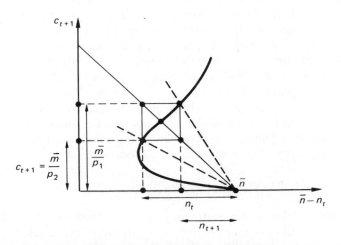

FIGURE 7.5 A two-periodic perfect foresight equilibrium

work to reduce labour supply and substitution effects work to increase labour supply. The conflict between these intertemporal income and substitution effects creates the possibility for the 'humped' offer curve and allows the possibility of periodic Walrasian equilibria (two-periodic in Figure 7.5), as follows. Suppose p_1 is the price in t and p_2 is expected in $t+1$. The young in t face a budget line of slope p_2/p_1 – the flatter dotted line – giving labour (and output) supply equal to n_t indicated in Figure 7.5. For p_1 to be the equilibrium in t needs $\bar{m}/p_1 = n_t$, which we assume. The young in t anticipate (and under perfect foresight will get) consumption in $t+1$ of $c_{t+1} = n_t p_1 p_2 = \bar{m}/p_2$, indicated in Figure 7.5, which is therefore output demand in $t+1$. In $t+1$ a new generation is born who face p_2 in their youth and expect p_1 in their old age, thus facing the steeper dotted budget line and giving labour and output supply in $t+1$ equal to the indicated n_{t+1}. Inspection now reveals that in the configuration of Figure 7.5, $n_{t+1} = \bar{m}/p_2$ and indeed there is equilibrium in $t+1$ at price p_2 on the expectation of p_1 in $t+2$. The two-period cycle p_1,p_2 then repeats indefinitely giving a two-periodic perfect-foresight Walrasian equilibrium.

In this example, a one-periodic cycle (the stationary solution) coexists with the two-period cycle; as the offer curve becomes more 'humped' more and more cycles emerge degenerating ultimately into what is known as *chaos*. In the presence of such multiple equilibrium solutions, attention turns to dynamics to choose between them. The natural perfect-foresight dynamic, $\bar{m}/p_t = n(p_t/p_{t+1})$ is, however, not appropriate out of (periodic) equilibrium, since there is then no 'pattern' to support, plausibly, perfect foresight. Instead consider the stationary state $p,p,p,\ldots$, of Figure 7.5, and assume that for histories of prices 'near' the stationary state agents have some common forecasting rule $p^e_{t+1} = \psi(p_t,p_{t-1},\ldots,p_{t-T})$ which respects stationarity – that is, $\psi(p,p,\ldots,p) = p$ – and which does not depend 'too much' on p_t (cf. Section 7.3). Then small disturbances from the stationary state lead the economy off on a sequence of temporary equilibria defined by:

$$\bar{m}/p_t = n(p_t/\psi(p_t,p_{t-1},\ldots,p_{t-T}))$$

Local stability of the stationary state can then be studied in this dynamic, the *dynamics with learning* in Grandmont (1985). Similarly the local stability in the dynamics with learning of the two-period cycle in Figure 7.5 can be studied assuming now that ψ respects this cycle – $\psi(p_1,p_2,\ldots p_1)=p_2$ and $\psi(p_2,p_1,\ldots p_1)=p_1$. It turns out that there is at most one locally stable solution in this sense, which, as the offer curve becomes more 'humped' is first the stationary solution, then the two-period cycle and then higher-order cycles. All this points towards the important conclusion that even under conditions of persistent Walrasian equilibrium and perfect foresight, an economy may find itself at or near a business cycle where both prices and output/employment oscillate regularly.

Following up this cyclical story, return to the two-period cycle in Figure 7.5. In t price is p_1 while last period then had price p_2; in t recent inflation has been $p_t/p_{t-1}-1=p_1/p_2-1>0$. And in t, output and employment are 'high' (n_t in Figure 7.5). In $t+1$ recent inflation is $p_{t+1}/p_t-1=p_2/p_1-1<0$ and output is 'low' (n_{t+1} in Figure 7.5). In the stationary state on the other hand inflation is 0 and output is in between 'high' and 'low' (see Figure 7.5). Across the set (here just two) of periodic equilibria there is an output–inflation trade-off with high (positive) inflation going with 'high' output and lower inflation going with lower output. Grandmont (1985) shows that there is indeed such a trade-off generally. And although money is neutral in that anticipated scalar (Ricardian) changes in the money stock have no real effect on the set of equilibria, the government can use monetary policy to guide the economy away from one equilibrium (say cyclical) back to another (say stationary), thus generating a real role for stabilisation policy.

If new classical macroeconomics points towards an emasculation of the power of economic policy, these periodic perfect-foresight Walrasian equilibria point towards an emasculation of new classical macroeconomics. It seems likely that further investigations along these lines will be an active research area in the near future.

7.7 DISEQUILIBRIUM AND OTHER NON-WALRASIAN APPROACHES

Models with Walrasian markets make the assumption that prices adjust very quickly at every date to equate desired supply and demand; involuntary unemployment, for instance, where a worker cannot find a job at the current wage although he is willing to work at this wage, is absent from all such models. Motivated by a desire to model involuntary unemployment and Keynesian ideas in general, a number of economists in the 1970s moved towards a polar extreme to the Walrasian price-flexibility assumption where, in the short run, prices were assumed exogenous to the model, not necessarily at their Walrasian values. At non-Walrasian prices agents will not all be able to execute their desired Walrasian trades and some will discover quantity restrictions on the amounts transactable. Various concepts of *equilibrium with quantity constraints or rationing* or *fixed-price equilibrium* have been proposed for this scenario. The literature is associated initially with Barro and Grossmann (1976), Benassy (1975), Dreze (1975) and Malinvaud (1977) and is often referred to as *macroeconomic disequilibrium theory* although models are based on a concept of non-Walrasian equilibrium. Although general models (arbitrary number of goods) exist we concentrate on the popular three-good structure of output, labour and money, familiar from earlier sections.

In a partial-equilibrium supply/demand model a natural postulate is that if prices are stuck at other than the equilibrium value, then the amount traded will be the lesser of the desired demand and supply at that price; for instance, if supply exceeds demand then every buyer has his demand satisfied but some suppliers will be rationed in the amount they can sell. In the three-good disequilibrium model to be spelt out below, this is the assumption made about labour and output transactions. However, rationing in the labour market, if it comes about, will affect the desired output transactions of those rationed: the unemployed worker demands less output than when employed. This was termed the *dual-decision hypothesis* by Clower (1965) in an early precursor of this literature. Ultimately equilibria were defined accommodating these disequilibrium spillover effects. In the sense of Benassy (1983) an equilibrium requires that each agent signals a supply or demand for labour and output; transactions then follow the minimum of supply and demand rule in labour and output; each agent's supply or demand for output is optimal given any quantity constraints perceived by that agent in labour; and each agent's supply or demand for labour is optimal given any quantity constraints perceived by that agent in output. The model to follow adds (for expositional convenience) the assumption that labour transactions chronologically precede output transactions so that labour supplies and demands are made in the light of anticipated output-quantity constraints and output-supplies and demands are signalled in the knowledge of previously observed labour constraints. The model is from Madden (1987) where further details can be found.

The model is short run, with given implicit expectation mechanisms. There is a representative firm producing output from labour according to a decreasing returns production function, $f(\ell)$. There is a representative consumer who supplies labour inelastically, $\bar{\ell}$. Profits will be made under decreasing returns and we assume they are paid out to the consumer within the short run, whose current income will then be the entire current value of output supply pq^s. The consumer has a money endowment $\bar{m}$ giving the current budget constraint:

$$q + m/p \leqslant q^s + \bar{m}/p \qquad (7.13)$$

The derived current-period utility-function (see Section 7.3) of the consumer is $U(q, m/p)$ which for simplicity we take to be homothetic and which is maximised subject to (7.13) giving the output demand of $\alpha(q^s + \bar{m}/p)$ for some constant $\alpha > 0$. The firm's labour demand, in anticipation of output demand q^d, will be the smaller of $f'^{(-1)}(w/p)$ and $f^{-1}(q^d)$ – the firm hires labour up to the point where the marginal product equals the real wage unless it cannot sell all the output then produced, when it hires just enough labour to produce what it can sell. The full model is then, with ℓ^s, ℓ^d, ℓ denoting labour supply, demand and transaction and similar notation for output:

$$\ell^s = \bar{\ell} \qquad (7.14)$$

$$\ell^d = \min\{f'^{(-1)}(w/p), f^{-1}(q^d)\} \qquad (7.15)$$

$$\ell = \min(\ell^s, \ell^d) \qquad (7.16)$$

$$q^s = f(\ell) \qquad (7.17)$$

$$q^d = \alpha(q^s + \bar{m}/p) \qquad (7.18)$$

$$q = \min(q^s, q^d) \qquad (7.19)$$

After some substitutions any solution to the model must satisfy

$$q = q^s = f(\ell) = \min[f(\bar{\ell}), f\{f'^{(-1)}(w/p)\}, q^d] \tag{7.20}$$

At the outset three potential non-Walrasian types of equilibrium can be identified from (7.20) when there is a unique smallest element under the min sign in (7.20) and depending on which element is then the smallest at that solution. If q^d is the smallest then there is (involuntary) unemployment since output q is then less than full employment output $f(\bar{\ell})$ and the factor restricting output is aggregate demand, q^d: this is *Keynesian unemployment* (KU). If $f\{f'^{(-1)}\}(w/p)\}$ is the smallest there is still unemployment but the restricting factor is now not demand but the real wage level; this is *classical unemployment* (CU). And if $f(\bar{\ell})$ is the smallest there is full employment ($q = f(\bar{\ell})$ with excess demand ($q^d > q$): this is *repressed inflation* (RI). When two or more elements under the min sign in (7.20) are equal-smallest various borderline cases occur: in particular when all three are the same, we have short-run *Walrasian equilibrium* (WE) since then $\ell^s = \ell^d = \ell$ and $q^s = q^d = q$. It turns out that this model has a *global uniqueness* property: for each value of the short-run exogenous parameters w/p and $\bar{m}/p$ there is a unique solution in output/employment to the model. Moreover the nature of the dependence of equilibrium output on w/p and $\bar{m}/p$ can be adequately summarised in Figure 7.6. Barro and Grossmann (1976) use a similar diagram: Malinvaud (1977) depicts the same information with w and p on the axes. Figure 7.6 indicates the

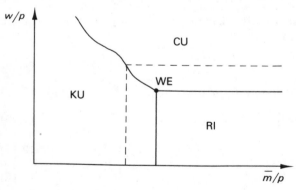

FIGURE 7.6   Regimes of non-Walrasian equilibria

solution 'regime' prevailing at the various w/p, $\bar{m}/p$ values. In the RI regime full employment output prevails. In KU and CU there is unemployment. Moreover output is constant along iso-output curves whose shape is that of the dotted, rotated L-shape in Figure 7.6, with the level of output increasing as we move south-east, reaching full employment at the RI border. The following stylised conclusions emerge from all this. If unemployment is Keynesian the reason is unsufficient demand, not too high real wages and the 'cure' is to boost demand; if unemployment is classical, however, the problem is too high a real wage and not insufficient demand. It is of further interest here to note that in KU, the equation defining equilibrium output is $q^s = q^d$ or aggregate supply equals demand. Thus in KU (at least when the real wage is less than its WE level) output is determined by the aggregate demand–supply or income–expenditure analysis of the introductory textbook. Adding a bond market produces IS–LM analysis (see Benassy, 1983; Varian, 1978). The disequilibrium approach thus leads to a micro-foundation for the elementary textbook 'Keynesian' macro models.

However, this short-run model carries the same implicit expectational deficiencies as that of Section 7.3 earlier. Moreover, the exogenous nature of wages and prices, whilst attractively allowing a relaxation of the auctioneer-based Walrasian assumption, leaves of itself too many possibilities for w and p. Some endogenous theory of non-Walrasian w and p determination ideally needs to be added. Remedial work on these deficiencies is an active area of current research. On the one hand, there are macroeconomic models with rational expectations and 'sticky prices' (see Fischer, 1977; Phelps and Taylor, 1977). On the other hand there are general equilibrium models where agents do not all treat prices as parametric and where some agents are endowed with the market power to influence prices. Following the leads of imperfect competition in (partial equilibrium) microeconomics, general equilibrium models in the style of Cournot oligopoly (especially Gabszewicz and Vial, 1972) and Bertrand oligopoly (especially Marschak and Selten, 1972) have been developed; a model which also has a macroeconomic disequilibrium flavour is Hart (1982), its links to the disequilibrium story being traced by Silvestre (1986). In endogenising price-setting and thus going beyond the Walrasian and fixed-price alternatives, this is likely to be an increasingly important area: see Hart (1985) for a survey.

7.8   CONCLUDING REMARKS

A number of themes have been addressed in the preceding pages, all of which fall, more or less, within the remit of the title. Coverage of these themes has been varied in extent, reflecting the author's own interests and views as to what is most important. Equally idiosyncratic must be any conclusions. Here it seems that short-run Walrasian theory is well understood. The long-run Walrasian story of periodic or cyclical equilibria (*à la* Grandmont) is not by any means complete. The influence of shocks and imperfect information (*à la* Lucas) on such a model and the merging of these two themes is not yet understood. However, the absence of involuntary unemployment from these models is, to some people, like the absence of the Prince of Denmark from Hamlet. Some kind of 'disequilibrium', probably via an imperfectly competitive equilibrium needs to be transplanted, as does some more convincing account of how agents form expectations. More generally and perhaps tritely, models which combine the themes of the preceding pages seem to provide an agenda of issues from which the most interesting insights will emerge in the near future.

8 Microeconometric Modelling and Microeconomic Policy Analysis*

IAN WALKER

8.1 INTRODUCTION

In recent years the empirical analysis of households with respect to expenditure patterns, labour-market behaviour and savings have increasingly been conducted using data on households. This is both a reflection of and is reflected in the increasing availability of such data, and the advent of more powerful computers and more accommodating software. It is also, I think, a consequence of the attraction of researching in an area where there is a close relationship between economic theory, model specification (both deterministic and stochastic) and estimation strategy.

Moreover while studies of expenditure patterns, of labour-market behaviour, and of savings have typically each been concerned with modelling their respective decisions in isolation from one another there has been some recent tendency to attempt to model these acts of decisions simultaneously. The motivation behind this tendency is that developments in public finance have highlighted the importance of the relationships between these sets of decisions for tax policy.

While working with micro data – i.e. data which relates to the behaviour of the agent under analysis – is attractive it does bring with it problems of its own. One pervasive feature of micro data is

209

that it is often the case that the agents' behaviour with respect to some decision is constrained – that is, behaviour cannot be described by a simple tangency position. This makes it necessary to extend both theory and estimation to accommodate the phenomenon.

This chapter is concerned with drawing together some of these developments in specifying, estimating and testing microeconometric behavioural models, in the relevant public finance theory, and in the use of microeconometric models for policy analysis.

Section 8.2 develops the point that it is possible, and generally desirable, to consider decisions over labour supply, savings and expenditure patterns as being made simultaneously. Section 8.3 considers the problem of having corner solutions arising from zero expenditures (or labour supplies) occurring in micro data. Section 8.4 outlines the relevant tax theory and demonstrates the power of separability in the context of optimal taxation, the income-tax treatment of the incomes of couples, and the debate concerning the choice of either income or expenditure as the tax base. In Section 8.5 we consider the possible use of microeconometric models for tax policy analyses and argue that separability makes a valuable contribution towards computational feasibility.

Thus separability considerations provide the common strand that binds the chapter together and the concluding section contains judgements about where it is essential to abandon it to be able to say anything meaningful and where it is essential to maintain it to be able to say anything at all.

8.2   LABOUR SUPPLY, EXPENDITURES AND SAVING

The ability to separate commodities by type, e.g. leisure on the one hand and food, clothing, etc. on the other, or by time period, e.g. consumption today versus consumption tomorrow, is a valuable and powerful one in econometric analysis since it enables research to be focused on a narrow area, for example, current labour-supply decisions, without concern about how to model other decisions. The most obvious way in which commodities can be brought together into separate groups is to appeal to two-stage budgeting. This idea stems from Gorman (1958) and essentially implies that the utility function must be weakly separable so that, if for example, $x_1, \ldots, x_N$ represents all commodities (including leisure) and $g_1, \ldots, g_G$ represents groups of commodities with which $x_1, \ldots, x_N$ can be uniquely associated then

$$U(x_1, \ldots, x_N) = F(U_1(g_1), \ldots, U_G(g_G)) \tag{8.1}$$

Thus $F(\cdot)$ describes preferences across groups, say between the group of commodities called 'goods' and the group called household leisure, while $U_j(g_j)$ describes preferences within a group, say between food and clothing. Weak separability implies two-stage budgeting since the allocation of expenditure to any x_i in g_k can be expressed as

$$p_i x_i = f_i(P^k, y_k) \tag{8.2}$$

where P^k is the vector of prices of the goods in group k and y_k is the allocation of total expenditure y to group k. That is, at the first stage y_k is determined and taken as given when making decisions on x_i at the second stage.

If g_1 contains goods such as food, clothing, etc. while g_2 contains leisure goods then (8.1) implies that food expenditure is determined by the prices of food, clothing, etc. and y_1 which is the allocation out of full income (income that would arise if household members worked all the hours available in a period) to consumption of goods. The remaining full income, y_2, is allocated to be 'spent' on leisure at the first stage. Thus expenditures depend on wages only to the extent that wages determine income. We can represent this example in Figure 8.1, where T hours of time are available, time can be sold to the market at a price of p_0 per hour. The household is also endowed with exogenous unearned income m so that full income $F = m + p_0 T$. Thus the first stage, maximising U_1 subject to p_0 and m, determines hours of work $(T - x_0)$ and hence income y_1. At the second stage y_1 is allocated between x_1 and x_2 so as to maximise U_2 subject to the constraint determined by p_1, p_2 and y_1.

This separation of decisions into labour supply on the one hand and commodity expenditures on the other has supported two separate and major industries in applied economics. The labour-supply-estimation literature (see Killingsworth, 1983, for an excellent survey) analyses the labour-supply function:

$$T - x_0 = f_0(p_0, m) \tag{8.3}$$

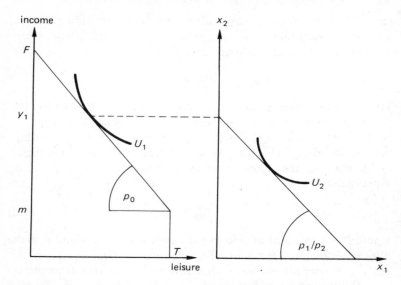

FIGURE 8.1 **Labour supply and commodity demands under two-stage budgeting**

while the applied-demand-analysis literature (see Phlips, 1974) analyses the demand equations

$$x_i = f_i(p_1, p_2, y_1) \tag{8.4}$$

The most famous example of forms for the above can be derived from a special case of the Gorman polar form indirect utility function

$$V(p_0, p, m) = \frac{F - a(p_0, p)}{b(p_0, p)} \tag{8.5}$$

where $a(p_0, p) = p_0 y_0 + py$, $py = \Sigma p_i y_i$ and

$$\log b(p_0, p) = \beta_0 \log p_0 + \sum_i \beta_i \log p_i$$

by applying Roy's identity to obtain

$$p_i x_i = p_i y_i + \beta_i (m + p_0 (T - y_0) - py) \qquad i = 1, \ldots, n \tag{8.6}$$

and

$$p_0(T - x_0) = (1 - \beta_0)p_0(T - y_0) - \beta_0(m - py) \tag{8.7}$$

In (8.6) the term in parenthesis is referred to as supernumerary income – defined as the (full) income left over after the individual has purchased the subsistence quantities y and the subsistence time $T - y_0$. Thus changes in p_0 (or p_j, $j = i$) in (8.6) give rise to an income effect on expenditure on good i but no substitution effect. Moreover, substituting (8.7) into (8.6) gives

$$p_i x_i = p_i y_i + \frac{\beta_i}{1 - \beta_0}[y - py] \tag{8.8}$$

where $y = m + p_0(T - x_0)$ is income, both unearned and earned. Thus separability supports the estimation of an expenditure system as a function of income and commodity prices in isolation as in (8.8). Similarly, in (8.7) since the p_is do not vary across households py is a constant, and it is only p_0 and m that is relevant for hours of work, $T - x_0$. In general, however, applying Roy's identity to (8.5) would give

$$x_i = a_i(p_0, p) + \frac{b_i(p_0, p)}{b(p_0, p)}[F - a(p_0, p)] \tag{8.9}$$

$$i = 0, 1, \ldots, N$$

where a_i and b_i are the ith price derivatives.

There are, in fact, few examples of estimated systems such as (8.9) in the literature. Blundell and Walker (1982) estimate a non-separable commodity demand and labour-supply system which strongly rejects the restrictions implied by separability. Blundell and Walker (1986) estimate a pair of labour-supply curves (for husbands and wives) and again reject separability both between the two labour supplies and between each labour supply and goods expenditure.

The second area where separability assumptions are widely used is that of intertemporal decision-making. Letting x_t be the period t choice vector, life-cycle utility, given separability, may be written as the discounted sum of period by period indices, $U_t(x_t)$. Thus, if L

is the length of life, r is the interest rate, and p is the discount rate then the problem can be written as

$$\text{Max}/U = \sum \frac{1}{(1+p)^t} U_t(x_t)$$

subject to

$$\sum_{t=1}^{t=1} \frac{1}{(1+r)^t} p_t x_t = A_0$$

where A_0 is the individual's initial assets. That is the individual has to allocate his assets over his life cycle to yield a stream of x_t's that maximise U. Intertemporal separability allows the problem to be broken down into allocating A_0 over time so that period t is allocated y_t, for example, followed by allocating y_t across goods at a point in time according to the usual vector of Marshallian demand equations:

$$x_{it} = F(p^t, y_t) \tag{8.9}$$

where p^t is a vector of prices reigning at time t. Thus intertemporal separability essentially allows demand analysis to ignore the fact that agents are making intertemporal decisions and to concentrate on just the atemporal ones.

Empirical work on life-cycle decision-making can be found in Blundell and Walker (1986) where estimates of a y_t conditional-labour-supply model are given; in Browning, Deaton and Irish (1985) where a constant-labour-supply model is estimated using the cohort means of successive cross-sections of data to form a pseudo-panel; and in Heckman and MaCurdy (1980) and MaCurdy (1981) who use US panel data to estimate constant-labour-supply models.

Thus, in principle, the relaxation of atemporal utility is feasible, requiring only data on expenditures and labour supplies; intertemporal separability is more difficult since it is usually invoked as a maintained hypothesis in estimation. Even in the atemporal case separability can be problematic because of the problem of corner solutions in household data.

8.3 CORNER SOLUTIONS, SEPARABILITY AND ESTIMATION

In data at the microeconomic level many observations would appear not to conform with the conventional theoretical characterisation of utility-maximising behaviour as a position where a marginal rate of substitution is equated to the relevant price ratio. Corner solutions occur with great frequency in any data set. In some cases such corner solutions arise because non-negativity conditions on behaviour are binding constraints at the given prices and wages. For example, the unskilled wife of a well-paid man who has young children will find that the market's valuation of the wife's time is low while the household's valuation of its use at home is high and the wife may choose not to work. A second example occurs in labour-supply analysis where the tax/benefit system induces non-linearities in budget constraints. A similar problem arises in the context of rationing, for example with housing in the short run because of transactions costs, or with male labour-supply where an institutionally determined length of working week is common. In other cases corner solutions may arise because some goods simply do not enter some individual's preference ordering at all and hence no price/income configuration would yield positive consumption; for example, cigarettes or alcohol. Finally, corner solutions may arise because, given transactions costs and individual characteristics, it has not been optimal in the survey period to make any expenditure on some good that is being consumed continuously but being purchased infrequently. The most important example here is durable goods.

The analysis of rationing and binding non-negativity constraints on behaviour is facilitated by the use of the consumer cost or expenditure function. Suppose good 0 is rationed at $\bar{x}_0$ then the individual's cost minimisation problem is

$$C^R(p,\bar{x}_0,\overline{U}) = \min\,(px - p_0\bar{x}_0|U > \overline{U})$$

where $p = p_1,\ldots,p_n$, $x = x_1,\ldots,x_n$. For example, in Figure 8.2 x_0 is rationed to be at least $\bar{x}_0$ so that $\overline{U}$ is attained. If x is the *numéraire* then the vertical axis can be given a monetary interpretation so that $C^R(p,\bar{x},\overline{U})$ is the rationed cost as defined above while $C(\bar{p}_0,\overline{U})$ is the

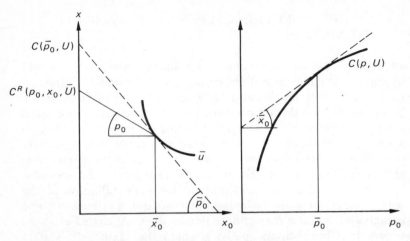

FIGURE 8.2   Rationed and unrationed cost functions

unrationed cost evaluated at the support (or virtual) price $\bar{p}_0$ required to attain $\overline{U}$. Thus:

$$C(\bar{p}_0, \overline{U}) = C^R(p_0, \bar{x}_0, \overline{U}) + (\bar{p}_0 - p_0)\bar{x}_0$$

i.e. the unrationed cost function at the virtual price equals the value of the rationed cost function at the market price plus the shadow value of the ration minus its cost. The derivatives of the rationed cost function define a (rationed) demand system for the unrationed goods, and when the ration is not binding, i.e. when $p_0 - \bar{p}_0$, $C(\bar{p}_0, \overline{U}) - C^R(x_0, p_0, \overline{U})$ the rationed and unrationed forms coincide.

Empirical examples of rationing can be found in Blundell and Walker (1982), and Lee and Pitt (1986). In Lee and Pitt (1986) it is only non-negativity constraints that are considered, i.e. $\bar{x}_1 = 0$, and this provides for some simplifications in their chosen form. In Blundell and Walker (1982) only one good – male labour supply – is rationed (at the observed level of hours) and the absence of separability makes the problem considerably more complicated. Essentially, labour-market rationing only has income effects on commodity-expenditure decisions if goods and leisure are separable. Similarly, a ration in one period under intertemporally separable preferences would only have an income effect on decisions in other periods via the amounts of life-cycle wealth that is allocated to each period.

The importance of wanting to maintain non-separability for policy analysis is outlined in the next section; the difficulty of maintaining it in estimation is that it implies that one cannot pool observations from the rationed regime with those from the unrationed. The problem is essentially one of switching regimes where if $p_0 \geqslant \bar{p}_0$ the unrationed model is relevant while if $p_0 < \bar{p}_0$ the rationed model is relevant. This would be difficult enough, even if $\bar{p}$ itself were not a stochastic function, but there are relatively few non-separable forms of preferences that yield a matched pair of rationed and unrationed systems. The problem can be partially circumvented by realising that unbiased estimates of all preference parameters can be recovered from only the unrationed observations, providing the sample selection bias associated with using a censored sample is corrected for, as in Blundell and Walker (1986). The problem of calculating utility for rationed individuals is then one of solving, perhaps numerically, for $\bar{p}_0$. This is a simple problem, but not one that one would want to solve for each observation in a large sample for each iteration of some maximum-likelihood algorithm. Nevertheless, Hausman and Ruud (1986) do estimate a model of male and female labour supply without separability using both regimes of data and this is made feasible by the fact that for the form chosen the reservation wage (the virtual price of female leisure at zero hours of work) is a quadratic function and can be easily solved.

Corner solutions that arise from purchase infrequency imply a divergence between consumption and expenditure that can be treated as measurement error. However it is a measurement error that would induce bias in OLS estimation since measurement error in the consumption of one good affects the total consumption measure, which is normally assumed to be measured without error in demand analysis. Nevertheless Keene (1986) has shown that an instrumental variable estimator can be used to remove the bias induced by this form of error. The case of zero expenditure arising because some goods do not enter the preferences of some individuals has been treated as an extreme form of purchase infrequency by Atkinson, Gomulka and Stern (1987) in their study of tobacco.

However, estimates of a general non-separable model of both labour supplies and expenditures that deal with corner solutions in a general way remains a difficult econometric prospect. Thus, in practice, separability seems like an essential, rather than just simplifying, assumption. This is especially the case in the intertemporal context.

8.4   TAXATION AND SEPARABILITY

The major feature of theories of optimal taxation is the derivation, under certain specific assumptions, of rules which the tax system should follow if it is to maximise social welfare. A full survey of the issues can be found in Atkinson and Stiglitz (1980), and a detailed examination of the role of separability can be found in Deaton (1981). Here I present a heuristic introduction to the area and discuss the application to three related and recurrent tax-policy issues: the choice of tax base between income and expenditure; the tax treatment of husbands and wives; and the degree of uniformity in indirect taxes.

It is convenient to abstract from distributional considerations by assuming a one-individual world with preferences $U = U(x_0, x)$ where x_0 is leisure and $x = x_1, \ldots, x_n$ are goods. The government wishes to collect R in tax revenue by imposing t_i tax on good i so that $\Sigma t_i x_i = R$. Assuming constant returns to scale producer prices are fixed so t_i is then the difference between consumer prices p_i and producer prices q_i. The government's problem is to maximise $U(x_0, x)$ subject to its revenue constraint which yields first order conditions

$$\sum_{i=1}^{n} U_i \frac{\partial x_i}{\partial t_k} + \mu \left[\sum_{i=1}^{2} t_i \frac{\partial x_i}{\partial l_k} + x_k \right] = 0 \quad k = 1, \ldots, n$$

Substituting from the individual's first order condition that $U_i = \lambda p_i$ and from the budget constraint we have

$$\sum t_i \frac{\partial x_i}{\partial t_k} = \left(\frac{\lambda - \mu}{\mu} \right) x_k = \sigma x_k, \quad k = 1, \ldots, n$$

Using the Slutsky equation and Slutsky symmetry we then get

$$\frac{\sum\limits_{i=1}^{n} t_i s_{ki}}{x_k} = \sigma + \sum_{i=1}^{n} t_i \frac{\partial x_i}{\partial y}, \quad k = 1, \ldots, n$$

where y is exogenous income and s_{ki} is the compensated effect of p_i on x_i. The left-hand side is the proportionate reduction in compensated demand for k arising from the taxes; the right side is the same for all k. Thus the rule implies equi-proportionate reductions in compensated demands. The rule can, for the two-commodity case, be rewritten as:

$$\frac{t_1/p_1}{t_2/p_2} = \left[\frac{(-\varepsilon_{11} + \varepsilon_{22}) - \varepsilon_{10}}{(-\varepsilon_{11} + \varepsilon_{22}) - \varepsilon_{20}} \right]$$

where ε_{ij} is the compensated cross-price elasticity. Since the own-price elasticities are negative this suggests that $t_1 < t_2$ if $\varepsilon_{10} > \varepsilon_{20}$, i.e. if good 1 is a better substitute for leisure than good 2. Weak separability implies that $\varepsilon_{10} = \varepsilon_{20}$ so that commodity taxes should be at a uniform rate; or alternatively commodity taxes should be zero and all income should be taxed at that rate instead. This is a powerful result and would come about if the researcher adopted two-stage budgeting for econometric convenience irrespective of the value of the elasticities that were estimated.

The taxation of the earnings of husbands and wives can be couched in the above framework as in Blundell and Walker (1982b). There it was shown that relative own- and cross-elasticities determine the optimal tax rates on male and female earnings. Of course, the feature of male and female earnings that distinguished them from expenditures on clothing and services, say, is that taxing earnings at different rates would, in most people's view, be a violation of horizontal equity while taxing expenditure at different rates would not. Nevertheless, given the marked differences in the elasticities of labour supply for men and women, taxing their earnings at the same rate might imply a significant deadweight loss relative to different increase tax rates. That is, ignoring cross-elasticities, the Ramsey rule reduces to

$$\frac{t_i}{p_i} = \frac{\sigma}{\varepsilon_{ii}}$$

the inverse elasticity rule, so that the highest tax rate should be levied on the good (labour supply) with the lowest compensated elasticity. In the absence of the ability to apply separate tax schedules to the earnings of men and women it seems likely that these efficiency considerations alone give rise to a case for applying an income-tax schedule that is a progressive function of individual earnings since men earn more than women on average. However, in the absence of separability, account needs to be taken of imposing a large deadweight loss by the imposition of a high tax rate on male earnings inducing a substantial compensated reduction in female labour supply. Moreover, when equity considerations are relevant, account must also be taken of the effect of the (positive) correlation between the wages of husbands and wives on the degree of inequality across household welfare levels.

The Ramsey rule may also be couched in a form suitable for addressing the choice of either income or expenditure as the tax base (see, for example Atkinson and Stiglitz, 1980, section 14.4). In this application the relevant cross-elasticities are those of labour supply with respect to the interest rate, and of savings with respect to the wage – magnitudes over which there is almost no empirical evidence given the assumption of intertemporal separability implicit in most econometric work. If we again neglect those cross-elasticities we are left with the inverse elasticity rule that the tax rate on earned income should be greater than that on interest income if the former is less elastic than the latter.

Despite the simplicity of the inverse elasticity rule it seems likely that the results of the more general Ramsey rule would be sensitive to changes in the cross-elasticities. Thus, it could well be crucial to employ a non-separable form in order to address the question of efficient taxation.

8.5   MICROECONOMIC POLICY ANALYSIS

In Section 8.4 we emphasised the importance of the form of preferences, and separability in particular, for optimal taxation. In practice policy interest is almost inevitably concerned with tax/ benefit reform rather than implementing an optimal tax scheme. Here separability is less crucial in the sense that assuming it does not necessarily generate specific directions of change for taxes. This is just as well since the direct tax/benefit system is, in the UK and elsewhere, rather complicated and results in a budget constraint in labour-supply space that is highly non-linear. Non-linearity in budget constraints will typically result in 'corner solutions' occurring at the kinks and policy analysis will require that individual utility-maximising problems be solved subject to such constraints. In Blundell, Meghir, Symons and Walker (1987) we argue that separability will, in general, make the evaluation of virtual prices at kinks in the budget constraint computationally difficult. Since the evaluation of utility may well require a knowledge of virtual prices this difficulty extends to analysing the behavioural effects of tax/benefit reform.

Thus, the problem for microeconomic policy analysis can be summarised as follows: non-separability between goods and leisure implies that indirect tax reform requires us to evaluate labour-supply consequences and this will, in general, be computationally difficult; non-separability between goods and separability across goods and leisure is the easiest of all worlds since the budget constraint is only non-linear in labour-supply space and not in goods space; separability between goods but not across goods and labour supply is a useful compromise for analysing direct tax reform since relative prices are kept constant and the only difficulty to deal with is the evaluation of virtual wages in labour-supply decisions.

Below we consider two examples. In the first we use a model of male and female labour supply which assumes that labour supplies are non-separable but that there is separability across goods. Thus, we can essentially ignore the allocation of income across goods and consider only the impact of the direct tax reform on labour supplies. In the second example we use a model of expenditure decisions that assumes that labour-supply decisions are separable from goods but that there is non-separability across goods. In this example, we consider a reform to the UK indirect-tax system on expenditure decisions assuming that labour supplies are unaffected.

Direct tax reform

In this example we use the model of household labour supplies in Blundell and Walker (1986) to simulate the effect of replacing the direct tax/benefit system in the UK by a simple proportional income tax using a microcomputer based program called Simulation Program for Analysing Incentives (SPAIN) that is designed to analyse any aspect of UK direct tax/benefit policy.

An important feature of the UK income system is the personal tax allowance. This serves to reduce the marginal tax rate faced by individuals with low earnings. In practice the vast majority of such individuals are married women. Employed married men almost invariably earn more than their tax allowance. Tax allowances and deductions, such as for mortgage-interest payments, clearly reduce tax revenue below the level that would be forthcoming in their absence. Thus, they imply that tax rates are higher than they would otherwise need to be. In addition to allowances and deductions in the income-tax system there are benefits (such as Child Benefit, Housing Benefit and Family Income Supplement) paid directly to certain households. Finally, National Insurance Contributions are levied on all earnings up to a certain level providing earnings are above some lower limit. Together the system of income taxation, National Insurance and means-tested benefits results in a budget constraint that is potentially very complicated and will always be characterised by several non-convexities.

Concern about the 'poverty trap' arising from the interaction between taxes, benefits and social security contributions has given rise to an interest in a tax-credit or negative income-tax system which involves a guaranteed lump sum but taxes all income at a rate sufficient to finance that amount. At the extreme a zero-guarantee level allows the minimum rate of tax and is efficient but inequitable. Here we apply our tax/benefit analysis routine to analyse the effects of this extreme case of reducing tax rates to their minimum (of 19.2 per cent) by abandoning all forms of income support and all tax allowances and deductions. Such a system has been proposed by advocates of 'flat' tax schedules.

Our simulation sample is a subset of the April to October 1981 *Family Expenditure Survey* data set which includes only married couples of working age with the husband an employee, and so will not be representative of the population as a whole. The data is brought up to April 1987 by reflating wages and prices by relevant indices and simulating the effects of the present tax system on this reflated data. This simulated sample then becomes the pre-reform sample for our analysis. Figure 8.3 shows a stylised pre-reform

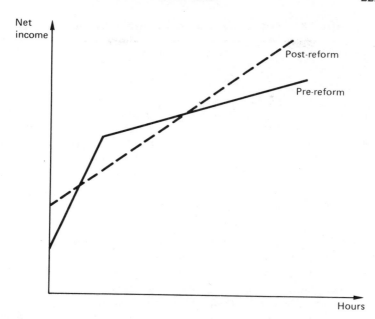

FIGURE 8.3   Pre- and post-reform constraints

budget constraint for a married women under the 1987 tax system. Earnings up to £46.63 per week are tax free, thereafter it is taxed at 27 per cent. Under the reform the budget constraint will be linear (since the allowance is abolished). The intercept of this constraint will depend on the effect of the change on the net income of the husband. Figure 8.3 shows the example of a husband with reasonably high earnings whose net income is greater after the tax change.

In Table 8.1 $dy|_h$ indicates the net income change that would occur if there were no behavioural responses to the reform, dy allows for behavioural response, dt is the change in the marginal tax rate, dh is the predicted hours change, $dh|_U$ is the compensated hours change, and EG is 'equivalent gain' – the money metric measure of the welfare change suggested by King (1983). Table 8.1 breaks down the effects for the whole sample into five subgroups: in the first column we give results for non-participating women ($h = 0$, where h is hours of work), in the second column are those working women in households which are better off but where the wife now faces a higher tax rate than before ($h > 0$, $dy|_h > 0$, $dt > 0$,

TABLE 8.1   Behavioural and welfare analysis by household type

	$h = 0$	$h > 0,$ $dy\vert_h > 0,$ $dt > 0$	$h > 0,$ $dy\vert_h < 0,$ $dt > 0$	$h > 0,$ $dy\vert_h < 0,$ $dt < 0$	$h > 0,$ $dy\vert_h > 0,$ $dt < 0$
$dy\vert_h$	-1.71	8.35	-11.22	-9.89	14.73
dt	0.14	0.17	0.17	-0.15	-0.17
dy	-1.42	4.30	-8.10	-4.90	11.94
$dh\vert_U$	—	-0.71	-0.86	0.54	0.58
dh	0.18	-2.19	1.76	1.96	-0.73
EG	-1.65	8.79	-11.05	-9.74	15.07
%	42	6	17	16	19

where dy is the change in income and dt is the change in marginal tax rate), in the third column are those in worse-off households where the wife faces a higher rate ($h > 0$, $dy\vert_h < 0$, $dt > 0$), in the fourth column are those worse-off households where the wife faces a lower rate ($h > 0$, $dy\vert_h < 0$, $dt < 0$), and in the fifth column are those better-off households where the wife faces a lower rate ($h > 0$, $dy\vert_h > 0$, $dt < 0$). The final row indicates the sample proportions.

Thus, for example, the final column shows the counteracting effects of the income and substitution effects of the reform on such individuals. The increase in net income leads to a reduction in labour supply that outweighs the substitution effect of 0.58 hours per week and the net effect is a reduction of 0.73 hours. This reduction gives rise to the income gain being £11.94 rather than £14.73. The EG of £15.07 is bounded by the $dy\vert_h$ of £14.73, and this is a general property if leisure is a normal good. The change in the deadweight loss of the tax system, DWL, is defined as minus the sum of the EGs plus the change in government revenue. Since this reform is designed to be revenue neutral

$$DWL = -\sum EG_i = \text{£0.69 per household per week}$$

Thus, far from promoting efficiency and work incentives, reducing the tax rate (and abolishing the allowances) decreases efficiency since the standard rate (albeit only 19.2 per cent) is imposed on all women not just on those with earnings above £46.63.

Now we turn to distribution effects. Clearly this reform is going

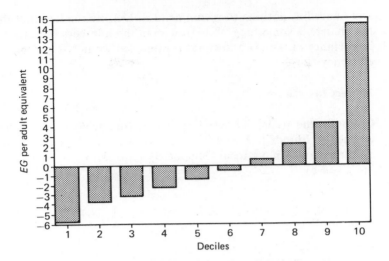

FIGURE 8.4 Distributional effects of proportional income tax

to lead to significant income losses for households on low net incomes and gains for those on high net incomes. However given our emphasis on the implications of the reform on labour supply we present the effects on the money metric measure of welfare used in the construction of *EG*. In Figure 8.4 households have been ranked by this money metric deflated by the number of adult equivalents in the household. The bars in Figure 8.4 show the average *EG* for each decile group. The adverse distributional effects depicted in Figure 8.4 are quantified in Table 8.2 in the form of Atkinson inequality and Gini indices.

Thus, the tax change produces an increase in inequality of 30 per cent or more as well as an increase in the *DWL* of the tax system,

TABLE 8.2 Atkinson equivalent income inequality indices before and after reform

Aversion parameter	1.0	2.0	3.0	4.0	5.0	Gini
Pre-reform inequality	0.08	0.14	0.20	0.25	0.29	0.23
Post-reform inequality	0.11	0.19	0.27	0.34	0.41	0.26

and hence has nothing to recommend it. Despite the fact that this tax change is something of a straw man the numbers indicate the importance of the tax allowance for married women in promoting efficiency.

Indirect tax reform

Credit for the model of household expenditure behaviour used here is due to Blundell, Pashardes and Weber, (1987) (BPW) who estimated an 'Almost Ideal Demand System,[1] whose budget shares are given by

$$w_i = \alpha_i + \sum_{j=1}^{n} \gamma_{ij} \log p_j + \beta_i \log (y/P) \qquad i = 1, \ldots, n$$

where w_i is the budget share of good i, p_i is the price of i, y is total expenditure on the n goods, and P is the Stone price index

$$\sum_{j=1}^{n} \alpha_{ij} \log p_j.$$

The estimates of BPW cover seven commodity groups: food, clothing, alcohol, fuel, transport, services and other goods and were obtained by applying a GLS technique proposed by Keene (1986) to correct for zero expenditures in the data arising from infrequency of purchase. The data used were the UK *Family Expenditure Surveys* from 1970 to 1984 – approximately 100 000 observations. Estimation was conducted one equation at a time and the cross-equation restrictions implied by symmetry, etc. were imposed using a minimum X^2 technique at a final stage. A broad idea for the sizes of elasticities is given in Table 8.3 which were calculated from the estimates in BPW and evaluated at the means of the relevant explanatory variables in the 1984 FES data. More detail of the estimation procedure and how the elasticities are distributed across households can be found in BPW.

In simulation we consider only the most recent sample at the time of writing, the 1984 FES which contains 7080 households. For simulation purposes the estimates are deficient in a number of respects. First, the seven commodity groups cover only 69 per cent of total expenditure according to the 1984 FES data since durables,

TABLE 8.3 Estimated elasticities

Pensioners

PRICE	Food	Alcl	Fuel	Cloth	Trans	Other	Servs
Food	−0.34	−0.02	0.03	−0.67	−0.12	−0.53	−0.78
Alcohol	−0.06	−1.89	0.74	−0.78	0.30	0.16	0.08
Fuel	−0.12	1.25	−0.52	0.06	0.13	−0.29	−0.34
Clothing	0.02	−0.35	0.03	−0.79	−0.05	0.00	−0.05
Transport	−0.15	0.58	−0.56	−0.06	−0.64	0.78	−0.53
Other goods	0.01	−0.99	0.33	5.20	−0.37	−0.36	−0.61
Services	−0.06	−0.11	−0.08	0.27	−0.44	0.55	−0.68
INCOME	0.62	2.18	0.48	1.54	1.29	1.06	1.84

Non-pensioners with children

PRICE	Food	Alcl	Fuel	Cloth	Trans	Other	Servs
Food	−0.62	0.04	−0.01	0.03	−0.05	0.00	−0.05
Alcohol	−0.19	−2.09	0.97	−0.20	0.58	−0.20	−0.81
Fuel	0.07	0.72	−0.86	−0.07	−0.04	−0.11	0.22
Clothing	−0.15	−0.07	−0.03	−0.89	−0.10	−0.17	0.09
Transport	−0.32	0.24	−0.32	−0.05	−0.73	0.04	−0.06
Other goods	−0.39	−0.09	−0.21	−0.21	−0.02	−0.94	−0.16
Services	−0.29	−0.39	−0.14	0.13	−0.06	0.25	−0.73
INCOME	0.65	1.93	0.33	1.33	1.20	1.70	0.95

Non-pensioners without children

PRICE	Food	Alcl	Fuel	Cloth	Trans	Other	Servs
Food	−0.57	0.06	−0.02	0.03	−0.05	0.01	−0.06
Alcohol	−0.10	−1.81	0.71	−0.14	0.41	−0.16	−0.59
Fuel	0.04	0.79	−0.85	0.07	−0.46	−0.10	0.24
Clothing	−0.15	−0.09	−0.03	−0.87	−0.12	−0.20	0.10
Transport	−0.27	0.20	−0.27	−0.04	−0.78	0.03	−0.05
Other goods	−0.30	−0.09	−0.17	−0.17	−0.04	−0.96	0.13
Services	−0.28	−0.38	0.14	0.13	−0.06	0.25	−0.73
INCOME	0.59	1.68	0.28	1.37	1.17	1.59	0.95

tobacco and housing expenditures are excluded from consideration. We incorporate these important commodity groups in simulation by assuming that the quantities of these goods are rationed at the levels implied by their observed 1984 expenditures and the 1984 price indices and separable from the community groups covered by the estimates. Thus, changes in the tax treatment of durables, tobacco or housing are treated as changes in total expenditure on the other seven commodities via the household budget constraint. That is, y is treated as the income remaining after the rationed levels of housing, tobacco and durables have been purchased, so that y will change as the tax treatment of the rationed goods changes. Secondly, the estimates may imply a predicted budget share outside the 0, 1 interval. While this does not occur using the prices reigning during 1984 it can occur at different prices implied by some tax change. In simulation we treat zero and unit budget shares as binding constraints and a prediction outside the unit interval would result in the prediction being set at the relevant bound and the additional implied income (which would be negative if the prediction were greater than unit budget share and positive if the prediction were for negative expenditure on a commodity group) reallocated to other goods in proportions given by their marginal budget shares. Finally, the estimated equations only allow the prediction of the behavioural responses of commodity groups such as clothing and not specific items, such as children's clothing. Since the latter are outside the VAT base while the former are within it we cannot appeal to the composite commodity theorem. Thus, the simulation routine assumes that the proportions of each commodity group expenditure spent on each item within the group are constant. Thus, taxing children's clothing reduces the quantity of clothing purchased but leaves the share of children's clothing in total clothing expenditure unchanged.[2]

In simulation, the estimated equations are used to reflate the 1984 data to June 1987 using the relevant components of the Retail Price Index. The tax changes on individual items are converted to commodity-group price-changes using weights derived from the 1984 FES data. Thus, an increase in petrol duty has no impact on the behavioural and welfare of households who do not own a car. Similarly, taxing children's clothing mainly affects households with children.[3] Further details of the simulation methodology can be found in Symons and Walker (1988).

The proposals for indirect taxation under consideration by the European Community imply quite radical changes in the structure of indirect taxation for the UK. Under the proposals zero-rated goods such as most food, domestic energy, etc., will be taxed at a new lower VAT rate for essential goods at, say, 4 per cent;

children's clothing seems likely to be subject to the standard rate of VAT which we assume will remain unchanged at 15 per cent. Excise duties on alcohol, tobacco and petrol will all be significantly reduced.

First we consider the implications of these changes on household expenditure decisions. In Table 8.4 we present the levels and percentage changes in expenditures obtained from simulation by averaging across all households. The final column shows the percentage change in expenditure that would arise if households did not change the quantities of the commodities that they consume. While this is the kind of analysis that might be conducted to obtain the very-short-run impact, the final figure in this column indicates that such expenditure changes would violate the household budget constraint in that total expenditure would fall by almost 1 per cent. Notice that fuel expenditure falls by nearly 15 per cent despite the 4 per cent tax rate imposed on it, while alcohol expenditure rises by 2 per cent despite the 20 per cent reduction in duty. Since tobacco is treated as a rationed commodity the 27 per cent reduction in expenditure mirrors exactly the 27 per cent reduction in price implied by harmonisation. Finally, in Table 8.4, expenditures on durables and housing are unchanged whether we allow for behavioural responses or not. This occurs because these commodities are both rationed and have their prices unaffected by harmonisation.

Clearly, behavioural changes of the order of magnitude suggested in Table 8.4 will have a pronounced effect on the calculation of government revenues. Table 8.5 gives a breakdown of the sources of government revenue in £ per household per week. Fuel and alcohol revenue figures differ considerably from the naive no-response figure because of the large behavioural changes shown in Table 8.4.[4] Thus, overall, the loss in government revenue from indirect taxation is 2.16 per cent of original revenue rather than a 3.68 per cent reduction. When 'grossed up' to the population this underestimation of government revenue would amount to more than £0.33 billion per year.

The greatest virtue of working with data at the household level is that it allows a comprehensive distributional analysis of the effects of tax changes. For example, it is possible to break down the indirect tax payments made by, say smokers and drinkers, compared with non-smokers and non-drinkers, as in Table 8.6. Clearly,

TABLE 8.4 Behavioural responses to harmonisation

Commodity group	1987 expenditure (£/hh/week)	Post-harmonisation expenditure (£/hh/week)	% change in expenditure	% change in expenditure (q fixed)
Food	36.35	36.81	1.27	1.03
Fuel	10.66	9.07	−14.92	4.00
Clothing	13.29	13.65	2.71	2.39
Transport	25.80	25.15	−2.52	1.06
Services	17.59	17.93	1.93	1.09
Other	14.64	14.68	7.62	1.01
Alcohol	7.38	7.53	2.03	−20.11
Tobacco	6.83	4.97	−27.23	−27.23
Durables	12.50	12.50	0.00	0.00
Housing	27.34	27.34	0.00	0.00
Total	171.39	171.39	0.00	−0.95

TABLE 8.5 Sources of tax revenue

Commodity group	Pre-harmonisation revenue	Post-harmonisation (fixed share)	Post-harmonisation (with responses)
Food	1.38	2.38	2.37
Fuel	0.00	0.42	0.35
Clothing	1.57	1.76	1.78
Transport	5.72	6.10	5.89
Services	1.63	1.50	1.51
Other	1.29	1.44	1.53
Alcohol	3.19	2.18	2.68
Tobacco	5.31	3.46	3.46
Durables	1.63	1.63	1.63
Housing	0.57	0.57	0.57
Total	22.26	21.44	21.78

Note: £ per household per week.

the nature of the proposals favour those households that spend a high proportion of their income on goods whose price falls – cigarettes and alcohol.

However, concern is usually with the impact of tax changes at different parts of the income distribution. In Figure 8.5 households have been ranked into deciles of the normal gross income distribution and shows the changes in indirect tax payments and indirectly the extent to which smoking (and, to a lesser extent, drinking) is concentrated towards the bottom of the income distribution.

Figure 8.5 does not, however, exploit the benefits of having an estimated welfare function for each household. For the 'AIDS' model the household expenditure function is given by

$$\log E(p,z,U) = \log A(p,z) + B(p)U \qquad (8.10)$$

where z is a vector of demographic characteristics and household variables that affect tastes. The functions $A(p,z)$ and $B(p)$ are given by

$$A(p,z) = a(z)_0 + \sum_i \sum_j \gamma_{ij} \log p_i \log p_j \qquad (8.11)$$

$$B(p) = \prod_{i=1}^{n} p^{B_i}$$

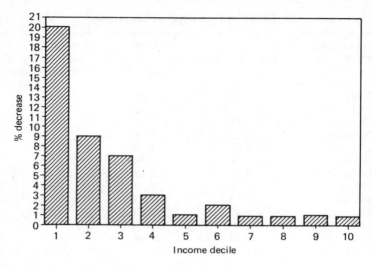

FIGURE 8.5   Tax reductions by income decile

Equation (8.10) allows the measurement of household utility (up to a monotonic transformation), and the calculation of measures of welfare changes. Thus, if p^0 is the original vector of prices and p^1 the new vector, then the compensating and equivalent variations can be defined as usual (see Hausman, 1982). The welfare-change measures known as compensating and equivalent gain (*CG* and *EG*) due to King (1983) are particularly useful in the present context since it allows for the impact of both price and lump-sum income changes arising from a fix charge. Since we are treating these commodities as rationed we can regard changes in their prices as lump-sum income changes. King (1983) defines *CG* and *EG* via the 'equivalent income' function as the income required to achieve the actual level of utility were the household to face the new prices. Thus, for the AIDS form the equivalent income function is given by

$$ YE = \exp \left[\left(\frac{B^1}{B^0} \right) \log \left(\frac{Y}{A^0} \right) + \log A^1 \right] $$

where $A^1 = A(p^1, z)$, $A^0 = A(p^0, z)$, $B^1 = B(p^1)$, and $B^0 = B(p^0)$. Then welfare change *EG* is defined as the change *EG* in income required

TABLE 8.6 **Reductions in indirect taxes paid**

EXCISE DUTY	Smokers	Non-smokers		
Drinkers	−1.90	−1.92	−1.90	
Non-drinkers	−1.45	−1.33	−1.38	
	−1.77	−1.66	−1.71	

VAT	Smokers	Non-smokers		
Drinkers	4.41	0.95	2.94	
Non-drinkers	2.39	−0.16	0.87	
	3.83	0.46	2.19	

TOTAL TAX	Smokers	Non-smokers		
Drinkers	2.51	−0.97	1.03	
Non-drinkers	0.94	−1.49	−0.51	
	2.07	−1.20	0.47	

to obtain the existing standard of living at the new prices as opposed to the existing prices, i.e.

$$EG = Y - YE$$

In Figure 8.6 we have ranked households by deciles of the original utility distribution and plotted the average EGs and changes in the tax payments for each decile group.

A more structured approach to inequality is provided by the familiar Atkinson Inequality Index (see Atkinson, 1970) which can be defined over equivalent incomes or households as:

$$I = \sum_{h=1}^{H} \frac{EY_h^{1-\varepsilon}}{1-\varepsilon}$$

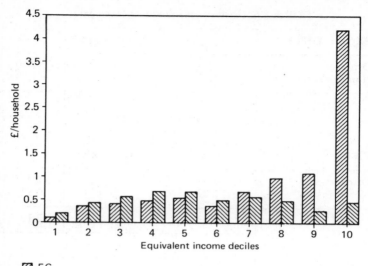

EG
Tax reduction

FIGURE 8.6   *EG* **and tax reductions by equivalent income decile**

where H is the number of households, ε is the value of inequality aversion, and EY_h is the level of equivalent income for household h. Table 8.7 gives the level of inequality in the existing equivalent income distribution and in that resulting from applying the harmonisation proposals for different levels at inequality aversions. The proposals unambiguously increase inequality at any level of aversion.

TABLE 8.7   **Atkinson equivalent income inequality indices before and after harmonisation**

Aversion parameter, ε	0.5	1.0	1.5	5.0	Gini
Pre-harmonisation	0.177	0.326	0.499	0.834	0.381
Post-harmonisation	0.120	0.334	0.511	0.855	0.386

TABLE 8.8   Social welfare change

ε	Change in W	% change in W
0.0	0.91	0.06
0.5	0.28	0.17
1.5	−0.76	−0.45
2.5	−1.60	−0.94
5.0	−3.44	−2.02

Defining inequality with reference to the Atkinson inequality index yields a natural definition of social welfare as:

$$W = \overline{EY}(1 - I)$$

i.e. the average living standard weighted by the level of equality. With ε = 0, no inequality aversion, $I = 0$ and social welfare is equal to the average welfare. King (1983) shows that the change in deadweight loss is ΣEG minus the change in government revenue.

In Table 8.8, we present social welfare change for different levels of inequality aversion. Given the increase in inequality implied by the harmonisation proposals ΔW eventually becomes negative at higher levels of ε because of the increasing weight given to the way unequally equivalent incomes are distributed. At zero inequality aversion the welfare change is £0.91 per household per week and, given the £0.47 decrease in government revenue, the decrease in deadweight loss is £0.44 per household.

The application here suggests that harmonisation would imply a welfare gain of £0.91 per household per week but together with increasing inequality in the distribution of welfare across households. Of course, against this has to be set the possible gains from reducing frontier barriers.

9 What's the Good of Equality?*

JOHN BROOME

9.1 INTRODUCTION

A country's income distribution can have many different shapes. It can be spread out or sharply peaked, skewed or symmetrical, perhaps even bimodal between the sexes. It is obviously impossible to capture all this variety in a single statistic such as the variance.

But this is *not* the difficulty in measuring inequality. The purpose of an inequality measure is not to compress a lot of information into one number. There is often no need to do that anyway. If someone wants to know, say, whether income is more equally distributed now than it was ten years ago, there may be no difficulty about presenting her with the whole distribution for each date. The difficulty is that, when she has all this information, she may *still* not know whether the distribution has become more or less unequal.

What more does she really want to know? Well, she could simply be interested in how she should use the term 'unequal' and apply it to this case. But if so the answer to her question may simply be that our notion of inequality is a pretty vague one, and she can use it how she wishes within broad limits. It is more likely that she wants to know whether inequality has grown better or worse. She is likely to be interested in the badness of the inequality rather than straightforwardly in the amount of it. And that is what I am going to be concerned with in this chapter. There is, of course, a distinction between the amount of inequality and the badness of it,

236

and it is a good idea to settle from the start which we shall be concerned with. Authors have not always made it clear which their 'measures of inequality' are supposed to be measuring,[1] and the ambiguity can be damaging.[2]

The question is, then: when is the inequality in one distribution worse than in another? But there is a wider question: when is one distribution worse than another? To ask the more specific question about inequality presupposes that the wider question can be split into two, one question about the relative goodness of the total income, and one about the relative badness of the inequality in its distribution. Is this a reasonable presupposition? Section 9.2 is about that.

9.2   TOTAL INCOME AND ITS DISTRIBUTION

Let me announce from the start that I am not going to try and deal with differences in population. That is a subject fraught with too many difficulties to broach in this paper.[3] I shall only try to compare distributions with the same population n. The distribution of income is the vector $y = (y_1, y_2, \ldots y_n)$, specifying each person's income. There is a relation, 'at least as good as' between different distributions. I shall call it, inaccurately, the 'betterness' relation. It is, as a matter of logic,[4] transitive and reflexive. It is commonly assumed to be a complete preorder. Then, provided it is continuous, it can be represented by a function $G(y)$. $G(y)$ says, up to an increasing transformation, how good the distribution y is. I shall call it a 'goodness function'. It only represents the betterness relation *ordinally*: $G(x) \geqslant G(y)$ if and only if x is at least as good as y. I doubt that such a function exists. As Sen (1973, 1978) tirelessly reminds us, it is likely that some pairs of distributions will not be comparable in terms of their goodness: neither better than the other, nor equally good either. If so, there will be no goodness function. Nevertheless, most authors have discussed inequality in terms of functions rather than incomplete relations, and for the sake of convenience and simplicity I am going to follow that practice.

The betterness relation will have to be indifferent to permutations of the distribution. Although we are comparing only populations with the same *number* of people, it would be an absurd restriction if we could only compare populations consisting of the very same people. This means we shall have to assume that the identities of the people do not matter. So it must be the case that $G(x) = G(y)$ whenever x is a permutation of y; $G(y)$ is symmetrical in the components of y.

This is forced on us, but there is a major assumption implicit in it. People differ, and some may make better use of income than others. In applying the betterness relation to *income* distributions, and then insisting on symmetry, I have made it impossible to take account of these differences. Everyone is being assumed to be the same apart from their income. To decide whether or not one distribution is at least as good as another, we really need to know more about the people receiving the incomes. A more thorough analysis would take account of people's characteristics (e.g. Fine, 1985). It might turn out that it is better to deal, not with income distributions but with distributions of some other variable that is itself a function of income and characteristics. Sen (1985) for instance, is interested in the distribution of 'capabilities', by which he means what people are able to do with their income. A characteristic that certainly makes a difference is how much income a person receives at other times in her life than the one at which we are looking now. Inequality of income is presumably less bad if the people at the bottom are not always at the bottom. So mobility is important, and it might be better to deal in lifetime income rather than current income.[5] Still, for better or worse, it is distributions of current income with which this chapter is concerned, and the anonymity assumption is unavoidable.[6]

We are interested in whether the betterness relation can usefully be split into something to do with total income and something to do with inequality in the distribution of income. One routine procedure for making a split of this sort has been popularised by Atkinson (1970). For a distribution y, take the *equal* distribution that is equally good: the distribution $\hat{\mu}e$ such that $G(\hat{\mu}e) = G(y)$ where e is the unit vector $(1, 1, \ldots 1)$. Let $\hat{M} = n\hat{\mu}$. $\hat{M}$ is an index of the distribution's goodness; better distributions will have a higher $\hat{M}$. It is, in fact, just another representation, like G, of the betterness relation. The difference between $\hat{M}$ and the total income M shows how much income is being wasted, as it were, as a result of the inequality; things could be just as good with that much less income, if only it were equally distributed.

The badness of the inequality may be measured as $I_a = (M - \hat{M})$. This is a measure in money terms. An alternative dimensionless measure is to take the ratio of I_a to M: $I_r = (1 - \hat{M}/M)$. Let us call I_a an 'absolute measure' of inequality and I_r a 'relative measure' – relative, that is, to the total.[7] Then

$$\hat{M} = M - I_a \tag{9.1}$$

$$\hat{M} = M(1 - I_r). \tag{9.2}$$

Since $\hat{M}$ measures the goodness of the distribution, this says that you can think of the distribution's goodness as made up of M measuring the goodness of the total, less I_a measuring the badness of the inequality. Or else you can think of it as M reduced by the fraction I_r. In this way the badness of inequality has been split off as a consideration on its own. The split may not be a very clean one, though. Nothing in the way that I_a and I_r are constructed guarantees that either of them will itself be in any sense independent of M.

Is I_a or I_r the better measure of inequality? This is a pretty sterile question. Suppose there has been a change that has made I_a go up and I_r go down. (There must have been an increase in M.) Has inequality got better or worse? Well, it has got worse in money terms and better relative to the total. There is not much more to be said. The notion of better or worse *simpliciter* applies to the distribution, not to its inequality. The notion applied to inequality depends on the context. It depends on how the badness of inequality is going to be put together with the other relevant consideration, the goodness of the total, in judging the overall goodness of the distribution. If they are to be put together in an additive way, then I_a is the right measure of badness; if in the fractional way shown in (9.2), I_r. Perhaps it is more natural to put goods and bads together additively. So the absolute measure may be a bit more natural.

There is, however, a substantive question that affects which measure is the more convenient to use (see Kolm, 1976). It can be put like this: should we expect either measure to be independent of total income, and if so which?

Take any distribution y and compare it with αy for some scalar $\alpha > 1$, a distribution where everyone's income is higher in the same proportion. Which distribution has the worse inequality? It has sometimes been suggested that the inequality is equally bad.[8] What people mean when they say this is that the relative measure I_r is the same in each. I_r, in fact, is homogeneous of degree zero in y. In this sense it is independent of total income. I_r may consequently be a convenient measure to use. But it would be a mistake to suggest that, if I_r has this property of homogeneity, a proportional increase in everyone's income leaves inequality *really* neither better nor worse. In absolute terms, measured by I_a, it makes it worse.

Now compare y with $(y + \alpha e)$ for some scalar $\alpha > 0$, a distribution where everyone's income is higher by the same amount. It might be suggested that the inequality in *these* two distributions is equally bad.[9] The suggestion here is that the absolute measure I_a is the same in each. I_a is then a nought-translatable function (i.e. has the property that $I_a(y + \alpha e) = I_a(y)$ for any $\alpha > 0$). In *this* sense I_a is independent of total income. This may make it a convenient measure to use. But again, it would be a mistake to suggest that a uniform increase in everyone's income leaves inequality *really* neither better nor worse. In relative terms, measured by I_r, it makes it better.

The conclusion I draw is that to argue in the abstract about the badness of different patterns of inequality is pointless.[10] The argument must be set in the context of a particular method of putting the badness of inequality into an assessment of the goodness of the distribution as a whole. What we are really concerned with is the form of the goodness function G. I shall concentrate on that, and not on measures of inequality. Once the form of G is settled, a measure of inequality can be split off from it in whatever way suits the context.

However, my discussion of the form of G will quickly reveal that I think inequality is in an important way a consideration on its own, distinct from other considerations that help to determine G. That is the main point of this chapter. To clear the way for it, I first need to raise an objection to an assumption that is commonly made about G.

9.3   SEPARABILITY OF THE BETTERNESS FUNCTION

The assumption to which I am going to object is that G is strongly separable. First I shall explain what this means. G is a function of the components of the vector y:

$$G(y) = G(y_1, y_2, \ldots y_n)$$

Pick out some collection of these components, say the first k: y_1, y_2, $\ldots y_k$. This collection is said to be *separable* in G if and only if the function G can be written in the form:

$$G(y) = \hat{G}[H(y_1, y_2, \ldots y_k), y_{k+1}, y_{k+2}, \ldots y_n]$$

This says that there is an ordering over the collection, represented by the function H, that is independent of the level of any of the other components of y, G is *strongly separable* if and only if every collection of components of y, not just the first k, is separable in G.

It turns out that G is strongly separable if and only if it is additively separable (Debreu, 1960). For G to be additively separable means that it is has the form:

$$G(y) = T[h_1(y_1) + h_2(y_2) + \ldots + h_n(y_n)]$$

where T is a positive transformation. Since G is only an ordinal representation of the betterness relation, we may as well divide out the transformation and take G itself to be

$$G(y) = h_1(y_1) + h_2(y_2) + \ldots + h_n(y_n) \tag{9.3}$$

Why should we think G is strongly separable? Authors who have adopted this assumption have not often tried to defend it. Dalton (1920) simply announces that it 'is reasonable in a preliminary discussion'. Atkinson (1970) says only that he is following Dalton. Rothschild and Stiglitz (1973) offer a half-hearted defence, concluding only that it is defensible but not compelling. They do little more than state the conditions for strong separability in two different forms, in the hope that one or the other will seem attractive. Strong separability seems to be recognised as an assumption that should be treated with caution. Nevertheless, it is still used (e.g. Fine, 1985; Kanbur and Stromberg, forthcoming). I want to establish that it has no place at all in the theory of inequality.

One thing that has *motivated* this assumption – however it might be justified – is an analogy with expected utility theory. For a moment reinterpret the distribution vector y, as a single person facing some uncertainty about what her income will be. Instead of n people, let there be n states of nature. Let each component of y stand for what the single person's income will be in a particular state of nature. A vector y then stands for a particular 'income prospect'. In expected utility theory the person is supposed to have preferences between prospects like this, and her preferences are supposed to conform to some axioms. Now look at strong separability as I defined it above and give it this new interpretation. Instead of the betterness relation think of the person's preference relation, and think of G as a utility function that represents it. Interpreted this way, strong separability is nothing other than the strong independence axiom or sure-thing principle, one of expected utility theory's fundamental axioms.

If we assume strong separability for income distributions then expected utility theory will be closely analogous to the theory of inequality. Risk-aversion will be analogous to inequality-aversion. Well-known facts about the former can be applied to the latter (see Atkinson, 1970). This makes strong separability an attractive assumption for income distributions. And Rothschild and Stiglitz's (1973) cautious defence of it uses arguments gleaned from expected utility theory.

But comparing it with the analogous assumption in expected utility theory also shows that, applied to income distributions, strong separability is very dubious indeed. In expected utility theory, this assumption has been under heavy fire since it was first developed. It can be defended against these attacks. But the analogous defence is not available at all in the theory of inequality.

Look at this example, which is a version of Allais's famous paradox.[11] Imagine one ticket out of a hundred is to be drawn at random. Consider four possible gambles, each determining your annual income according to which ticket is drawn. The prizes are shown in Table 9.1 (the states of nature are ticket numbers). It turns out that a lot of people, when asked to choose between these gambles, prefer w to x, and also z to y But this is not consistent with strong separability. To see this, look at equation (9.3) and substitute into it the components of w, x, y and z. It will become obvious that if $G(w)$ is greater than $G(x)$ then $G(y)$ has to be greater than

TABLE 9.1   States of nature or people

		1 (£)	2–10 (£)	11–100 (£)
	w	50 000	50 000	50 000
Prospects or	*x*	1 000	150 000	50 000
distributions	*y*	50 000	50 000	1 000
	z	1 000	150 000	1 000

$G(z)$. Allais offers this explanation. Strong separability assumes that what happens in one state of nature can be valued independently of what happens in other states. Equation (9.3) makes this clear. But actually, says Allais, there may be interactions or complementarity between states. In the example, gamble *w* makes it *certain* that your income will be £50 000. It eliminates uncertainty, and there is a special value attached to this. It gives *w* an advantage over *x* that *y* does not have over *z*. But this fact of certainty is only visible when all the states of nature are looked at together. If you try to value the prize in each state taken separately, it does not appear. According to Allais, then, strong separability is a bad assumption because it ignores interactions between what happens in different states.

But there is a defence against this argument. (Whether it succeeds or fails is irrelevant. See Broome, 1988b.) It has to be conceded that in practice people's preferences are not always strongly separable; Allais's example (and many others) show this. But strong separability can be defended as a condition of *rationality* for preferences. A rational person should realise that there is really no room for interactions between different states of nature. What happens in one state should not affect the value of what happens in another, because if one state comes about the other does not. As Samuelson (1952) says: 'Within the stochastic realm, independence has a legitimacy that it does not have in the nonstochastic realm. Why? Because either heads *or* tails must come up: if one comes up the other cannot.'

Now look again at the example in Table 9.1 but interpret *w*, *x*, *y* and *z* now as alternative distributions of income for a hundred people. It is not implausible to think the distribution w is better than x, whereas z is better than y. This conflicts with strong separability. Strong separability requires that distributions should be valued one person at a time,[12] just as in the alternative interpretation it required that prospects should be valued one state at a time. But in support of the view that w is better than x and z better than y, one might point out that w has income equally distributed, and this is a merit that is not shared by y. The equality in w will not emerge if you try to value it one person at a time. Because equality is valuable, there is an interaction between what happens to different people. So strong separability must be rejected.

All this is analogous to Allais's argument. But in the context of inequality the reply I described is not available. Whether or not it was successful, it could obviously only get off the ground because we were dealing with states of nature, and only one of them would actually happen. With an income distribution, each of the different incomes will be received by someone, and all these people will live in one society. We cannot possibly rule out interactions between the incomes of different people.

9.4   UTILITARIANISM AND EGALITARIANISM

Indeed, I think we can go further. It is not simply that we cannot insist on strong separability. To assume strong separability is actually to repudiate a concern, of an appropriate sort, for equality. This claim needs some explaining, since people have often tried to capture the value of equality by means of a strongly separable goodness function. Two related but distinct theories support them in this. In this section and section 9.5 I shall explain why I think both are unsuccessful. And in section 9.5 also I shall explain why I think, quite generally, that true egalitarianism is incompatible with strong separability.[13]

The first theory is straightforward utilitarianism. Suppose that $g_i(y_i)$ is the amount of good the ith person derives from her income y_i. Utilitarianism identifies the overall goodness of a distribution with the total of people's good.[14] So we can write:

$$G = g_1(y_1) + g_2(y_2) + \ldots g_n(y_n)$$

Suppose now that all the functions g_i are the same, and also strictly concave. Then:

$$G = g(y_1) + g(y_2) + \ldots g(y_n) \qquad (9.4)$$

where g is strictly concave. This is a strongly separable goodness function that has some egalitarian tendency. For any given total of income, it says it is better for it to be equally distributed rather than unequally. Utilitarianism is against inequality here because it is inefficient in a sense. Units of income are more efficiently used to generate good if they go to the poor rather than the rich.

However, it is well known that utilitarianism has only a very weak tendency to favour equality.[15] It happens to do so if everybody's function g_i is the same and strictly concave, but otherwise it may not. That the function is strictly concave is traditional and plausible wisdom; income has diminishing marginal benefit. That everybody's function is the same is not plausible at all.[16] It is much more plausible to think that some people, the handicapped and people with expensive tastes for instance, derive less benefit from a given amount of income than others. If there is a given amount of income to distribute, the utilitarian formula will then recommend that these people should get less of it than others. Handicapped people, it will say, who need more income than others to achieve the same level of good, should actually receive less. This is not egalitarian. That utilitarianism has egalitarian implications in equation (9.4) is really no more than an accident. And even when its implications are egalitarian, utilitarianism does not capture the spirit of egalitarianism at all. An egalitarian believes that inequality is unfair or unjust. But according to utilitarianism the most that can be wrong with it is that it is inefficient.[17] 'As a framework for judging inequality' says Sen (1973), 'utilitarianism is indeed a non-starter.' I do not need to dwell on this point.

It is possible to move away from utilitarianism in an egalitarian direction, whilst keeping the goodness function strongly separable. This leads to the second theory I mentioned above. I shall call it 'modified utilitarianism'. It starts out from the thought that the reason utilitarianism is not fundamentally egalitarian is because it does not care about equality in the distribution of *good*. To put that right it transforms each person's good by a strictly concave function before adding up:

$$G = t(g_1) + t(g_2) + \ldots + t(g_n) \qquad (9.5)$$

where g_i is i's good and t is strictly concave. If there is a given amount of good to be distributed, this formula will favour distributing it equally.

If each person's good is a function $g_i(y_i)$ of her income, then

$$G = \hat{g}_1(y_1) + \hat{g}_2(y_2) + \ldots + \hat{g}_n(y_n)$$

where $\hat{g}_i(y_i)$ is $t(g_i(y_i))$. If each function g_i is the same:

$$G = \hat{g}(y_1) + \hat{g}(y_2) + \ldots + \hat{g}(y_n) \qquad (9.6)$$

where $\hat{g}(y_i)$ is $t(g(y_i))$. Provided g is concave, or not convex enough to outweigh the strict concavity of t, $\hat{g}$ will be strictly concave. Equation (9.6) will be indistinguishable in practice from (9.4).[18] And modified utilitarianism need be no more egalitarian in its practical implications than ordinary utilitarianism. It may, for instance, still recommend giving handicapped people less income than others. Nevertheless, modified utilitarianism does seem more genuinely egalitarian in spirit than the unmodified version. It does, for one thing, care directly about the distribution of good. And second, the function $\hat{g}_i$ depends, not just on g_i, which shows how much good i derives from income, but also on the transformation t. If this is very concave, the differential effect of different g_i functions will be small, and the egalitarian tendency will in practice be strong.

All the same, I do not think that modified utilitarianism represents adequately the value of equality. I shall spell out my reason in section 9.5. But before that I also want to mention a doubt I have about the intelligibility of the theory itself (see Broome, 1987).

In equation (9.5), g_i stands for i's good. But $t(g_i)$ rather than g_i is the quantity that is added to others to make up overall good. What does $t(g_i)$ stand for? Well, evidently it is the amount that i's good *counts* in judging overall good. The theory relies on a distinction between the quantity of i's good and how much her good counts in overall judgments. I am not convinced that this distinction can really be maintained. When it comes to a choice between two actions, the theory will sometimes say that one of them does more good but the other brings about the best result. This is *prima facie* puzzling.

To be sure, a distinction between good and how much it counts very often makes clear sense. My family's good, for instance, may count for more than other people's in determining what is right for me to do. But this is one specific context. Modified utilitarianism, on the other hand, makes the very general claim that *whenever* it comes to judging overall good, every individual's good must always be transformed by the function *t* before being added to those of others. In aggregating across people, a quantity of good never appears in the calculation as its own naked self. This makes me wonder what can be meant by the quantity of a person's good as distinct from the transform of it that appears in the calculations. If the transform is the only thing that ever counts, I suspect it must really be the good itself, and that the untransformed version is a sham.

Perhaps modified utilitarianism has been deceived by a sham. But I am not sure. What a modified utilitarian needs to do is produce a way of giving the quantity of a person's good a meaning independently of how much it counts in aggregations across people. Perhaps this can be done. The way to do it is to find a different context – not the aggregation of good across people – where quantities of good are put together *without* being transformed. This could be the context where the notion of the quantity of good gets its meaning. Such a context might, for instance, be the intertemporal aggregation of the good that comes to a person at different times of her life. But there is a difficulty, about finding another context to serve this purpose (see Broome, 1987). Until this is overcome, I shall continue to doubt that modified utilitarianism is really intelligible.

I find it hard to understand for another reason too (or it may be another aspect of the first reason). Suppose we have succeeded in making the necessary distinction between good and how much good counts. It is then a puzzle to know *why* one person's good should count differently from another's. With ordinary utilitarianism it is easy to understand why one person's income should count differently from another's. That is because it does that person a different amount of good. With modified utilitarianism, though, good itself counts differently. Why? The answer can only be that we care about equality, and this is the way that equality is given a value in modified utilitarianism. We give less weight to the good of better-off people. But this is a feeble answer. If equality is valuable, we ought to be able to explain why it is valuable, and then express its value in a way that properly represents the reason. Certainly the reason has something to do with fairness, so an account of fairness will be required. Modified utilitarianism just takes for granted that equality is valuable and finds an *ad hoc* way of fitting its value into a formula. It chooses this particular way, presumably, because it makes the smallest departure from utilitarianism. Nothing in it suggests to me that it is even trying to capture the idea of fairness. It seems to be activated by a fond attachment to strong separability.

9.5   INEQUALITY AND INCOME COMPARISONS

I do not believe the value of equality can be properly captured by any additively separable function of incomes, modified utilitarianism's or any other. What is wrong with inequality (if anything) is a comparative matter: some people have less income than others. To assess the badness of inequality you must therefore compare together different people's incomes. It is hopeless to try and represent its badness by a function that explicitly eschews such comparisons. I shall elaborate this point.

Imagine a society containing just two people. Compare two alternative prospects for the society, shown in Table 9.2. The brackets show the incomes of the two people. Prospect U gives each person an equal chance of getting one unit of income or two units. So does prospect V. So both people's prospects of income are the same under U and V. Under U, however, it is certain that income will be distributed unequally. Under V it is certain that it will be distributed equally. True egalitarianism therefore implies that V is better than U.

What does modified utilitarianism have to say about this example? From equation (9.6):

$$G(1,2) = (G(2,1) = (G(1,1) + G(2,2))/2.$$

So the expectation of G is the same under both U and V. It may look as if this immediately commits a modified utilitarian to thinking that these prospects are equally good. But that is not so. The function G only represents the betterness relation ordinally.

TABLE 9.2   Income distributions

	States of nature (equally probable)	
	1	2
Prospects *U*	(1,2)	(2,1)
V	(1,1)	(2,2)

Nothing says it can be put straight into an expected utility calculation. It is open to a modified utilitarian to be risk-loving about *G*. That way prospect *V* would come out better than *U*. And, given equation (9.6), this is the only way it is going to come out better. Since egalitarianism implies *V* really is better than *U*, this is the only way modified utilitarianism can hope to accommodate egalitarianism.

But this is a desperate measure. It is obvious that to take on a risk-loving attitude about *G* is not really going to achieve what is needed. It happens that in the particular example of Table 9.2, equality in income goes along with risk to *G*, so a risk-loving attitude happens to lead to equality. But there is no reason why it should do so in general.[19]

The real trouble is that for *V* to be better than *U* is inconsistent with something I shall call *weak prospect separability*. Each prospect such as *U* or *V* gives each person an income prospect. *U*, for instance, gives the first person the prospect (1,2). For generality, write the first person's prospect Y_1, the second person's Y_2, and so on. Suppose there are *n* people. Let *Y* be the vector $(Y_1, Y_2, \ldots Y_n)$; this is a way of writing prospects such as *U* and *V*. *U* is, in fact, ((1,2), (2,1)). *V* is ((1,2), (1,2)). Each component of *Y* is itself a vector. These prospects *Y* will be related by a betterness relation, and if that relation is complete it can be represented by a goodness function *F(Y)*. Weak prospect separability says that each component Y_i is separable in this function. That is to say, for every *i*

$$F(Y) = \hat{F}(Y_1, Y_2, \ldots Y_{i-1}, f_i(Y_i), Y_{i+1}, \ldots Y_n)$$

This immediately implies that F has the form

$$F(y) = \hat{F}(f_1(Y_1), f_2(Y_2), \ldots f_n(Y_n)).$$

F, in fact, depends only on each vector Y_i taken as a whole. So there is no interaction amongst the components, taken separately, of different vectors.

Weak prospect separability, then, implies that the goodness of U and V in particular will be given by $\hat{F}(f_1(1,2), f_2(2,1))$ and $\hat{F}(f_1(1,2), f_2(1,2))$. These amounts could only be different if $f_2(2,1)$ were different from $f_2(1,2)$. But that is not possible because both the prospects $(2,1)$ and $(1,2)$ mean that the second person has an equal chance of one unit of income or two units. These prospects must therefore have an equal value. So weak prospect separability implies that U and V are equally good.

But according to egalitarianism they are not equally good. Egalitarianism is therefore incompatible with weak prospect separability. Could it still be compatible with strong separability? I think not. In one way weak prospect separability is a weaker condition than strong separability. It only requires the individuals to be separable one at a time, whereas strong separability requires any arbitrary group of them to be separable. In another way, though, weak prospect separability is stronger, because it applies to uncertain prospects rather than just to incomes received for certain. There is no doubt that extending separability to prospects is a big step (see Broome, 1987). But I should be surprised if a believer in strong separability could hold back from taking this step. Since she believes income distributions should be judged taking one person at a time, it would be hard for her to deny that prospects should be judged that way too. Besides, her only escape from the example of Table 9.2, even if she is willing to abandon weak prospect separability, is to take on the bizarre attitude to risk which I described. I think, therefore, that this example is enough to rule out strong separability as an acceptable bedfellow for egalitarianism. If equality is valuable, strong separability has to go.[20]

Sen's comment about utilitarianism needs to be extended to modified utilitarianism too: as a framework for judging inequality it is a non-starter. I agree wholeheartedly with Temkin (forthcoming):

The problem with this view is clear. It is not concerned with equality. Equality describes a relation obtaining between people that is essentially comparative. People are more or less equal relative to one another. The view in question is concerned with how people fare, but not with how they fare relative to each other.

9.6 FAIRNESS AND THE VALUE OF EQUALITY

If we are to accommodate the value of equality properly in a goodness function, the first step should be to decide just what, if anything, is valuable about equality in the first place. Too much work on inequality consists of trying out various axioms or various functions to see where they lead, without giving much attention to what could justify them. So I am next going to offer a theory about the value of equality. It will be a theory of fairness, since fairness is the central notion of egalitarianism.

The principal evidence I have to offer in support of my theory is that it is the only adequate way of explaining the fairness of random selection. It often happens that there are several candidates to receive an indivisible good, but not enough is available to go round them all. Haemodialysis is an example. On some occasions like this, it seems that the best way to choose between the candidates is by a random lottery. The advantage of a lottery must be that it is fair way of making the choice. My account of fairness explains why this is so, and I can find no other adequate explanation. So I think that understanding the fairness of a lottery is a useful way of coming to understand fairness in general (see Broome, 1988a).

Suppose some good, divisible or not, is to be distributed amongst a number of candidates. It might, for instance, be income to be distributed amongst a population. For each candidate there will be reasons why she should have the good, or some of the good. One reason why a person should have some income, for instance, might be that she would derive some benefit from it. This is a straightforward utilitarian reason. It would need to be spelled out more fully by specifying her good as a function of the income she gets. Another reason might be that she is entitled to income because she has worked for it. All these reasons have some part to play in determining who should have how much of the good.

But what part? One might simply weigh up the reasons against each other. Take the good to be distributed one unit at a time. (If it is divisible take very small units, if not take its natural units.) For each unit weigh each person's reasons why she should have it against those of other people. Award the unit to the person with the strongest reasons on balance. Then do the same for the next unit. A utilitarian, for instance, would award each small unit of income to the person who would derive most good from it. The effect is to maximise good overall. Equation (9.4) embodies the results of this process. A modified utilitarian would do much the same, but weight reasons differently. The effect is still to end up maximising some function of the distribution; equation (9.6) specifies it. Generally, if reasons work in a decently coherent fashion, this process will end up maximising some function of the distribution. The process might be said to achieve the maximum satisfaction of reasons.

Weighing reasons, or maximising the satisfaction of reasons, is undoubtedly one consideration that comes into determining the best distribution of the good. I shall call it the 'aggregative' consideration. But it ignores fairness.

To take account of fairness we must start by dividing the reasons why a person should get a good into two classes: 'claims' and other reasons. By a claim to the good I mean a duty owed to the candidate herself that she should have it. Many reasons are not claims. Imagine, for instance, that someone has to be sent on an unpleasant and very dangerous – probably fatal – mission. One person out of a group must be chosen to go. And one of them has special talents that make her more likely than the others to accomplish the mission well. So there are stronger reasons why she, rather than one of the others, should go. The good to be distributed here is the good of being left behind. There are stronger reasons for giving this good to the untalented candidates. But their lack of talent does not give them a stronger *claim* to this good. It is not *owed* to them that they should be left behind.

Claims, and not other reasons, are the object of fairness. Fairness is concerned only with mediating between the claims of different people. If there are reasons why a person should have a good, but she does not get it, no unfairness is done her unless she has a claim to it.

But when it mediates between people's claims, what exactly does fairness require? Does it require simply that claims should get their proper weight when they come to be weighed against other reasons and the claims of other people? This cannot be enough because *all* reasons should get their proper weight. So does it require, perhaps, that claims should be given extra heavy weight? This would be inadequate too. In the example of the dangerous mission, suppose everybody has the same claim to the good of being excused. So claims are exactly matched. But there is a separate reason why the talented person should not get this good: she would accomplish the mission better. So if claims are simply weighed up, however much weight they are given, the result will be that the talented person gets sent. But it is unfair that she should be required to endanger her life just because of her special talents. She might make this plausible complaint. She has as strong a claim to the good of being excused as anybody else. But because of her talents, the weighing-up of reasons simply amounts to overriding her claim. It is never even on the cards that she might get what she has a claim to. This is not giving her claim the recognition it deserves.

When claims conflict, I believe that what fairness requires is not that they be weighed against each other and other reasons, but that they actually be satisfied in proportion to their strength.

This formula, to be honest, has more precision than I really intend. The essential point is that fairness prescribes how far each person's claim should be satisfied *relative* to the satisfaction of other people's claims. Stronger claims require more satisfaction and equal claims require equal satisfaction. Also, weaker claims cannot simply be overridden by stronger ones: if a stronger claim is satisfied to some extent, then so should a weaker one be to a lesser extent. Fairness is a relative matter. It is not at all concerned with the total satisfaction of claims. If everyone has an equal claim to some good, they are all treated perfectly fairly so long as they all get the same amount of it, even if the amount is small or even none at all. Of course, the more they get the *better*, but not the fairer. There is at least one reason for each of them to have the good; this is the reason that constitutes a claim. On *aggregative* grounds, therefore, it is better for them to get more. But *fairness* does not require this.

In the example of the dangerous mission claims are equal. Fairness therefore requires that either everyone goes or no one. Assume that neither of these alternatives is possible. Then the requirement of fairness cannot be satisfied. Some unfairness is inevitable because someone has to go when others, who have no stronger claim to be excused, stay behind. I argued in my other paper (Broome, 1988a) that the unfairness might be mitigated by holding a lottery. Or it may be right simply to send the talented candidate. This will be unfair to her, but fairness is not an overriding end. It might be right to sacrifice it for other goals on this occasion. One more point. Fairness is a personal good, and unfairness is a personal harm. If a distribution is not fair, that is because someone's claim has not been satisfied in proportion to its strength. This is a harm done specifically to her. Fairness is not some sort of suprapersonal good.

To summarise: There are two sorts of consideration that go into judging the distribution of a good, the aggregative consideration and fairness. The former has to do with maximising the satisfaction of the reasons why people should have the good. The latter is concerned only with some of these reasons, namely claims. And it is not concerned with the aggregate satisfaction of claims, but only with proportionality in their satisfaction. Now to apply this to judging the distribution of income. It will become obvious immediately that what I have been saying leaves some very large issues still to be settled. One of the issues that remains to be settled is what reasons are claims, and that forms the title of Sen's (1980) paper 'Equality of What?' What is it that we should be aiming to distribute equally? This has been much argued over,[21] and implicitly the argument has been about claims.

I cannot pursue this argument. Instead, for the sake of illustration only, I shall adopt an assumption that I hope is not ridiculous. I shall assume that everyone has an equal claim to income. This is only a vague statement. It does not say, for instance, what happens when people start with unequal amounts of income: does a richer person have no claim until all the poorer people have caught up? But this vague statement is enough to get us going. It is meant to be a gesture in the direction of the view that people have a claim to resources rather than to the good or welfare they derive from resources.[22] Income is standing in as a surrogate for resources. Plainly I am ignoring differences in the amounts people work. It is also meant to be a gesture towards the view that because claims are part of the overt commerce of the world, people's claims must be to overt things like income rather than private things like welfare.

Fairness, then, will require that income should be equally

distributed. If it is not, then some unfairness is done. How much? This is another issue which my theory leaves open. This chapter began with the question of how bad is the inequality in a particular distribution of income. We have now arrived at the question of how much unfairness does it do, and we have no answer to that yet. This may not look like progress. But actually we have learned something. First, this unfairness is definitely not a matter of inefficiency or a failure to maximise good; all of that has gone into what I called the aggregative consideration. Second, the unfairness is relative, a matter of how each person fares relative to others. Third, it is a personal harm, suffered specifically by individuals.

This last point gives us a start. We can consider how much unfairness is done to each person. I like the term introduced by Temkin (forthcoming) who calls the amount of unfairness suffered by person i her 'complaint' c_i. A person's complaint will be a function $c_i(y)$ of the distribution. More specifically (the second point above), it will be determined by how much her income is less than other people's. She has the same claim as other people, so unfairness is done her if she ends up with less. But this still leaves open many questions. Is unfairness done to a person whenever she gets less than someone else? Or is she only treated unfairly when she gets less than the mean, which is what she would have got in a perfectly fair distribution? Questions like these and their implications for measuring inequality have been investigated very thoroughly by Temkin (forthcoming). I have nothing to add to his discussion. I shall just mention a couple of examples. Person i's complaint might simply be how far she falls short of the mean μ:

$$c_i(y) = \max\{0, \mu - y_i\} \tag{9.7}$$

Or it might be the total of the differences between her income and the income of each person who is better off:

$$c_i(y) = \Sigma_j \max\{0, y_j - y_i\} \tag{9.8}$$

A person's complaint need not represent how badly she *feels* about unfairness; nor need she actually complain. Unfairness is a harm that is done her, but not all harms are necessarily bad feelings. Unfairness is not necessarily connected with envy.

Overall unfairness will be some sort of aggregate $C(c_1, c_2, \ldots c_n)$

of the complaints. To determine the overall goodness of the distribution, this unfairness has to be put together with the other consideration, the aggregative one. The latter will value the distribution according to some function $F(y_1, y_2, \ldots y_n)$, so overall goodness will be:

$$G = \hat{G}(F(y_1, y_2, \ldots y_n), C(c_1, c_2, \ldots c_n)).$$

What this says is that the goodness function $G(y)$ may be written

$$G = \tilde{G}(y_1, y_2, \ldots y_n, c_1, c_2, \ldots c_n)$$

and in this function $(y_1, y_2, \ldots y_n)$ and $(c_1, c_2, \ldots c_n)$ are both separable in $\tilde{G}$.

Now I am going to assume that each pair (y_i, c_i) is also separable in $\tilde{G}$. My grounds are these. First, I take it that person i's good is entirely determined by y_i and c_i. So it can be written $g_i(y_i, c_i)$. This amounts to assuming that any interaction or complementarity in determining i's good between i's income and that of other people has been taken up into c_i; there is no other source of interaction besides fairness and c_i accounts for that. Second, I take it that the overall goodness of a distribution is entirely determined by the good of the people. I call this the 'principle of personal good', and I have argued for it elsewhere (Broome, 1987). It means that G is a function of individual good:

$$G(y) = \mathring{G}[(g_1(y_1, c_1), g_2(y_2, c_2), \ldots g_n(y_n, c_n)]$$

And this says that each (y_i, c_i) is separable in G.

The principle of personal good is often called 'individualism' (though other principles are often called 'individualism' too). Earlier I said that egalitarianism is incompatible with the view that overall good is separable between individuals' *incomes* or prospects of income. But it is compatible with individualism. It can accept that overall good is separable between individuals' *good* and prospects of good.

By a theorem of Gorman (1968) all this separability implies that G can be transformed into this additively separable form:

$$G = \bar{g}_1(y_1) + \ldots + \bar{g}_n(y_n) - w_1(c_1) - \ldots - w_n(c_n)$$

Symmetry requires all the $\bar{g}_i$ functions and all the w_i functions to be the same:

$$G = \Sigma_i \bar{g}(y_i) - \Sigma_i w(c_i) = \Sigma_i (\bar{g}(y_i) - w(c_i)) \tag{9.9}$$

In equation (9.9) the amount $\bar{g}(y_i) - w(c_i)$ is the value given to i's good in the overall evaluation of the distribution. It would be technically possible to suppose this amount is some transform of i's good, but I think it is most reasonably taken to be her good itself. The reason is the one I mentioned in section (9.4). This amount is definitely how much i's good *counts* in the evaluation, and it is hard to see how an intelligible distinction can be made here between how much her good counts and her good itself. Furthermore, there is no point in maintaining a distinction between i's complaint and how much that complaint counts. We may *define* her complaint as just the amount that the unfairness done her should count (negatively) in evaluating the distribution. So $w(c_i)$ is just c_i. Person i's good is $\bar{g}(y_i) - c_i$; $\bar{g}(y_i)$ is her good apart from the matter of fairness, and from that you have to subtract the harm done her by unfairness. So

$$G = \Sigma_i \bar{g}(y_i) - J = \Sigma_i (\bar{g}(y_i) - c_i) \tag{9.10}$$

where J is total unfairness $\Sigma_i c_i$.

G, which represents the betterness relation,[23] turns out in equations (9.9) and (9.10) to be the total of people's good. So these equations are utilitarian in a broad sense. Evidently Sen's stricture that utilitarianism is a non-starter as a framework for judging inequality does not apply if utilitarianism is interpreted broadly enough. Utilitarians only need to recognise the specific sort of harm that inequality does: namely unfairness.

However, my theory of fairness is decidedly non-utilitarian in another way. It agrees that the best distribution is the one with the greatest total of good, taking account of unfairness. However, it denies that when there is a choice to be made between alternative distributions, the right one to choose is necessarily the best. Suppose the distribution is at present unequal, and a little more income becomes available. The best result would be achieved by letting this income go to the poorest person. And this would be the best way of reducing the total of unfairness J. But, nevertheless, this may not be what fairness requires. The poorest person has the strongest claim to the extra income. But other people may have claims too. And if so, these claims should be satisfied in proportion to their strength. At least they should be satisfied to some extent. So other people should get some share of the extra income. The theory I have given, then, must not be understood as just another maximising theory, with a different conception of good to be maximised. But it does *have* a different conception of good, and that is what this chapter is about. The fact that it need not always be in favour of maximising good does not concern us now.

9.7 A MEASURE OF UNFAIRNESS

What will the unfairness measure J be like? This depends on what determines each person's complaint. I mentioned some examples. If c_i is given by equation (9.7), then

$$J = \Sigma_i c_i = \Sigma_i \max\{0,\ \mu - y_i\} = (1/2)\Sigma_i |\mu - y_i|$$

This is half the absolute mean deviation. If c_i is given by equation (9.8), then

$$J = \Sigma_i c_i = \Sigma_i \Sigma_j \max\{0,\ y_j - y_i\} = (1/2)\Sigma_i \Sigma_j |y_j - y_i|$$

This is the 'absolute' Gini coefficient, the common or relative Gini coefficient multiplied by the mean μ (Donaldson and Weymark, 1980).

These two are amongst the many measures of inequality that have been endlessly argued over. Naturally, objections have been made to them. The main objection to the absolute mean deviation is that it does not satisfy Dalton's (1920) principle of transfers. This principle says that a transfer of income from a richer person to a poorer makes the inequality less bad. But it does not increase the absolute mean deviation unless these people are on opposite sides of the mean. The main objection to the Gini coefficient is, I think, best explained by Blackorby and Donaldson (1978). This measure is always in favour of a transfer from a richer person to a poorer, but the value it attaches to such a transfer is independent of the inequality of the distribution. It is plausible perhaps (I am not sure myself) that the worse the inequality to start off with, the more valuable is a transfer.

These objections are to the consequences of the measures. Until some ground has been given for them, there is no way to judge the measures except by their consequences. But I have suggested a way they might be grounded. I hope this may open up a new approach to judging them.

In any case, I suggested these measures only as examples. They derive from very specific assumptions chosen to illustrate the theory. There are many other possibilities. For instance a person's complaint might be a non-linear function of the difference between her income and the mean. And different people's complaints might not be aggregated simply by adding. More broadly, it may be that people do not have equal claims to income in the first place. We might simply not have any claim to income, in which case an issue of fairness would not arise in the distribution of income. The only issue would be inefficiency. Or our claims might be determined by our labour. And so on. (A most important possibility is mentioned in section 9.10).

Evidently the theory I have described allows a lot of freedom. But there are some things it does not allow. For instance, if the goodness of an income distribution has anything to do with fairness, it is not going to allow the goodness function to be strongly separable. Another example: in recent years various authors (e.g. Mehran, 1976; Donaldson and Weymark, 1980; Yaari, 1987) have proposed to generalise the Gini coefficient. Now, evidently some generalisations of the Gini coefficient would fit nicely into the framework of claims and complaints. But so far as I can tell, the ones that have been proposed are incompatible with it. I have offered a theory of inequality that could underlie the ungeneralised Gini. What theory, I wonder, could underlie these generalisations?

Equation (9.10) shows that unfairness need not be whole badness of inequality. Diminishing marginal benefit of income is still a plausible story, and that will appear as strict concavity in the function $\bar{g}(y_i)$. Inequality will then do two sorts of harm. First it will create unfairness. Second it will cause the total of good apart from fairness to be less than it would have been if the same income had been equally distributed. It will be inefficient in the sense I mentioned in section (9.4). So inequality can be both inefficient and unfair.

It is possible to quantify the inefficiency on a scale comparable to the other harm J. Let

$$I_d = G(\mu e) - G(y) = n\bar{g}(\mu) - \{\Sigma_i \bar{g}(y_i) - J\}$$

where μ is the mean of y. I_d is the difference between what G would be if income were equally distributed and what it actually is. G now measures total good. So I_d is a measure of the badness of the inequality. It is an absolute measure, like I_a described in section 9.2, but in units of good rather than money. It is actually the absolute version of the inequality measure originally proposed by Dalton (1920).[24] Now let

$$I = I_d - J = n\bar{g}(\mu) - \Sigma_i \bar{g}(y_i)$$

I is the difference between what G would be if income were equally distributed, and what it actually is, ignoring unfairness. So it is a measure of inefficiency.

$$G(y) = G(\mu e) - I_d = G(\mu e) - I - J$$

Actual good is equally distributed good, less inefficiency and unfairness.

I hope that the separation of inefficiency and unfairness may be useful. Atkinson's (1970) measure, which is derived from either (9.4) or (9.6) above, is evidently aimed at inefficiency. The Gini coefficient is aimed at unfairness.

9.8 FAIRNESS, INEQUALITY AND POVERTY

I shall close this paper with some inchoate remarks about poverty. In section 9.7 I examined the implications of supposing that everyone has an equal claim to income. Now suppose alternatively that we all have an equal claim to enough income to satisfy our basic needs. Needs are, indeed, one of the most plausible sources of claims.[25] Perhaps this is the only claim we have on income,[26] perhaps it is a particularly strong claim and we also have a weaker claim to higher levels of income. Let us call the level of income needed to satisfy a person's basic needs the 'poverty line'.

Almost all the analysis in section 9.7 is still applicable. If everyone has the same income, either below or above the poverty line, no unfairness is done. If people have different incomes, but they are all below the poverty line, the analysis of section 9.7 is unaltered. If some people are below the line and some above, then new issues arise. But they will only require us to alter our formula for a person's complaint.

When someone is poor and other people have more income than her, she is being treated unfairly because they have no stronger claim to income than she has. If, in addition, some of them are above the poverty line, then the unfairness done her is much greater. Above the poverty line they have either no claim at all on income or a much weaker claim than hers. Yet they have income that she needs. Her complaint, then, depends very much on the number of people above the poverty line and how much they are getting. The tradition in the literature on measuring poverty, initiated by Sen (1976), has been to make the measures depend on the incomes of the poor only. This may be because the aim has been to produce a measure of the amount of poverty, rather than of its badness. But what I said in section 9.1 about inequality is also true of poverty: we are more likely to be interested in its badness than in its amount.[27] The unfairness of poverty is a part of its badness, and it depends strongly on the incomes of the nonpoor.

Unfairness is not the only thing wrong with poverty. Another is simply that living in poverty, without one's basic needs satisfied, is not a good life. Let us assume that a person's good falls precipitously if she drops below the poverty line, so the function $\bar{g}$ in equation (9.10) is very concave around that income. If everyone is below the poverty line, then things are bad because total income in the society is low, and if there is also inequality there will be unfairness and inefficiency of the sort described in section 9.7. If, on the other hand, some people are above the line and some below, there is much greater unfairness as I have explained. There will also be a lot of inefficiency because of the concavity of $\bar{g}$.[28]

I think, then, that the badness of poverty can be accounted for within the framework I have already developed. The goodness of a distribution can be split into three components, one positive and two negative: the level of the mean or total income, the inefficiency and the unfairness. Inefficiency and unfairness are the result of inequality. Poverty can add poignancy to all three components, and it can make inequality particularly bad. But the only analytic innovation it calls for is to recognise the especial claim of needs.

10. Institutional Economics

ROBERT A. SOLO

10.1 INTRODUCTION

This chapter is addressed to the student who has worked through this book, who has mastered and feels at home with the microeconomic model, and who would like know how 'institutional economics' relates to what he has already learned; to answer, in effect, what it is about institutional economics that might interest the fledgling economist flushed from a neoclassical nest.

There are today two dominant modes of thought about the economy: the neoclassical and the Marxist. Each of the two develops from a few basic assumptions, a closed model that would encompass and explain the operation of an entire economy. Some believers will claim universality for their model in the interpretation of behaviour and event. Institutional economics, on the other hand, is not an integral system. It offers no encompassing model that would explain the operation of an entire economy. It can be understood rather as clusters of thought that supplement, complement and challenge mainstream economics; clusters of thought that evolved piecemeal and pragmatically in response to perceived inadequacies of the neoclassical paradigm. Institutional economics, reform-oriented rather than revolutionary, reflecting experience where class has a quite different meaning from that in Europe, is perhaps the only significant non-Marxist critique of modern capitalism.

We will try here to comprehend and explain at least the character if not the substance of institutional economics as an offset and a challenge to perceived inadequacies of the neoclassical model. To do that we must specify what those inadequacies are: which is to say, we must make clear what is the essential character of mainstream theory, and what, given its character, it can and cannot explain. But note this: we understand institutional economics to mean not the work of a specifiable group of economists, but clusters of thought that fill in the spaces left uncovered by the neoclassical paradigm, regardless of the academic pedigree or ideological affiliation of those who produced that thought.

10.2 THE MAINSTREAM PARADIGM

The two essential assumptions of the neoclassical model are:

1. *individualised* choice, i.e. the choice of rational, autonomous, self-seeking individuals deciding on a course of action that will best suit their personal goals;
2. the interaction of these individuals through exchange in *price-directed markets* where the free movement of price guides the deployment of resources.

Deduced from the twin assumptions of individualised choice and price-directed markets, a powerful analytic is developed to explain the determination of price, hence the allocation of resources, therefore the distribution of income.

The neoclassical approach admits of certain variants wherein the self-same, self-seeking individuals operate in altered market contexts; thus the theories of monopoly, oligopoly or imperfect or monopolistic competition. These are considered as exceptional cases, peripheral to the price-directed market. The condition of pure competition is taken as the core and essence of economic reality; as indeed it must be if the neoclassical model is to offer a viable, general explanation of the economy.

10.3 THE SYSTEMS OF POWER

The price-directed market envisaged by neoclassical economics is a system of exchange. It is also a system of power: the power to deploy resources, to command labour, to organise production and to produce, to innovate, to select items for consumption and to consume, hence the power to determine output priorities and to select from among input potentials. Here power resides in the prerogatives of private property, an instrument uniquely suited to the exercise of power by autonomous individuals and the only form of power with which the neoclassical analytic is equipped to deal. But private property is not a simple existence. Any and every item of private property consists of some set of rights, variously bundled, never 'given' but rather in a more or less constant state of flux and transformation. And every change in a constituted set of property rights is liable to affect market relationships and the consequences of market transactions.

The two founding fathers of institutional economics were John R. Commons and Thorstein Veblen. The brand of institutional economics associated with John R. Commons is focused on the variable character of property rights.

Property-based exchange coexists with another system of power, and both systems, a market system and a political system, bear upon the determination of economic event. The two encompass the same population and the same cultural complex, but between the one system and the other the nature of power, the distribution of power and the character of choice, are very different. It is the political system, nominally sovereign, that must arbitrate and settle conflicting claims to or concerning property rights in the market system. It is the political system which, through the law and under the aegis of the courts, must articulate, legitimise, protect, revise, sustain and enforce property rights in the market system, thereby affecting market outcomes. Its focus on this intersection of the political and the market systems brings a number of issues to the fore as problems of institutional economics:

1. The market system is no longer seen as autonomous and closed, but as linked to the political system. The back and forward interactions of power in the two systems become subject to the institutionalist's inquiry.
2. The institutionalist's analytic seeks to explain and predict the market consequences of alternative distributions of property rights. Such rights are understood to include any prerogative, privilege, or position of value. The various forms of land tenancy, condemnation proceedings, bankruptcy laws, the privilege of incorporation, patents, access or non-access to

information, workman's compensation, are examples of state policies and sanctioned rules that determine a distribution of property rights and hence a distribution of wealth and income.

3. A spotlight on the alternative distributions of property rights and especially on the consequences of the changes in the distribution of property rights induced by law or the decisions of the courts, leads to an evaluation of those laws or decisions and the principles they embody, and to the devising of institutional means for deliberately affecting property rights in order to achieve sought-for public purposes. Hence the institutionalist tack leads perforce to a concern with public policy and economic reform.

4. The institutionalism of John R. Commons related not only to transactions in the neoclassical domain of individualised choice in price-competitive markets, but also to rights and transactions both in the political system and in the quasi-political realm of corporate organisation; and to the norms of reasonableness wherein these negotiated rather than exchange transactions can find their equilibrium.

5. Since the mid-1930s, neoclassical economics has tried to detach itself from any value commitment. So long as neoclassical practitioners opt for the *status quo* in the distribution of income and privilege, and are satisfied that the privately held values (i.e. the 'preferences') that can be expressed through consumer demand, are proper and sufficient as a guide to the allocation of resources, they need hardly engage in value-related discourse. But for the institutional economist focused on points of conflict in the distribution of rights (and hence of wealth and income) and on the formation of public policy, it would be difficult to maintain even the appearance of detachment from the process of value judgement.

6. Hence institutional economics offers a refuge and a haven for those who reject logical positivism's anathema on value judgement, and the confines of Pareto-optimality. Among institutionalists there does exist an active discourse concerning norms and values and their policy implications. The dilemmas implicit in that discourse remain unresolved.

7. Historically institutional economists have approached the market economy from the side of a positive state, seeking the

replacement, control or reform of market relationships through collective choice, public policy and the instrumentalities of government. That effort has, of course, been strongly resisted by neoclassical thinkers with their *laissez-faire* tradition. As a consequence a considerable literature has evolved with a contribution from both sides of the ideological frontier concerning the criteria possibly appropriate in defining a 'public good' and the proper boundaries of public intervention, taking cognisance of such considerations as 'external economies and diseconomies' where real benefits and costs escape the entrepreneurial calculus, and the corollary costs of excluding the 'free rider', and the sheer costs of the market transaction as an offset to the benefits of exchange, and the occasional impossibility of fully realising economies scale (or the optimal use of such outputs as information produced through research) in price-competitive markets.

In recent decades by a curious twist conservative, even ultra conservative *laissez-faire* ideologues have entered the zones of institutional thought in attacking the operation of the processes of democratic governance as an essentially retrograde form of the exchange economy, where interest groups bargain for self-advantage at the expense of, and as parasitical upon, the general interest. Here the reformers seek to extend the operation of the market system into the domain of the political authority, e.g. the proposals of Milton Friedman to substitute educational vouchers through which subsidised individuals can buy their own schooling, for an administered system of public education, or of Jane Jacobs to replace the construction and administration of public housing with vouchers distributed to the poor that recipients could use on the free market in lieu of rental payments. Gary Becker applied the market calculus in the analysis of racial discrimination and of the matrimonial ties. Gordon Tulloch applied it in an analysis of crime and punishment, and James Buchanan, of the social contract.

10.4 INDIVIDUALS AND ORGANISATIONS

Neoclassical economics is a theory of *individualised* choice. It rests on and cannot do without the assumption of the self-seeking, self-optimising choice of autonomous individuals. No doubt such choice exists and can account for observed behaviour in important sectors of the economy. But also there are decisions that are a function not of such individualised choice, but that emanate rather through the policy-making processes of large, complex organisations. The greatest of these organisations are those of the state, e.g the political parties, the electoral system and parliament or congress, the executive agencies and the courts.

Organisational decision-making prevails also in the megacorporations and the great trade unions at the heart of modern capitalism. Organisational choice as something other than the self-seeking choice of the autonomous individual falls outside the scope of neoclassical theory; and neoclassical theorists have failed to recognise the difference. Just as the lawyers, the judges and the courts have regarded the great corporation to be an (artificial) individual, indistinguishable before the bar from any Joe Smith or Mary Jones, so the economists have perceived the production function of the firm as the simple projection of self-interested will of the entrepreneurial individual, precisely the same for General Motors or Royal Dutch Shell as for the greengrocer's shop across the street from the cinema.

Hence as another institutionalist response to limitations that inhere in the neoclassical paradigm, is in efforts to comprehend political–organisational or corporate–organisational choice and policy formation.

To give some concreteness to the importance of differentiating between organisational and individualised choice, and of the consequence of the failure to understand the former, consider Keynesian macroeconomics. Neoclassical theory absolutely requires the autonomous power of free-moving price to direct the flow of resources and to equilibrate markets. Keynesian macroeconomics absolutely requires rigid prices to account for mass unemployment (and mass re-employment) as a function of the upward and downward flux of aggregate demand. It was the virtue of Keynes's *General Theory* that its key assumption was consistent with the experience of the Great Depression, that it could account for the phenomenon of mass unemployment and that it offered the basis for a full employment policy. But price rigidity which is a keystone of Keynesian thought and mass unemployment which is the objective of Keynesian policy, were not universal phenomena even during those depression years. In American agricultural markets, for example, when demand dropped, prices plunged and employment increased. The experience of rigid pricing was particular to one part of the modern capitalist economy: the corporate-organisational sector where the megacorporations and the great trade unions hold sway.

These two points then are:

1. the key assumption of Keynesian macroeconomics is totally in contradiction with that of neoclassical microeconomics, and
2. Keynesian macroeconomics is specifically about the massive organisations of the corporate-industrial sector.

Keynesians did not recognise the sectorial particularity of their assumption. They did not probe the behavioural specifics of that corporate-industrial sector, to which their theory must refer. They did not challenge the universal claims of neoclassical economics. Dealing in aggregates, they assumed that at the level of the firm, prices moved and markets worked just as neoclassical theory said they did, though no trick of statistics can equate price declines in response to falling demand on the part of all individual firms with price rigidity for all the firms taken together. It was made to seem that the economist could have his cake and eat it too. Via Keynesian macro-theory he could take up the cudgels against the phenomenon of mass unemployment, without surrendering his commitment to neoclassical thought. That of course made it easier for a discipline already enfolded in the neoclassical paradigm to accept the new Keynesian macro-theory. Proclaiming a Keynesian revolution, economists rushed into the public arena shouting an answer to mass unemployment without having to recant an older confessional. For decades the discipline accepted a curiously schizophrenic micro–macro vision of the economy. Open one eye and see a macro universe of fixed and unchanging prices. Close that eye and open the other to a world where price is in flux and motion.

If this deception and self-deception had its advantages in enabling the quick and easy triumph of Keynes's message, it also had its price. Later it would account for the quick and easy collapse in the support for Keynesian theory.

That corporate-organisational prices held firm for years in the face of a catastrophic drop in demand cannot be dismissed as a mere imperfection of price-directed markets. It signalled rather a different system entirely for the determination of price. Because Keynes and his followers did not go beneath the observation of aggregated behaviour to comprehend its causal roots, they missed the obvious. Simply that pricing in the organisational sector is a function of organisational policy. Since all the policies of all organisations can and frequently do change, in order to explain, predict or control the price policies of corporate organisations and the wage policies of the great trade unions, it would be necessary first to comprehend and then perhaps to act upon these policy-making processes.

During the years of the depression when the megacorporation and the great trade union stood precariously at the edge of an abyss, their policy was to hang on, to hold tight. Prices and wages were rigid. In the benign environment of the decades after the Second World War the sense of desperation vanished, and price–wage policy was geared to rising income expectation among all classes. So long as the rate of rising expectations was matched by the pace of rising productivity, prices remained stable. When rising expectations ceased to be matched by the rise in productivity, price 'rigidity' went out of the window. Instead prices (and nominal wages) still geared to those built-in expectations, started their inflationary climb. Under the circumstances of stable aggregate demand, that policy-based rise in prices and wages must generate unemployment. Such was the phenomenon of stagflation that toppled Keynesian macroeconomics. The simultaneous rise in unemployment and of the price level was quite beyond the explanatory scope of an economics that relied on the assumption of 'rigid pricing' for the aggregate and on the free-moving prices of pure competition in the particular. Keynesian macro-theory seems to have perished quite simply because its practitioners never recognised, let alone explained the behaviour of the megaorganisations to which their theory referred.

What then has been contribution of those outside the mainstream to an understanding of organisational behaviour and the formation of corporate-organisational policy?

Because he recognised that the realities of corporate policy are not compatible with the neoclassical notion of profit maximisation as indicator of business choice, Herbert Simon tried to reconcile corporate policy-making with the individualised entrepreneurial choice of neoclassical theory by substituting for maximising, 'satisficing'. For that he won a Nobel Prize. Suppose one hypothesised that the firm is motivated simply to satisfice some or other objective. Absent a specification of what that objective is, and a specification of the scale by which to measure satisficing–dissatisficing, and a further specification as to whose satisficing–dissatisficing is to be measured, such an hypothesis would be as impossible to refute (and as empty) as the observation that firms do what they do.

John R.Commons noted the essentially negotiated (hence indeterminate) character of inter- and intra-corporate relations. John Kenneth Galbraith has emphasised:

1. the planning function, broadly encompassing a time-extended complex of activities within the corporate enterprise, with planning extended beyond the firm in its efforts to develop or stabilise its product outlets and supply sources;
2. and the critical components of the technostructure, as enclaves rendered inherently autonomous and self-perpetuating by a specialised, high-level knowledge and mastery that escapes the comprehension, evaluation and control by any power outside itself.

Gunnar Myrdal and Seymour Melman among others have explored the power interactions and overlap of the corporate-industrial power and the political systems.

Underlying the neoclassical schemata (and that of ideological liberalism) is the idea of society as a social grid, a kind of endless chequerboard, with each space a private domain, its boundaries defined by the ownership of property, wherein the individual in possession can do as he will and is free to enter into relations of exchange and social intercourse with others, each within the freedom of his enclave, where such exchange or intercourse is considered by those concerned to be to their advantage. The soaring vision of Kenneth Boulding has replaced the modern habitat from a space on the socioeconomic grid to a niche in a system of operations. Indeed in this universe of complex organisations, we each of us occupy a niche in a number of coexisting systems, wherein we do not choose as autonomous individuals do, but where we may participate in a process of collective choice, and where the niche we occupy defines and determines our obligations, prerogatives, opportunities, and roles.

Economics, broadly understood and including both the neoclassical and the Marxist brands, operates through the analysis of the interaction and consequences of competitive or conflictual choice by autonomous entities, individuals in the one instance and economic classes in the other. This is but one of the two modes of thought currently prevailing in the social sciences. It is a mode of thought that can, as we have seen, be applied not only to the market economy but in the analysis of other social systems as well. The other mode of thought (in general to be associated with sociology, and which we will call here the 'sociological mode') relies on the perception and projection of recurrent patterns of behaviour. It is a mode of thought that has been applied by those who consider themselves institutionalists and others who do not, to deal with certain phenomena outside the reach of the neoclassical analytic. It was and is used, for example, by Max Weber and those who followed him in the study of bureaucracy – an essential component of all large organisations. It was used by Wesley Mitchell and his colleagues and followers at the National Bureau for Economic Research in their studies of business cycles and business indicators. It was used by Edwin Mansfield, following rural sociologists, tracing out patterns in the corporate-industrial acceptance of technological innovations. Keynes used it in his postulating a particular form of consumption propensity.

It has also been used in the effort to comprehend and predict organisational behavior, by Max Weber in his studies of bureaucracy, by Alain Cotta in devising a matrix of corporate-industrial responses with the grooved-in and hence predictable relationships and responses of e.g. leaders and followers, of independents, of adventurers, of inventors, innovators, adaptors and laggards. I used it in the section above to explain wage–price policy and behaviour as a function of income expectations in relation to productivity changes in the corporate industrial sector.

For a deeper understanding of that which forms and transforms organisational policy, one must look to the cultural/cognitive context and the psychic roots of organisational and of individual behaviour.

10.5 CULTURAL/COGNITIVE SYSTEMS, IDEOLOGY, AND THE STRUCTURES OF THE PSYCHE

When Thorstein Veblen, back in 1899, published *The Theory of the Leisure Class* and when Kenneth E. Boulding published *The Image* in 1961 they departed fundamentally from the mechanics of rational choice, the motor-force of neoclassical economics, and from the projection of observed patterns of behaviour in the sociological mode. Instead they formulated hypotheses concerning the framework of thought, and within that framework, concerning the operation of the mind. While that approach remains alien to economics and sociology in the USA and the UK, it has in recent years been at the forefront of advance in other disciplines – e.g. the psychology of Jean Piaget, the anthropology of Lévi-Strauss, the history and philosophy of science of Thomas Kuhn and Michel Foucault, and the linguistics of Noam Chomsky. It is an approach, moreover, that seems to us essential for an understanding of policy and its transformations in the complex organisations of the corporate industrial sector or in the political system.

In *The Image*, Boulding postulates that any organisation, large or small, can only operate effectively within the boundaries of a *public image*. Some years ago I taught for a term at the University of Grenoble in France. I provoked a minor riot in my classroom by asking a student to come to the front of the room and solve a problem on the blackboard. Students pounded the desks and stood on the benches and shouted that that 'wasn't the French way.' Evidently those students and I did not share in a public image of the role and obligations of the professor, of the expectations and obligations of the students, of the norms of practice and of civility. Without that we could not gear together; our activities could not mesh. For that reason the classroom did not work. It would be the same for the relations of foreman and worker on the shop-floor of a factory, for the apparent chaos of speculators bidding in the securities exchange, for the army drill field, or for the business of parliament or congress.

The effective operation of voluntary associations (or 'groups') needs more than a public image in order to operate. There must also be a shared purpose. The shared idea of what is and what ought to be, constitutes an *ideology*. Every voluntary association or group is at base a community of ideological commitment. We, each one of us, possess and are possessed by ideas of what is and what ought to be with respect to family, friend and foe, with respect to economy and polity, with respect to god and country, with respect to the house, the business, the school. From whence come these public images and ideologies that possess and control us? We, individually, did not invent them. They were learned and inculcated in a thousand ways through what one might call the cognitive and cultural systems of society.

Consider the 'state', largest and most complex, but also the prototype of modern organisations, and the enormous changes that have occurred in its economic and social policies and practices in the UK, say, between the period of Stanley Baldwin and that of Clement Attlee, and between Attlee's time and that of Margaret Thatcher, or in the USA from the administration of William Howard Taft to that of Franklin D. Roosevelt, and from Roosevelt to Ronald Reagan. Those changes can only be understood as expressing the transformation of prevailing ideologies. And that transformation (we have elsewhere demonstrated) is a complex process rooted in social experiences and is, in that sense, the product of social learning.

It is not very different among the megaorganisations of the market system. The industrial economy in the USA has fallen upon relatively hard times of late. Its technology and productivity that not long ago were beyond the reach of the rest of the world, have now been equalled and surpassed by many others. Its great industrial bastions in steel, automobiles and machine tools have bowed to the force of foreign competition. Such is the fact; and such has been the experience. What response? The proud American industrial system, following an ideology and blueprint most clearly formulated by Frederick Winslow Taylor, that for generations dominated American industrial practice in the organisation of work, in the character of control and in the relations between management and labour, is under fire. Japan is the new model. The pot boils in a ferment of ideological transformation, expressed in the work of Seymour Melman, Robert Reich, Michael Piore, Charles Sabel, Chalmers Johnson.

Thorstein Veblen conceived the essential social and economic conflict not as between different classes, but as between different modes of thought; between that of the engineer and that of the financier, between the productive and the predatory, between the technological and the manipulative. That Veblenian vision, suddenly currently relevant, casts a harsh and clear light on the phenomenon of industrial decline in the corporate-organisational economy of American and perhaps of British capitalism today. For the pace of conglomerate mergers has brought the asset manipulators to the apex of corporate power, with technologies shuffled in and out of the corporative pack like cards on the gambling table, and with no viable linkage of knowledge or commitment between the élites who command from the apex and the technologies with their peculiar potentials, that operate at the base.

10.6 CHANGE AND EVOLUTION

Keynes credited his mentor Alfred Marshall with having brought to its culmination the conception of the economy where 'all the elements of the universe are kept in their places by mutual counterpoise and interaction'. In that idea of the economy, as in the Newtonian cosmos, there is movement but no development. The neoclassical model cannot explain or comprehend an economic system becoming something other than it was. Evolution is beyond its scope. Marshall was quite aware of this as a limit and a failing of his theory, and he pointed to Darwinian evolution as the Mecca for economists. Marshall never made the pilgrimage to his Mecca. Nor did any of his followers. They could not. The forbidden city was beyond their ingrained mode of thought.

Others have found explanations for that evolutionary process whereby an economic system becomes something genuinely other than it was. Karl Marx certainly did, but also Thorstein Veblen, Clarence Ayres, and Joseph Schumpeter. In every instance technology was at the heart of their explanation. Alike they relied on the incursion of new technology as the motor-force of evolutionary change.

Neoclassical theory is neutral with respect to technology. It has no opening wherein to take the specific consequences of the introduction of new technologies into account. The theory, explaining production and productivity as a function of resource combination coupled with the law of diminishing marginal return, would operate in the same way in the context of a stone age or of a space age technology.

While for Marx, Veblen, Ayres and Schumpeter, the advent of new technology was the key to the evolution of systems, they all understood the advent of new technology as an incursion from outside the economy. It was for them an historical phenomenon, a stormy parameter, a random and exogenous force, and they focused on its consequences, benign or malignant, and the transformations it set in train. Joseph Schumpeter, for example, when he wrote *The Theory of Capitalist Development* in Austria in the years before the First World War, conceived of potential new technologies as something in the air, waiting to be seized upon. Schumpeter's concern was with the capacity of an economy to exploit those latent potentials, and he saw the rationale and virtue of capitalism as providing a form of (property) power that enabled the heroic individual innovator to undertake the risks, to swim against the tide, to buck the deep resistances of vested interests, and to impose a new technology, forcing it into the structures of the system. It was this installation of new technology that created investment opportunity. By reference to the unfolding potentials of major new technologies and then the ultimate exhaustion of those potentials, Schumpeter explained the long swings of the business cycle.

Schumpeter's theory conveyed the reality of the world seen from Vienna at the turn of the century. But when Schumpeter at Harvard wrote *Capitalism, Socialism and Democracy* in the days of the Second World War, observing the corporate-organisational core of modern capitalism, he noted a profound change, one that in his view destroyed the rationale of capitalism. The autonomous corporate organisation (Galbraith's technostructure) had 'routinised' innovation, replacing the individual innovator with private property as his power base.

A profound change indeed. For the first time in history, not simply innovation, but the whole process of technological advance has been tamed, harnessed, directed. Hence, as another facet of institutional economics (one might find examples in work done at the University of Sussex in Great Britain) is the effort to understand the process of technological advance as endogenous, as seen from the inside, a system to be controlled, manipulated and managed as an instrument of corporate and of public policy.

End-Notes

CHAPTER 2

* Reprinted with some changes and deletions from the *Journal of Economic Perspectives*, Summer 1987. Copyright 1987, American Economic Association. I am grateful to Brian Binger, John Conlisk, Jim Cox, Vincent Crawford, Gong Jin-Dong, Elizabeth Hoffman, Michael Rothschild, Carl Shapiro, Vernon Smith, Joseph Stiglitz, Timothy Taylor, the editor of this volume, and especially Joel Sobel for helpful discussions on this material, and the Alfred P. Sloan Foundation for financial support.

1. E.g. von Neumann and Morgenstern (1947) and Savage (1954) (axiomatics); Arrow (1965), Pratt (1964) and Rothschild and Stiglitz (1970) (analytics); Akerlof (1970) and Spence and Zeckhauser (1971) (information).

2. For reasons of space, references have been limited to the most significant examples of and/or most useful introductions to the literature in each area. For further discussions of these issues see Arrow (1982), Machina (1983a, 1983b), Sugden (1986) and Tversky and Kahneman (1986).

3. Such transformations are often used to *normalise* the utility function, for example to set $U(0) = 0$ and $U(M) = 1$ for some large value M.

4. Thus, for example, a $\frac{2}{3}:\frac{1}{3}$ chance of \$100 or \$20 and a $\frac{1}{2}:\frac{1}{2}$ chance of \$100 or \$30 both stochastically dominate a $\frac{1}{2}:\frac{1}{2}$ chance of \$100 or \$20.

5. Thus if $x_1 = \$20$, $x_2 = \$30$ and $x_3 = \$100$, the prospects in Note 4 would be represented by the points $(p_1, p_3) = (\frac{1}{3}, \frac{2}{3})$, $(p_1, p_3) = (0, \frac{1}{2})$ and $(p_1, p_3) = (\frac{1}{2}, \frac{1}{2})$ respectively. Although it is fair to describe the *renewal of interest* in this approach as 'modern', versions of this diagram go back to Marschak (1950) at least.

6. This follows since the slope of the indifference curves is $[U(x_2) - U(x_1)]/[U(x_3) - U(x_2)]$, the slope of the iso-expected value lines is $[x_2 - x_1]/[x_3 - x_2]$, and concavity of $U(\cdot)$ implies $[U(x_2 - U(x_1)]/[x_2 - x_1] > [U(x_3) - U(x_2)]/[x_3 - x_2]$ whenever $x_1 < x_2 < x_3$.

7. Algebraically, these cases are equivalent to the expression $[0.10 \cdot U(5\,000\,000) - 0.11 \cdot U(1\,000\,000) + 0.01 U(0)]$ being negative or positive, respectively.

8. The Allais paradox choices a_1, a_2, a_3, and a_4 correspond to b_1, b_2, b_4 and b_3, where $\alpha = 0.11$, $x = \$1\,000\,000$, p is a $\frac{10}{11}$: $\frac{1}{11}$ chance of $\$5\,000\,000$ or $\$0$, P^* is a sure chance of $\$0$, and P^{**} is a sure chance of $\$1\,000\,000$. The name of this phenomenon comes from the 'common consequence' P^{**} in $\{b_1, b_2\}$ and P^* in $\{b_3, b_4\}$.

9. As Bell (1985) notes, 'winning the top prize of $\$10\,000$ in a lottery may leave one much happier than receiving $\$10\,000$ as the lowest prize in a lottery'.

10. In a conversation with the author, Kenneth Arrow has offered an alternative phrasing of this argument: 'The widely maintained hypothesis of decreasing absolute risk aversion asserts that individuals will display more risk aversion in the event of a loss, and less risk aversion in the event of a gain. In the common consequence effect, individuals display more risk aversion in the event of an *opportunity loss*, and less risk aversion in the event of an *opportunity gain*.'

11. The former involves setting $p = 1$, and the latter consists of a two-step choice problem where individuals exhibit the effect with $Y = 2X$ and $p = 2q$. The name 'common ratio effect' comes from the common value of $\mathrm{prob}(X)/\mathrm{prob}(Y)$ in the pairs $\{c_1, c_2\}$ and $\{c_3, c_4\}$.

12. Having found that ξ_1 which solves $U(\xi_1) = (\frac{1}{2}) \cdot U(M) + (\frac{1}{2}) \cdot U(0)$, choose $\{x_1, x_2, x_3\} = \{0, \xi_1, M\}$, so that the indifference curve through $(0, 0)$ (i.e. a surge gain of ξ_1) also passes through $(\frac{1}{2}, \frac{1}{2})$ (a $\frac{1}{2} : \frac{1}{2}$ chance of M or 0). The order of ξ_1, ξ_2, ξ_3 and ξ_1^* and ξ_1^{**} in Figure 2a is derived from the individual's preference ordering over the five distributions in Figure 2b for which they are the respective certainty equivalents.

13. Roughly speaking, the subject states a value for the item, and then the experimenter draws a random price. If the price is above the stated value, the subject forgoes the item and receives the price. If the drawn price is below the stated value, the subject keeps the item. The reader can verify that under such a scheme it can never be in a subject's best interest to report anything other than his or her true value.

14. Economic theory tells us that income effects could cause an individual to assign a lower *bid* price to the object which, if both were free, would actually be preferred. However, this reversal should not occur for either selling prices or the Becker, DeGroot and Marschak elicitations. For evidence on sell-price/bid-price disparities, see Knetsch and Sinden (1984) and the references cited there.

15. When $r(x,y)$ takes the form $r(x,y) \equiv v(x)\tau(y) - v(y)\tau(x)$, this model will reduce to the (transitive) model of equation (6). This is the most general form of the model which is compatible with transitivity.

16. In this model the indifference curves will all cross at the same point. This point will thus be indifferent to all lotteries in the triangle.

17. A final 'twist' on the preference reversal phenomenon: Holt (1986) and Karni and Safra (1987) have shown how the procedures used in most of these studies will only lead to truthful revelation of preferences under the added assumption that the individual satisfies the independence axiom, and have given examples of transitive *non*-expected utility preference rankings which lead to the typical 'preference reversal'

choices. How (and whether) experimenters will be able to address this issue remains to be seen.

18. Subjects were asked to choose either (a) a sure gain of \$240 or (b) $\frac{1}{4}:\frac{3}{4}$ chance of \$1000 or \$0 (zero) and to choose either (c) a sure loss of \$750 or (d) a $\frac{3}{4}:\frac{1}{4}$ chance of $-\$1000$ or zero. 84 per cent chose (a) over (b) and 87 per cent chose (d) over (c), even though (b) + (c) dominates (a) + (d), and choices over the combined distributions were unanimous when they were presented explicitly.

19. Fischhoff (1983, pp. 115–16). Fischhoff notes that 'If one can only infer frames from preferences after assuming the truth of the theory, one runs the risk of making the theory itself untestable.'

20. A wonderful example, offered by my colleague Joel Sobel, are milk advertisements which make no reference to either price or a specific dairy. What could be a more well-known commodity than *milk*?

CHAPTER 3

* I am grateful to Brian Ferguson, Mike Hoy, and Clive Scuthey for helpful discussions on the subject of this chapter. They bear no responsibility for the final result, of course.

1. Thus note that (3.6) can be arranged to give the equation

$$W_2 = \frac{\overline{W^0}}{p} - \frac{(1-p)W_1}{p}$$

2. For example, if a bookmaker is offering odds of 10 to 1 against a particular horse winning a race, this means that he will give you \$10 if the horse wins and you will give him \$1 if the horse loses. Thus, $(1-p)/p = 10$, and so $p = 0.091$ is the probability the bookmaker is placing on the event of the horse winning.

3. If the individual's utility function $u(\cdot)$ is strictly concave (risk aversion), then the expected utility function, a weighted sum of concave functions, is also concave, and so is strictly quasi-concave, i.e. has convex-to-the-origin indifference curves. Alternatively differentiate the contour $(1-p)u(W_1) + pu(W_2) = u$ twice to obtain:

$$dW_2/dW_1 = -(1-p)u'(W_1)/pu'(W_2) < 0$$

$$d^2W_2/dW_1^2 = -\left\{ \frac{(1-p)u''(W_1) - (dW_2/dW_1)^2 pu''(W_2)}{pu'(W_2)} \right\} > 0$$

implying that the contours have a negative slope, and are convex to the origin if $u'' < 0$.

4. Since $dW_2/dW_1 = -(1-p)u'(W_1)/pu'(W_2)$, $W_1 = W_2$ implies $u'(W_1) = u'(W_2)$ and so $dW_2/dW_1 = -(1-p)/p$ at such a point.

5. To see this note that the marginal utility of wealth is constant in this case, and so cancels out in the expression for dW_2/dW_1 (see previous note) leaving $dW_2/dW_1 = -(1-p)/p$.

6. However, it could be shown that if we increase the numbers of individuals of each type shown in the figure, the contract curve will shrink until in the limit it converges to the fair premium point e^0. This is a straightforward application of the theorem of the 'shrinking core' (for an exposition at about this level see Gravelle and Rees, 1981, ch. 10), noting that in the present model e^0 is the Walrasian equilibrium. This can be shown by taking the offer curves for each individual as derived in the previous section, and showing that they must intersect at e^0. This is left as an exercise.

7. Note that there are $N(N-1)$ possible pairs of individuals in a population of size N.

8. Note that the assumption of identical risks implies that if $\rho \neq 0$ then it must be positive, since $\text{var}(W^0) > 0$.

9. Thus positive transactions costs would have to be covered by a 'loading' on the premiums, making it higher than the fair premium, so inducing individuals to buy less than full insurance.

10. To derive (3.17), let n_L and n_H be the (very large) numbers of low- and high-risk types respectively, so that $\lambda = n_L/(n_L + n_H)$. Then, total premium income will be $n_L p C_L + n_H p C_H$, and dividing through by $n_L + n_H$ gives premium income per contract.

11. Thus, total claims would be on average $n_L p_L C_L + n_H p_H C_H$, and so dividing through by $n_L + n_H$ gives the average claim per contract.

12. Recall that the indifference curves at a point on the certainty line must have slopes $-(1-p_L)/p_L$ and $-(1-p_H)/p_H$ respectively.

13. It is usual to make the assumption that indifference between lying and telling the truth will result in choice of the truth. If this were not the case, the solution would be to choose a point slightly below e_L on E^L, so that high-risk types strictly prefer their contract.

14. Note that the absolute value of the slope of an expected value line corresponding to the pooled probability p can be written

$$\frac{(1-\bar{p})}{p} = \frac{(1-p_H+\lambda(p_H-p_L))}{p_H-\lambda(p_H-p_L)}$$

Then, since $p_H > p_L$, increasing λ increases the numerator and decreases the denominator, thus steepening the expected value line.

15. This could be generalised in two ways. We could think of possible expenditures as taking on any value $a \geq 0$, rather than simply 0 or a fixed value a. We could also think of a not as expenditure but rather as some other variable such as effort, which creates disutility for the individual. However, the simple assumption made here suffices to bring out the main points.

16. For example, insurance policies often specify that the buyer must incur some specified expenditure, e.g. installation of a burglar alarm, to obtain a particular favourable premium, it being understood that the installation can be checked by the insurance company (though presumably at some cost).

17. It would be possible, by choosing a greater value of a, and/or a smaller difference $p_0 - p_a$ (slope of E^a closer to slope of E^0), to have point c in Figure 3.8 to the *left* of point b. This implies that it would never be worthwhile to incur expenditure a, and the analysis of this section is irrelevant. The condition under which it would be worth spending a, given in either case the availability of full insurance, is $(1 - p_a)(W_1^0 - a) + p_a(W_2^0 - a) \geqslant (1 - p_0)W_1^0 + p_0 W_2^0$ since points b and c are simply expected values of wealth in the two situations. Rearranging this, recalling that $W_2^0 = W_1^0 - L$, gives the condition

$$(p_0 - p_a)L \geqslant a.$$

The lefthand side gives the incremental benefit of spending a as the reduction in expected value of loss, and this must be at least as great as a for the expenditure to be worthwhile. Note that this condition can be expressed in terms of expected values because of the assumption that full insurance is available at a fair premium, which is in turn due to the assumed absence of information asymmetries. when this assumption is relaxed, the condition changes, as we shall see below.

18. Note that at the premium $p_a C$, buyers who do not spend a would prefer to over-insure, i.e. be above point d on the expected value line E^m. The *true* probability they face is $p_0 < p_a$, and so their marginal rate of substitution at any point on the certainty line is $-(1 - p_0)/p_0$, as Figure 3.8 indicates.

19. Or at least one version of it. The term moral hazard also refers to the case in which the existence of insurance reduces the buyer's incentive to keep down the value of the loss associated with the insured event, e.g. a patient being treated by a doctor whose charges will be fully covered by insurance has no incentive to ensure that unnecessary costs are avoided. The general nature of the results for this case is however similar to that considered here.

20. Note that here we make the important assumption that if the individual is indifferent between spending and not spending a, then he *does* spend it. This assumption is essentially for analytical convenience. If we wanted to dispense with it, we would have to say that the insurance contract should offer compensation slightly less than C^*, i.e. the individual should be slightly below point e in the figure, and then he will positively prefer to spend a. This point is further considered in connection with Figure 3.10.

21. To see this, note that in Figure 3.9, increasing C^* from 0 to L means moving along E^a and E^m from g and W^0 to c and d, passing through higher and higher indifference curves on the way. Alternatively, note that

$$\frac{\overline{du}_a^*}{dC^*} = p_a(1 - p_a)[u_2' - u_1']$$

where u_2' is marginal utility of wealth in state 2 and u_1' is that in state 1. But wealth is lower in state 2 than in state 1 when $C^* < L$, and so $u_2' > u_1'$, implying that $d\overline{u}_a^*/dC^* > 0$ for $C^* < L$. A similar argument implies that $d_C^*/dC^* >$ over the same range. However, when $C^* = L$ both derivatives are zero.

22. Thus with $C^* = L$, $\overline{u}_a^* = u(W_1^0 - p_a C^* - a)$, and $\overline{u}_0^* = u(W_1^0 - p_a C^*)$, and so $\overline{u}_0^* > \overline{u}_a^*$. As Figure 3.8 showed, it is this inequality that creates the moral hazard problem.

23. The continuity of the utility functions ensures this.

24. Note that an intersection point in Figures 3.10 and 3.11 can only be an equilibrium if the $\overline{u}_a$ curve cuts the $\overline{u}_0$ curve from above. In the converse case, it would be possible to offer a contract with slightly higher C^*, and this would still satisfy the condition $\overline{u}_a^* > \overline{u}_a^*$, and so an intersection point where $\overline{u}_a$ curve cuts the $\overline{u}_0$ curve below cannot be an equilibrium.

25. Note that a problem here could be that an individual could take out insurance with a number of different insurers, thus achieving any degree of coverage he might want, in the aggregate. This clearly presents problems for the solutions to the moral hazard and adverse selection problems presented here. For a discussion of the implications of this see M. V. Pauly (1974). In practice insurance contracts usually contain a clause stating that compensation will be reduced to take account of any compensation paid by other insurers, and clearly it would be possible for insurers to centralise information on insurance contracts (though this begins to undermine the assumption of competition, perhaps).

CHAPTER 4

1. Rational expectations was introduced into macroeconomics in a blaze of controversy, largely because it was first applied to oversimplified, crude models of the labour market which inevitably threw up the implausible conclusion that involuntary unemployment could not exist. Had equally crude Keynesians been first to introduce rational expectations, then the force of fiscal·policy would have been enhanced by rational expectations, and not neutered by it. For instance, in the simplest $Y = C + I + G$ model with exogenous investment and $C = a + by$, an increase in G would not need to await the laborious knock-on effects of the multiplier for consumption to increase and income with it: the rational expectation of income increases would entice consumers to raise demand immediately to its new equilibrium level. The reason for mentioning this is not to advance a particular macro model, but to divorce the analytical method from the policy stance.

2. Von Neumann and Morgenstern (1944) used the terms 'complete information' and 'incomplete information' games respectively. We follow modern terminology.

3. The NE is unique in this example. However, were 2's pay-off to (c_1, c_2) 5 instead of 0 then that would also be a pure strategy NE, as well as (a_1, b_2). In such cases of multiple equilibria, the game theorist is unable to say which is more likely to arise. Pre-play communication might help 1 and 2 to focus on one or the other, but unless one NE Pareto dominates the other (which it does not in this example) communication may be of little use.

4. Alternatively, if firm 1 thinks about playing $\hat{s}_1$ and duplicates 2's thought process expecting her to reason in the same way and set output B_2, then the conclusion would be that each would have higher than Cournot outputs and neither would be making best replies. This would also give worse profits than the NE. Interestingly, the Pareto suboptimality of mutual Stackelberg leadership is not always the case. With upward-sloping best-reply curves, as typically arise from price competition, higher profits may obtain for both players as Stackelberg leadership involves higher prices. Nevertheless, this does not get round the essential point that best replies are not being played. These points relate to the simultaneous choice of strategies. See the text for the case where the 'follower' is a genuine follower in that she chooses her strategy sequentially after the leader has declared his.

5. Incidentally, the pay-offs to entry and acquiescence in the example correspond to the linear Cournot game with parameter values $(a - c)^2 / b = 72$ and fixed costs of 5. Actual fighting corresponds to setting price equal to marginal cost, c.

6. The recent game-theoretic literature on oligopoly has become known as the 'New IO' (New Industrial Organisation). Both price and quantity have been utilised as strategic variables. For instance, much of the game-theoretic work on technological competition (see Dasgupta, 1987, for a good review) has firms choosing R&D expenditures to determine costs (i.e. process innovation) combined with Cournot quantity competition in the product market.

7. We have specified a three-stage game with sequential entry followed by pricing, because this yields a pure strategy equilibrium. If 1 and 2 must simultaneously decide on entry before they know what the other has done, we have a two-stage game but mixed strategies are required for equilibrium (see Fudenberg and Tirole, 1986). Mixed strategies are discussed in the pricing context later in this section.

8. If capacity costs are only a proportion of c and the remainder of costs can be postponed until a later date, this does not affect the problem from the point of view of the first stage.

9. This is an example of the so called 'folk theorem' which states that any individually rational outcome is sustainable in an infinitely repeated game without discounting (see Friedman, 1986, or Binmore and Dasgupta, 1986, for further references). Individual rationality eliminates only those strategies for which an alternative could guarantee the

player a higher pay-off regardless of what rivals do. It is a very weak definition of rationality and generally permits multiple equilibria (e.g. both (a_1, a_2) and (b_1, b_2) in the one-shot prisoners' dilemma are individually rational equilibria). In the present, infinitely repeated example, trigger collusion, perpetual play of (b_1, b_2), and many other equilibria are possible. Many game theorists are very wary of this Pandora's box of equilibria opened up by the folk theorem; though others are content that multiple equilibria are a more accurate reflection of real world situations.

10. It was earlier suggested that the practice of promising to match a rival's price could help deter entry. At the same time, in the present context, the same practice can help facilitate non-cooperative collusion between existing firms because it speeds up a price-cutting response by making it automatic. Thus, a superficially competitive strategy, in fact, reduces the incentive to cut price.

11. That we have $d > 0.5$ for both collusion and immediate remorse to be profitable is a contrivance of this particular example, but the general principle should be clear.

12. As such, it can claim to be the 'best' equilibrium amongst the set given by the folk theorem (which can be modified to include discounting: see Fudenberg and Maskin, 1986).

13. Remember, d may be frighteningly low – it was only 0.5 in one of earlier examples!

14. See Farber & Bazerman (1987) for a recent survey of arbitration theories.

15. Aumann and Kurz (1977) present a similar interpretation of Nash's solution.

16. Here it is assumed that meetings are instantaneous consisting of one offer followed by either acceptance or rejection.

17. Consider a case of haggling between a buyer and a seller over the price of a commodity. The buyer is offering 200 while the seller demands 250. if an outside option became available to the seller, it would, according to Nash, invariably shift the threat point in the seller's favour. In Rubinstein's analysis, however, it would only do so if its expected value exceeded 200.

18. One-sided asymmetric information bargaining models such as Fudenberg and Tirole (1986) have been modified to account for industrial disputes. For example, see Hayes (1984) and Tracy (1987).

19. The only way of deriving a single solution is by devising suitable restrictions on the players' beliefs. The model-builder has to find a fine balance between too strong and too weak restrictions or, otherwise, between non-existent and multiple equilibria. See Kreps (1986).

20. A parallel can be drawn here with the inheritance division game. Rubinstein shows that, in the presence of full information, the two relatives will come to an immediate agreement even if there is the possibility of many future, albeit instantaneous, negotiating stages separated by an exogenously fixed 'delay'. Uncertainty about each other – for example, concerning their discount rates – yields a positive

probability of more than one stage before agreement. However, if we now allow them to enter the room and only come out when they have agreed, despite the presence of two-sided uncertainty, the probability of wasteful disagreement vanishes as there will be no need for a second meeting.

21. This type of myopia is not dissimilar to Zeuthen's implicit assumption that, at every round, bargainers fail to learn from past experience that since concessions have already been made by their opponents, further concessions may be forthcoming.

22. See Varoufakis (1987) where the Cross model is extended as a theory of strikes by incorporating two optimisation structures, one for each side. The crucial interdependence between bargainers – which is absent in models such as Ashenfelter and Johnson (1969) – is then restored as expectations on the opponent's concession rates, and therefore offers vary. Furthermore, strategic delay in conceding is explicitly modelled along the lines of models discussed in Part III Section 5 of Varoufakis (1987).

23. Finite horizons can be invoked for a number of reasons. For example, it may be that a politician's term has an upper bound (R. Reagan ?) or that it is common knowledge that, whatever protectionist measures from which a firm may be benefiting in an EEC country today, come 1992 it will be removed. Some oligopolistic games may thus be repeated over a finite period. In the analysis that follows T is assumed to be fixed. This need not be the case: Hargreaves-Heap and Varoufakis (1987) present a version of the models with stochastic horizons.

24. $0(\delta t)$ terms will be ignored throughout so as not to put off the non-technical student.

25. From equation (4.1) it can be shown that if the union's reputation (p_t) exceeds the value implicit in f, the firm will abstain from challenging.

CHAPTER 8

* I am grateful to Richard Blundell, Costas Meghir and Elizabeth Symons for allowing me to draw on our jointly authored work.

1. See Deaton and Muellbauer (1980) for background to the 'AIDS' model.

2. Clearly, one could develop the accuracy and sophistication of the simulation by disaggregating further until the point is reached where commodities correspond to items that are subject to specific tax treatment. Thus, for example, alcohol could be disaggregated into, say, beer, wine and spirits. Two-stage budgeting implied by separability would be a useful assumption to appeal to since it could allow the estimation of subsystems of equations for each commodity group.

3. Households without children do on average record a small amount of expenditure on children's clothing; presumably as gifts.

4. In Table 8.5 we interpret no-response as no change in budget share. This ensures that the budget constraint is satisfied.

CHAPTER 9

* I am very grateful to Angus Deaton and Jan Graaf for their helpful comments, and especially to Larry Temkin for the magnificent set of comments he sent me. Many of Temkin's comments go so deep that I have not been able to take account of them adequately, I am sorry to say.

1. E.g. Dalton (1920), Atkinson (1970).
2. See Sen (1978). I do not mean to suggest that measuring the amount of inequality, as opposed to its badness, is a pointless enterprise. But it is not the subject of this paper.
3. Many authors have considered the effect of differences in population on judgements about inequality, e.g. Donaldson and Weymark (1980) and Temkin (forthcoming). But how differences in population should influence our judgements about the state of society is a notoriously intractable problem. See Parfit (1984) Part IV. And judgements about inequality are not immune from the difficulties.
4. See, for instance, Morton (1987). However, an important paper by Larry Temkin (1987) challenges the transitivity of the betterness relation. I am sorry to say that I have not yet come to terms with Temkin's argument. It is concerned with questions to do with changing population. Since this paper assumes the population is fixed, I hope it may escape Temkin's objections.
5. This point has been the stimulus for interesting recent work on evaluating mobility, for instance Atkinson (1981), Kanbur and Stiglitz (1986), Kanbur and Stromberg (forthcoming). I regret that I have no space for it in this paper.
6. We are forced to make judgements between income distribution without knowing the relevant facts about characteristics. An idea of Lerner's (1944) – see also Sen (1973) pp. 83–4 – is to make it explicit that we have to judge in ignorance. Lerner argues that egalitarian consequences follow.
7. This terminology is Kolm's (1976). The terms are used rather differently in Blackorby and Donaldson (1978), (1980) and Donaldson and Weymark (1980).
8. Atkinson (1970) p. 251 points out that nearly all the conventional measures of inequality have this implication (if they are understood as measures of the badness of inequality). He suggests a measure of his own (p. 275) that also has it, but he does not commit himself to this measure.
9. I do not know of anyone who has actually made this claim, but Kolm (1976) entertains it seriously.
10. I am puzzled by Kolm's (1976) attitude. Kolm recognises very well the distinction between relative and absolute measures. Yet he calls the opinion that I_r is homogeneous of degree zero 'rightist' and the opinion that I_a is nought-translatable 'leftist' as though they betray obviously conflicting political stances. In fact these opinions are not even inconsis-

tent with each other; there are goodness functions that have both properties (Blackorby and Donaldson, 1980; Donaldson and Weymark, 1980). To support his terminology, Kolm tells us than in 1968 French radicals felt bitter and cheated when, as a result of a strike, everybody's pay was increased in the same proportion. But these radicals had no reason to quarrel with the opinion Kolm calls rightist. According to a rightist, the proportional pay rise made inequality no worse in relative terms, but it certainly made it worse in absolute terms. And that is what the radicals were complaining about. The radicals presumably also thought it would have been better to have an absolutely equal pay rise. And Kolm's rightist would agree about that too. An absolutely equal pay rise would have made inequality better in relative terms, whereas in her view the proportional rise did not make it better. Therefore, for any given increase in total income, she would agree that the absolutely equal rise would have been better overall. In this context, Atkinson (1983a) tells another story about an absolutely equal pay cut in the British Navy. Apparently it caused a mutiny. I am not sure what moral Atkinson intends to draw, but this story is no more relevant than Kolm's to the issue between Kolm's rightists and leftists. The mutineers might have held either opinion; either implies that a proportional pay cut would have been better. A recent paper by Eichhorn (1986) continues this puzzling argument.

11. Allais (1979) p. 89. My formulation of the example is more like Savage's (1972) p. 103. There is an example of the same sort in Sen (1973) p. 41.

12. We are not necessarily comparing distributions over the same people. But the anonymity requirement says that the relative values we set on the distributions are as they would be if the people were the same.

13. By 'true egalitarianism' I mean the view that inequality is unfair or unjust, not merely inefficient. The distinction will become clearer later.

14. It is more common in these discussions to talk of a person's welfare rather than her good. But it is clear that her welfare is taken to encompass everything that is good for her. I think, however, that there are sorts of good that cannot decently be included under welfare. Fairness is one I shall be talking about. So I use the more general term.

15. At least since Edgeworth (1881) pp. 78–9, justified by utilitarianism 'aristocratical privilege – the privilege of man above brute, of civilised above savage, of birth, of talent and of the male sex'. His argument was based on differences in capacity for pleasure. He quoted Tennyson:

Woman is the lesser man, and her passions unto mine
Are as moonlight unto sunlight and as water unto wine.

16. Of course it is forced on us by the anonymity assumption. But the point is that utilitarianism is not *generally* egalitarian.

17. Utilitarianism is sometimes said to be itself a theory of fairness, for instance by Griffin (1985). But I am unconvinced.

18. Atkinson (1983a) p. 5 remains non-committal between utilitarianism and modified utilitarianism.

19. Let $\bar{\mu}$ be the equally distributed equivalent income of (1,2). According to modified utilitarianism this means that $\hat{g}(\bar{\mu}) = (\hat{g}(1) + \hat{g}(2))/2$. Consider these prospects:

	States	
	1	2
W	$(\bar{\mu}, \bar{\mu})$	$(\bar{\mu}, \bar{\mu})$
X	$(1, \bar{\mu})$	$(\bar{\mu}, 2)$

W is equally as good as U. To be risk-loving about G implies that X is better than W. This is bizarre if the aim is to capture the value of equality, since W leads to equality and X does not. To be sure, X has a greater expectation of income if $\bar{\mu}$ is less than 1.5. But that has already been taken account of in defining $\bar{\mu}$; X has the *same* expectation of $\hat{g}$ as W. X has a *lower* expectation of income than U, yet it has to be reckoned better than U too.

20. Atkinson now seems ready to concede this point. See Atkinson (1983a) pp. 5–6.

21. In Dworkin (1981) particularly and in much of Sen's work on capabilities such as Sen (1985). See also Roemer (1986).

22. E.g. Dworkin (1981). Of course, some authors (e.g. Nozick, 1974) argue that people's claims to income or resources are not equal at all.

23. W was originally an ordinal representation only, but Equation (9.9) has picked out a specific representation unique up to positive linear transformations.

24. Atkinson (1970) objects to Dalton's measure because it is not invariant with respect to linear transformations of the goodness function. The absolute measure I_d does not have this failing. Changing the origin of the function leaves it unaltered. Changing the *scale* of good will change the measure, of course, because it is in units of good.

25. This idea has been thoroughly examined by Wiggins (1985). He says: 'The indispensable role of the concept of need is precisely to assist us in singling or marking out those very interests that have to be the *special* concern of social justice.'

26. There will still be reasons why we should have greater income, but they will not be claims.

27. Besides it is clear that the measures proposed have really been intended to reflect the badness of poverty as well as its amount. See, for instance, Sen's (1976) justification for his 'axiom of relative equity'.

28. In Lewis and Ulph's theory (1987) the function drops vertically at the poverty line and then flattens out. The result is actually a non-concavity at the line. This means that inequality can be more efficient than equality. But inequality is still unfair.

References

Abreu, D. Pearce, F. and Stacchetti, E. (1986) 'Optimal Cartel Equilibria with Imperfect Monitoring', *Journal of Economic Theory*, 39, pp. 251–69.

Abreu, D. (1986) 'Extremal Equilibria of Oligopolistic Supergames', *Journal of Economic Theory*, 39, pp. 191–225.

Admarti, A. and Perry, M. (1985) 'Strategic Delay in Bargaining', mimeo, Stanford University, Graduate School of Business.

Akerlof, G. A. (1970) 'The Market for "Lemons": Quality Uncertainty and the Market Mechanism'. *Quarterly Journal of Economics*. August, 84, pp. 488–500.

Akerlof, G. A. (1980) 'A Theory of Social Custom of which Unemployment May Be One Consequence', *Quarterly Journal of Economics*, 94, pp. 749–75.

Alger, Daniel, (1987) 'Laboratory Tests of Equilibrium Predictions with Disequilibrium Data', *Review of Economic Studies*, 54, pp. 105–46.

Allais, Maurice (1953) 'Le Comportement de l'Homme Rationel devant le Risque: Critique des Postulates et Axiomes de l'Ecole Americaine', *Econometrica*, October, 21, pp. 503–46.

Allais, Maurice (1979) 'The Foundations of a Positive Theory of Choice Involving Risk and a Criticism of the Postulates and Axioms of the American School', in Allais and Hagen (1979).

Allais, Maurice and Hagen, Ole (eds) (1979) *Expected Utility Hypotheses and the Allais Paradox* (Dordrecht, Holland: D. Reidel).

Allen, Beth (1987) 'Smooth Preferences and the Local Expected Utility Hypothesis', *Journal of Economic Theory*, April, 41, pp. 340–55.

Arkes, Hal R. and Hammond, Kenneth R. (eds) (1986) *Judgement and Decision Making: An Interdisciplinary Reader* (Cambridge: Cambridge University Press).

Arrow, K. J. (1963) 'Uncertainty and the Economics of Medical Care', *American Economic Review*, 53, pp. 941–73.

Arrow, K. J. (1951) 'Alternative Approaches to the Theory of Choice in Risk-Taking Situations', *Econometrica*, October, pp. 404–37. Reprinted in Arrow (1965).

Arrow, K. J. (1958) 'Le Rôle des Valeurs Boursières pour la Répartition le meilleure des risques', *Econometrie*. Colloques Internationaux du Centre National de la Recherche Scientifique, Paris, 40, pp. 41–7. English translation: *Review of Economic Studies*, April 1964, 31, pp. 91–6.

Arrow, K. J. (1953/1964) 'Le Role des Valeur Boursieres pour La Repartition le meillure des risques', *Econometrie*. Colloques Internationaux du Centre National de la Recherche Scientifique Paris, 40, pp. 41–7. English translation: *Review of Economic Studies*, 31, pp. 91–6.

Arrow, K. J. (1965) *Aspects of the Theory of Risk-Bearing* (Helsinki: Yrjo Jahnsson Saatio).

Arrow, K. J. (1982) 'Risk Perception in Psychology and Economics', *Economic Inquiry*, January, 20, pp. 1–9.

Arrow, K. J. and Hahn, F. H. (1971) *General Competitive Analysis* (Edinburgh: Oliver & Boyd).

Arrow, K. J. and Hurwicz, Leonard (1972) 'An Optimality Criterion for Decision-making under Ignorance', in C. F. Carter and J. L. Ford (eds) *Uncertainty and Expectations in Economics* (Oxford: Basil Blackwell).

Ashenfelter, O. and Johnson, G. E. (1969) 'Bargaining Theory, Trade Unions and Industrial Strike Activity', *American Economic Review*, 59, pp. 35–49.

Atkinson, A. (1970) 'On the Measurement of Inequality', *Journal of Economic Theory*, 2, pp. 244–63.

Atkinson, A., Gomulka, S. and Stern, W. H. (1984) 'Household Expenditure on Tobacco, 1970–1980', LSE ECERD discussion paper, 57.

Atkinson, A. and Stern, N. (1980) 'On the Switch from Direct to Indirect Taxation', *Journal of Public Economics*, 14, pp. 195–224.

Atkinson, A. and Stiglitz, J. (1980) *Lectures in Public Economics* (New York: McGraw-Hill).

Atkinson, A. B. (1981) 'The Measurement of Economic Mobility', in Eigelshoven and van Gemerden (1981), pp. 9–24, reprinted in Atkinson (1983b), pp. 61–75.

Atkinson, A. B. (1983a) 'Introduction to Part I' in Atkinson (1983b), pp. 3–13.

Atkinson, A. B. (1983b) *Social Justice and Public Policy* (Brighton: Wheatsheaf, and Boston, Mass.: MIT).

Aumann, R. J. and Kurz, H. (1977) 'Power and Taxes', *Econometrica*, 45, pp. 1137–61.

Axelrod, R. (1984) *The Evolution of Co-operation* (New York: Basic Books).

Ayres, Clarence E. (1944) *The Theory of Economic Progress* (Chapel Hill: University of North Carolina Press).

Ayres, Clarence E. (1952) *The Industrial Economy* (Boston: Houghton Mifflin Co.).

Azariadis, C. (1981) 'A Re-examination of Natural Rate Theory', *American Economic Review*, 71, pp. 946–60.

Bar-Hillel, Maya (1973) 'On the Subjective Probability of Compound Events', *Organizational Behavior and Human Performance*, June, 9, pp. 396–406.

Bar-Hillel, Maya (1974) 'Similarity and Probability', *Organizational Behavior and Human Performance*, April, 11, pp. 277–82.

Barro, R. J. and Grossmann, H. I. (1976) *Money, Employment and Inflation* (Cambridge: Cambridge University Press).

Battalio, Raymond C., Kagel, John H. and MacDonald, Don N. (1985)

'Animals' Choices over Uncertain Outcomes', *American Economic Review*, September, 75, pp. 597–613.

Becker, Gary Stanley (1971) *The Economics of Discrimination* (Chicago: University of Chicago Press).

Becker, Gary Stanley (1981) *A Treatise on the Family* (Cambridge, Mass.: Harvard University Press).

Becker, Selwyn W. and Brownson, Fred O. (1964) 'What Price Ambiguity? Or the Role of Ambiguity in Decision-Making', *Journal of Political Economy*, February, 72, pp. 62–73.

Becker, Gordon M., DeGroot, Morris H. and Marschak, Jacob (1964) 'Measuring Utility by a Single-Response Sequential Method', *Behavioral Science*, July, 9, pp. 226–32.

Bell, David E. (1982) 'Regret in Decision Making Under Uncertainty', *Operations Research*, September–October, 30, pp. 961–81.

Bell, David E. (1985) 'Disappointment in Decision Making Under Uncertainty', *Operations Research*, January–February, 33, pp. 1–27.

Benassy, J. P. (1975) 'Neo-Keynesian Disequilibrium Theory in a Monetary Economy', *Review of Economic Studies*, 42, pp. 503–23.

Benassy, J. P. (1983) 'The Three Regimes of the IS–LM model – a non-Walrasian analysis', *European Economic Review*, 50, p. 23.

Benoit, J. -P. and Krishna, V. (1987) 'Dynamic Du-poly: Prices and Quantities', *Review of Economic Studies*, 54, pp. 23–35.

Berg, Joyce E., Dickhaut, John W. and O'Brien, John R. (1983) 'Preference Reversal and Arbitrage', manuscript, University of Minnesota, September.

Berg, Joyce E., Dickhaut, John W. and O'Brien, John R. (1985) 'Preference Reversal and Arbitrage', in V. L. Smith (ed.) *Research in Experimental Economics*, vol. 3, pp. 31–72.

Bernheim, B. D. (1985) 'Rationalizable Strategic Behaviour', *Econometrica*, 52, pp. 1007–28.

Bernoulli, Daniel (1738/1954) 'Specimen Theoriae Novae de Mensura Sortis', *Commentarii Academiae Scientiarum Imperialis Petropolitanae*, 1738, 5, 175–92. English translation: *Econometrica*, January 1954, 22, pp. 23–36.

Binmore, K. G. (1987) 'Nash Bargaining Theory I–III', in Binmore, K, and Dasgupta, P. (eds) *Essays in Bargaining Theory* (Oxford: Basil Blackwell).

Binmore, K. G. and Dasgupta, P. (eds) (1986) *Economic Organisations as Games* (Oxford: Basil Blackwell).

Bishop, R. L. (1963) 'Game Theoretic Analyses of Bargaining', *Quarterly Journal of Economics*, 77, pp. 559–602.

Bishop, R. L. (1964) 'A Zeuthen–Hicks Theory of Bargaining', *Econometrica*, 32, pp. 410–17.

Blackorby, Charles and Donaldson, David (1978) 'Measures of Relative Equality and their Meaning in Terms of Social Welfare', *Journal of Economic Theory*, 18, pp. 59–80.

Blackorby, Charles and Donaldson, David (1980) 'A Theoretical Treatment of Indices of Absolute Inequality', *International Economic Review*, 21, pp. 107–36.

Blundell, R., Meghir, C., Symons, E., and Walker, I. (1987) 'Labour Supply Specification and the Empirical Evaluation of the Tax Reforms', IFS Working Paper 8714.

Blundell, R., Pashardes, P. and Weber, G. (1987) 'A Household Expenditure Model for Indirect Tax Analysis', IFS mimeo.

Blundell, R. and Walker, I. (1982) 'Modelling the Joint Determination of Household Labour Supplies and Commodity Demands', *Economic Journal*, 92, pp. 351–64.

Blundell, R. and Walker, I. (1982b) 'On the Optimal Taxation of Two-Person Households', *Economics Letters*, 25, pp. 371–377.

Blundell, R. and Walker, I. (1986) 'A Life Cycle Consistent Empirical Model of Family Labour Supply Using Cross Section Data', *Review of Economic Studies*, 53, pp. 539–58.

Blyth, Colin R. (1972) 'Some Probability Paradoxes in Choice from Among Random Alternatives', *Journal of the American Statistical Association*, June, 67, pp. 366–73.

Bonanno, G. (1987) 'Product Proliferation and Entry Deterrence Revisited', *Review of Economic Studies*, 54, pp. 37–64.

Boulding, Kenneth E. (1961) *The Image* (Ann Arbor: University of Michigan Press).

Boulding, Kenneth E. (1968) *The Organizational Revolution* (Chicago: Quadrangle Books).

Boulding, Kenneth E. (1978) *Ecodynamics* (Beverly Hills: Sage Publications).

Braithwaite, R. B. (1955) *Theory of Games as a Tool for the Moral Philosopher* (Cambridge: Cambridge University Press).

Broome, John (1987) 'Utilitarianism and Expected Utility', *Journal of Philosophy*, 84, pp. 405–22.

Broome, John (1988a) 'Fairness and the Random Distribution of Goods', in Elster (1988).

Broome, John (1988b) 'Rationality and the 'Sure-thing Principle', in Meeks (1988).

Browning, M., Deaton, A., and Irish, M. (1985) 'A Profitable Approach to Labour Supply and Commodity Demands over the Life-Cycle', *Econometrica*, 53, pp. 503–44.

Buchanan, J. M. and Tulloch G. (1962) *The Calculus of Consent* (Ann Arbor: University of Michigan Press).

Burns, Penny (1985) 'Experience and Decision Making: A Comparison of Students and Businessmen in a Simulated Progressive Auction', in V. L. Smith (ed.) *Research in Experimental Economics*, vol. 3, pp. 139–57.

Chamberlin, E. H. (1933) *The Theory of Monopolistic Competition* (Cambridge, Mass: Harvard University Press).

Chamberlin, Edward (1948) 'An Experimental Imperfect Market', *Journal of Political Economy*, 56, pp. 95–108.

Chari, V. (1983) 'Involuntary Unemployment and Implicit Contracts', *Quarterly Journal of Economics*, 98 (Supplement), pp. 107–22.

Chatterjee, K. and Samuelson, L. (1987) 'Bargaining with Two-Sided Incomplete Information: An Infinite Horizon Model with Alternating Offers', *Review of Economic Studies*, 53, pp. 709–24.

Chew, Soo Hong (1983) 'A Generalization of the Quasilinear Mean With Applications to the Measurement of Income Inequality and Decision Theory Resolving The Allais Paradox', *Econometrica*, July, 51, pp. 1065–92.

Chew, Soo Hong, Karni, Edi and Safra, Zvi (1987) 'Risk Aversion in the Theory of Expected Utility with Rank Dependent Probabilities', *Journal of Economic Theory*, August, 42, pp. 370–81.

Chew, Soo Hong and Waller, William (1986) 'Empirical Tests of Weighted Utility Theory', *Journal of Mathematical Psychology*, March, 30, pp. 55–72.

Cho, I. K. and Kreps, D. (1987). 'Signalling Games and Stable Equilibria', *Quarterly Journal of Economics*, CII, pp. 179–221.

Clower, R. W. (1965) 'The Keynesian Counter-Revolution: a Theoretical Appraisal', in *The Theory of Interest Rates*, ed. Hahn, F. H. and Brechling, E. (London: Macmillan).

Colman, Andrew (1982) *Game Theory and Experimental Games: The Study of Strategic Interaction* (Oxford: Pergamon Press).

Commons, John R. (1934) *Institutional Economics* (Madison: University of Wisconsin Press).

Commons, John R. (1950) *The Economics of Collective Action* (New York: Macmillan).

Commons, John R. (1968) *Legal Foundations of Capitalism* (Madison: University of Wisconsin Press).

Coppinger, Vicki, Smith, Vernon and Titus, Jon (1980) 'Incentives and Behavior in English, Dutch and Sealed-Bid Auctions', *Economic Inquiry*, 18, pp. 1–22.

Cotta, Alain (1970) *Les Choix Economiques de la Grande Entreprise* (Paris, Dunod).

Cox, James, Roberson, Bruce, and Smith, Vernon (1982) 'Theory and Behavior of Single Object Auctions', in V. L. Smith (ed.) *Research in Experimental Economics*, vol. 2, pp. 1–43.

Crampton, P. C. (1984) 'Bargaining with Incomplete Information: An Infinite Horizon Model with Continuous Uncertainty', *Review of Economic Studies*, 51, pp. 579–94.

Crawford, V. P. (1982) 'A Theory of Disagreement in Bargaining', *Econometrica*, 50, pp. 607–37.

Crawford, V. P. and Sobel, J. (1982) 'Strategic Information Transmission', *Econometrica*, 50, pp. 1431–51.

Crocker, K. J. and Snow, A. (1986) 'The Efficiency of Competitive Equilibria in Insurance Markets with Asymmetric Information', *Journal of Public Economics*, 26, 2, pp. 207–220.

Cross, J. (1969) *The Economics of Bargaining* (New York: Basic Books).

Dalton, Hugh (1920) 'The Measurement of the Inequality of Incomes', *Economic Journal*, 30, pp. 348–61.

Dasgupta, P. (1987) 'The Theory of Competition', in Stiglitz, J. and Matthewson, G. F., *New Developments in the Analysis of Market Structure* (Basingstoke: Macmillan).

Dasgupta, P. and Maskin, E. (1971) 'Existence of Equilibrium in Discontinuous Economic Games: 1 and 2', *Review of Economic Studies* 53, pp. 1–41.

Dasgupta, Partha, Sen, Amartya and Starrett, David (1973) 'Notes on the Measurement of Inequality', *Journal of Economic Theory*, 6, pp. 180–7.

Dasgupta, P. and Stiglitz, J. (1988) 'Learning by Doing', *Oxford Economic Papers*, 40, pp. 246–68.

D'Aspremont, C., Gabszewicz, J. Jaskold and Thisse, J. F. 'On Hotelling's "Stability in Competition"', *Econometrica*, 47, pp. 1145–50.

Dawes, Robyn (1980) 'Social Dilemmas', *Annual Review of Psychology*, 31, pp. 169–93.

Deaton, A. (1981) 'Optimal Taxes and the Structure of Preferences', *Econometrica*, 49, pp. 1245–60.

Deaton, A. and Muelbauer, J. (1980) *Economics and Consumer Behaviour* (Cambridge: Cambridge University Press).

Debreu, Gerard (1959) *Theory of Value: An Axiomatic Analysis of General Equilibrium* (New Haven: Yale University Press).

Debreu, G. (1960) 'Topological Methods in Cardinal Utility', in Karlin and Suppes (1960).

Diamond, Peter A. and Yaari, Menahem (1972) 'Implications of the Theory of Rationing for Consumers Under Uncertainty', *American Economic Review*, June, 62, pp. 333–43.

Dierker, E. (1982) 'Regular Economies', in K. J. Arrow and M. D. Intriligator (eds) *Handbook of Mathematical Economics*, vol. II (Amsterdam: North-Holland).

Dixit, A. (1980) 'Recent Developments in Oligopoly Theory', *American Economic Review, Papers and Proceedings*, 72, pp. 12–17.

Dixon, H. (1988) 'Oligopoly Theory Made Simple', in Davies, S. and Lyons, B. *et al.*, *Surveys in Industrial Organisation* (London: Longman).

Donaldson, David, and Weymark, John A. (1980) 'A Single Parameter of the Gini Indices of Inequality', *Journal of Economic Theory*, 22, pp. 67–87.

Dreze, J. H. (1975) 'Existence of an Exchange Equilibrium under Price Rigidities', *International Economic Review*, 16, pp. 301–20.

Dworkin, Ronald (1981) 'What is Equality?', *Philosophy and Public Affairs*, 10, pp. 185–246 and 283–345.

Edgeworth, F. Y. (1881) *Mathematical Psychics* (London: Kegan Paul).

Edwards, Ward (1954) 'The Theory of Decision Making', *Psychological Bulletin*, July, 51, pp. 380–417.

Edwards, Ward (1955) 'The Prediction of Decisions Among Bets', *Journal of Experimental Psychology*, September, 50, pp. 201–14.

Edwards, Ward, Lindman, Harold and Savage, Leonard J. (1963) 'Bayesian Statistical Inference for Psychological Research', *Psychological Review*, May, 70, pp. 193–242.

Eichhorn, Wolfgang (1986) 'On a Class of Inequality Measures', typescript.

Eigelshoven, P. J. and van Gemerden, L. J. (eds) (1981) *Incomensverdeling en Openbare Financiën* (Uitgeverij: Het Spectrum).

Ellsberg, Daniel (1961) 'Risk, Ambiguity and the Savage Axioms', *Quarterly Journal of Economics*, November, 75, pp. 643–69.

Elster, Jon (ed.) (1988) *Justice and the Lottery* (Cambridge: Cambridge University Press).

Epstein, Larry (1985) 'Decreasing Risk Aversion and Mean-Variance Analysis', *Econometrica*, 53, pp. 945–61.

Farber, H. S. (1978) 'Bargaining Theory, Wage Outcomes, and the Occurrence of Strikes: An Econometric Analysis', *American Economic Review*, 68, pp. 262–71.

Farber, H. S. and Bazerman, M. H. (1987) 'Why is there Disagreement in Bargaining?', *American Economic Review*, 77, pp. 347–52.

Farquhar, Peter (1984) 'Utility Assessment Methods', *Management Science*, 30, pp. 123–30.

Fellner, William (1961) 'Distortion of Subjective Probabilities as a Reaction to Uncertainty', *Quarterly Journal of Economics*, November, 75, pp. 670–89.

Fine, Ben (1985) 'A Note on the Measurement of Inequality and Interpersonal Comparability', *Social Choice and Welfare*, 1, pp. 273–7.

Fischer, S. (1977) 'Long-term Contracts, Rational Expectations and the Optimal Money Supply Rule', *Journal of Political Economy*, 85, pp. 191–205.

Fischhoff, Baruch (1983) 'Predicting Frames', *Journal of Experimental Psychology: Learning, Memory and Cognition*, January, 9, pp. 103–16.

Fishburn, Peter C. (1982) 'Nontransitive Measurable Utility', *Journal of Mathematical Psychology*, August, 26, pp. 31–67.

Fishburn, Peter C. (1983) 'Transitive Measurable Utility', *Journal of Economic Theory*, December, 31, pp. 293–317.

Fishburn, Peter C. (1984) 'SSB Utility Theory: An Economic Perspective', *Mathematical Social Sciences*, 8, pp. 63–94.

Fishburn, Peter C. (1986) 'A New Model for Decisions Under Uncertainty', *Economics Letters*, 21, pp. 127–30.

Foster, James E. (1984) 'On Economic Poverty: A Survey of Aggregate Measures', *Advances in Econometrics*, 3 (1984), pp. 215–51.

Freixas, X., Guesnerie, R. and Tirole, J. (1985) 'Planning Under Incomplete Information and the Ratchet Effect', *Review of Economic Studies*, 52, pp. 173–91.

Friedman, J. W. (1971) 'A Non-cooperative Equilibrium for Supergames', *Review of Economic Studies*, 28, pp. 1–12.

Friedman, J. W. (1977) *Oligopoly and the Theory of Games* (Amsterdam: North-Holland).

Friedman, J. W. (1985) 'Cooperative Equilibria in Finite Horizon Non-Cooperative Supergames', *Journal of Economic Theory*, 35, pp. 390–8.

Friedman, J. W. (1986) *Game Theory with Applications to Economics* (Oxford: Oxford University Press).

Friedman, Milton (1955) 'The Role of Government in Education', in Robert A. Solo (ed.) *Economics and the Public Interest* (New Brunswick: Rutgers University Press).

Friedman, M. (1968) 'The Role of Monetary Policy', *American Economic Review*, 58, pp. 1–17.

Friedman, Milton and Savage, Leonard J. (1948) 'The Utility Analysis of Choices Involving Risk', *Journal of Political Economy*, August, 56, pp. 279–304.

Fudenberg, D. and Maskin, E. (1986) 'The Folk Theorem in Repeated Games with Discounting or with Incomplete Information', *Econometrica*, 54, pp. 533–54.

Fudenberg, D. and Tirole, J. (1986) 'A Theory of Exit in Duopoly', *Econometrica*, 54, pp. 943–60.

Fudenberg, D. and Tirole, J. (1987) 'Understanding Rent Dissipation: On the Use of Game Theory in Industrial Organisation', *American Economic Association Papers and Proceedings*, May, vol. 77, pp. 176–83.

Gabszewicz, J. J. and Vial, J. P. (1972) 'Oligopoly "a la Cournot" in a General Equilibrium Analysis', *Journal of Economic Theory*, 4, pp. 381–400.

Gabszewicz, J. J. and Thisse, J. F. (1980) 'Entry (and Exit) in a Differentiated Industry', *Journal of Economic Theory*, 22, pp. 327–38.

Gabszewicz, J. J., Shaked, A., Sutton, J. and Thisse, J. F. (1981) 'International Trade in Differentiated Products', *International Economic Review*, 22, pp. 527–35.

Gorman, W. (1958) 'Separable Utility and Aggregation', *Econometrica*, 27, pp. 469–81.

Gorman, W. M. (1968) 'The Structure of Utility Functions', *Review of Economic Studies*, 36, pp. 605–9.

Grandmont, J. M. (1977) 'Temporary general equilibrium theory', *Econometrica*, 45, pp. 535–72.

Grandmont, J. M. (1983). *Money and Value* (Cambridge: Cambridge University Press).

Grandmont, J. M. (1985). 'On endogenous competitive business cycles', *Econometrica*, 53, pp. 995–1046.

Gravelle, H. S. E. and Rees, R. (1981) *Microeconomics* (London: Longman).

Green, E. J. and Porter, R. H. (1984) 'Non-cooperative Collusion under Imperfect Price Information', *Econometrica*, 52, pp. 87–100.

Green, J. R. and Kahn, C. (1983) 'Wage Employment Contracts', *Quarterly Journal of Economics*, 98 (Supplement), pp. 173–88.

Green, J. R. and Stokey, N. L. (1983) 'A Comparison of Tournaments and Contracts', *Journal of Political Economy*, 91, pp. 349–64.

Grether, D. M. (1980) 'Bayes Rule as a Descriptive Model: The Representativeness Heuristic', *Quarterly Journal of Economics*, 95, pp. 537–57.

Grether, D. M. and Plott, C. R. (1979) 'Economic Theory of Choice and the Preference Reversal Phenomenon', *American Economic Review*, 69, pp. 627–38.

Griffin, James (1985) 'Some problems of fairness', *Ethics*, 96, pp. 100–18.

Grossman, S. J. and Hart, O. D. (1981) 'Implicit Contracts, Moral Hazard and Unemployment', *American Economic Review papers and proceedings*, 71, pp. 301–8.

Grossman, S. J. and Hart, O. D. (1983) 'An Analysis of the Principal–Agent Problem', *Econometrica*, 51, pp. 7–45.

Gul, F. and Sonnenschein, H. (1985) 'One-Sided Uncertainty Does Not Cause Delay', mimeo, Stanford University, Graduate Business School.

Gul, F., Sonnenschein, H. and Wilson, R. (1985) 'Foundations of Dynamic Oligopoly and the Coase Conjecture', mimeo, Stanford University, Graduate Business School.

Hagen, Ole (1979) 'Towards a Positive Theory of Preferences Under Risk', in Allais and Hagen (1979).

Hahn, F. H. (1971) 'Equilibrium with Transactions Costs', *Econometrica*, 39.

Hahn, F. H. (1973) 'On Transaction Costs, Inessential Sequence Economies and Money', *Review of Economic Studies*, 40.

Hall, R. E. (1982) 'The Importance of Lifetime Jobs in the US Economy', *American Economic Review*, 72, pp. 716–24.

Hargreaves-Heap, S. and Varoufakis, Y. (1987) 'Multiple Reputations in Games with Uncertain Horizons', Discussion Paper No. 22, *Economics Research Centre*, University of East Anglia.

Harsanyi, J. (1961) 'On the Rationality Postulates underlying the Theory of Cooperative Games', *Journal of Conflict Resolution*, 5, pp. 179–96.

Hart, O. D. (1982) 'A Model of Imperfect Competition with Keynesian Features', *Quarterly Journal of Economics*, 97, pp. 109–38.

Hart, O. D. (1983) 'Optimal Labour Contracts Under Asymmetric Information: An Introduction', *Review of Economic Studies*, 50, pp. 3–35.

Hart, O. D. (1985) 'Imperfect Competition in General Equilibrium: An Overview of Recent Work', in K. J. Arrow and S. Honkapohja (eds) *Frontiers of Economics* (Oxford: Basil Blackwell).

Hart, O. D. and Holmstrom, B. (1985) 'The Theory of Contracts', in T. Bewley (ed.) *Advances in Economic Theory*, (Cambridge: Cambridge University Press).

Hausman, J. (1981) 'Exact Consumer's Surplus and Deadweight Loss', *American Economic Review*, 73, pp. 662–76.

Hausman, J. and Ruud, P. (1986) 'Family Labour Supply with Taxes', *American Economic Review*, 74, pp. 242–8.

Hausman, Jerry and Wise, David (1987) *Social Experimentation* (Chicago: University of Chicago Press).

Hay, D. A. (1976) 'Sequential Entry and Entry-Deterring Strategies in Spatial Competition', *Oxford Economic Papers*, 28, pp. 240–57.

Hayes, B. (1984) 'Unions and Strikes and Asymmetric Information', *Journal of Labour Economics*, 2, pp. 57–83.

Heckman, J. and MaCurdy, T. (1980) 'A Life Cycle Model of Female Labour Supply', *Review of Economic Studies*, 47, pp. 47–74.

Heiner, Ronald (1985) 'Experimental Economics: Comment', *American Economic Review*, 75, pp. 260–3.

Hershey, John C. and Schoemaker, Paul J. H. (1980) 'Risk-Taking and Problem Context in the Domain of Losses – An Expected Utility Analysis', *Journal of Risk and Insurance*, March, 47, pp. 111–32.

Hershey, John C. and Schoemaker, Paul J. H. (1985) 'Probability Versus Certainty Equivalence Methods in Utility Measurement: Are They Equivalent?', *Management Science,* October, 31, pp. 121–33.

Hey, John (1984) 'The Economics of Optimism and Pessimism: A Definition and Some Applications', *Kyklos* (Fasc. 2) 37, pp. 181–205.

Hicks, J. R. (1932, reprinted in 1966) *The Theory of Wages* (London: Macmillan).

Hicks, J. R. (1946) *Value and Capital* (Oxford: Oxford University Press) 2nd edn.

Hildenbrand, W. and Kirman, A. P. (1976) *Introduction to Equilibrium Analysis* (Amsterdam: North-Holland).

Hirshleifer, Jack (1966) 'Investment Decision Under Uncertainty: Applications of the State-Preference Approach', *Quarterly Journal of Economics*, May, 80, pp. 252–77.

Hirschleifer, J. and Riley, J. G. (1979) 'The Analytics of Uncertainty and Information – An Expository Survey', *Journal of Economic Literature*, XVII, 4, pp. 1375–1421.

Hogarth, Robin (1975) 'Cognitive Processes and the Assessment of Subjective Probability Distributions', *Journal of the American Statistical Association*, June, 70, pp. 271–89.

Hogarth, Robin and Kunreuther, Howard (1986) 'Decision Making Under Ambiguity', *Journal of Business*, 4, pp. 225–50.

Hogarth, Robin and Reder, Melvin (1987) *Rational Choice: The Contrast Between Economics and Psychology* (Chicago: University of Chicago Press).

Holmstrom, B. (1982) 'Moral Hazard in Teams', *Bell Journal of Economics*, 13, pp. 324–40.

Holt, Charles (1986) 'Preference Reversals and the Independence Axiom', *American Economic Review*, 76, pp. 508–15.

Honderich, Ted (ed.) (1985) *Morality and Objectivity* (London: Routledge & Kegan Paul).

Hong, James and Plott, Charles (1982) 'Rate Filing Policies for Inland Water Transportation: An Experimental Approach', *Bell Journal of Economics*, 13, pp. 11–19.

Hotelling, H. (1929) 'Stability in Competition', *Economic Journal*, 39, pp. 41–57.

Hoy, M. (1982) 'Categorizing Risks in the Insurance Industry', *Quarterly Journal of Economics*, XCVII, pp. 321–36.

Ippolito, P. and Scheffman, D. (1986) *Empirical Approaches to Consumer Protection Economics* (Federal Trade Commission).

Jacobs, Jane (1961) *The Death and Life of Great American Cities* (New York: Vintage Books).

Johnson, Chalmers (1982) *Miti and the Japanese Miracle* (Stanford: Stanford University Press).

Johnston, J. (1972) 'A Model of Wage Determination under Bilateral Monopoly', *Economic Journal*, 82, pp. 837–52.

Kagel, John and Levin, Dan (1986) 'The Winner's Curse and Public Information in Common Value Auctions', *American Economic Review*, 76, pp. 894–920.

Kahneman, Daniel, Knetsch, Jack and Thaler, Richard (1986) 'Fairness as a Constraint on Profit Seeking: Entitlements in the Market', *American Economic Review*, 76, pp. 728–41.

Kahneman, Daniel, Slovic, Paul and Tversky, Amos (1982) *Judgement Under Uncertainty: Heuristics and Biases* (Cambridge: Cambridge University Press).

Kahneman, Daniel and Tversky, A. (1973) 'On the Psychology of Prediction', *Psychological Review*, 80, pp. 237–51.

Kahneman, Daniel and Tversky, Amos (1979) 'Prospect Theory: An Analysis of Decision Under Risk', *Econometrica*, 47, pp. 263–91.

Kanbur, S. M. (Ravi) and Stiglitz, Joseph E. (1986) 'Intergenerational mobility and dynastic inequality', typescript.

Kanbur, S. M. (Ravi) and Stromberg, J. O. (forthcoming) 'Income Transitions and Income Distribution Dominance', *Journal of Economic Theory*.

Karlin, S. and Suppes, P. (eds) (1960) *Mathematical Methods in the Social Sciences* (Stanford: Stanford University Press).

Karmarkar, U. S. (1974) 'The Effect of Probabilities on the Subjective Evaluation of Lotteries', MIT Sloan School Working Paper.

Karmarker, U. S. (1978) 'Subjectively Weighted Utility. A Descriptive Extension of the Weighted Utility Model', *Organisational Behaviour and Human Performance*, 21, pp. 61–72.

Karni, Edi and Safra, Zvi (1987) ' "Preference Reversal" and the Observability of Preferences by Experimental Methods', *Econometrica*, 55, pp. 675–85.

Keene, M. (1986) 'Zero Expenditures and the Estimation of Engel Curves', *Journal of Applied Econometrics*, 1, pp. 277–86.

Keller, L. R. (1982) 'The Effects of Decision Problem Representation on Utility Conformance' MS, University of California, Irvine.

Ketcham, Jon, Smith, Vernon and Williams, Arlington (1984) 'A Comparison of Posted-Offer and Double-Auction Pricing Institutions', *Review of Economic Studies*, 51, pp. 595–614.

Keynes, John Maynard (1933) *Essays in Biography* (New York: Harcourt & Brace).

Keynes, John Maynard (1936) *The General Theory of Employment, Interest and Money* (New York: Harcourt & Brace).

Killingsworth, M. (1983) *Labour Supply* (Cambridge: Cambridge University Press).

King, M. (1983) 'Welfare Analysis of Tax Reforms Using Household Data', *Journal of Public Economics*, 21, pp. 183–214.

Knetsch, Jack. L. and Sinden, J. (1984) 'Willingness to Pay and Compensation Demanded: Experimental Evidence of an Unexpected Disparity in Measures of Value', *Quarterly Journal of Economics*, 99, pp. 507–21.

Knez, Marc and Smith, V. (1986) 'Hypothetical Valuations and Preference Reversals in the Context of Asset Trading', University of Arizona, mimeo.

Knez, Peter, Smith, Vernon and Williams, Arlington (1985) 'Individual Rationality, Market Rationality and Value Estimation', *American Economic Review*, 75, pp. 397–402.

Kolm, Serge-Christophe (1976) 'Unequal Inequalities', *Journal of Economic Theory*, 12, pp. 416–42 and 13, pp. 82–111.

Krelle, W. and Shorrocks, A. A. (eds) (1978) *Personal Income Distribution* (Amsterdam: North-Holland).

Kreps, D. (1986) 'Out of Equilibrium Beliefs and Out of Equilibrium Behaviour', mimeo, Stanford University, Graduate Business School.

Kreps, D., Milgrom, P., Roberts, J. and Wilson, R. (1982). 'Rational Cooperation in the Finitely Repeated Prisoner's Dilemma', *Journal of Economic Theory*, 27, pp. 245–52.

Kreps, D. and Scheinkman, J. A. (1985) 'Quantity Precommitment and Bertrand Competition Yield Cournot Outcomes', *The Bell Journal of Economics*, pp. 326–77.

Kreps, D. and Wilson, R. (1982a) 'Reputation and Imperfect Information', *Journal of Economic Theory*, 27, pp. 253–79.

Kreps, D. and Wilson, R. (1982b) 'Sequential Equilibria', *Econometrica*, 50, pp. 863–94.

Krugman, P. (ed.) (1986) *Strategic Trade Policy and the New International Economics* (Boston, Mass: MIT Press).

Kunreuther, Howard (1987) 'Comments on Plott and on Kahneman, Knetsch and Thaler', in R. M. Hogarth and M. W. Reder (eds) *Rational Choice*, pp. 145–59.

Laffont, J.-J. and Tirole, J. (1987) 'Comparative Statics of the Optimal Dynamic Incentive Contact', *European Economic Review*, 31, pp. 901–26.

Lane, W. (1980) 'Product Differentiation in a Market with Endogenous Sequential Entry', *Bell Journal of Economics*, 11, pp. 237–60.

Lazear, E. P. and Rosen, S. (1981) 'Rank–Order Tournaments as Optimum Labor Contracts', *Journal of Political Economy*, 89.

Lee, L. F. and Pitt, M. (1986) 'Microeconometric Demand Systems with Binding Non-Negativity Constraints: The Dual Approach', *Econometrica*, 54, pp. 1237–42.

Lerner, Abba (1944) *The Economics of Control* (Basingstoke: Macmillan).

Levitan, R. and Shubik, M. (1972) 'Price Duopoly and Capacity Constraints', *International Economic Review*, February, vol. 13, pp. 111–22.

Lewis, G. W. and Ulph, D. T. (1987) 'Poverty, Inequality and Welfare', typescript.

Lichtenstein, S. and Slovic, P. (1979) 'Reversal of Preferences Between Bids and Choices in Gambling Decisions', *Journal of Experimental Psychology*, 89, pp. 46–55.

Lindman, H. (1971) 'Inconsistent Preferences Among Gambles', *Journal of Experimental Psychology*, 1989, pp. 390–7.

Loewenstein, George (1987) 'Anticipation and the Valuation of Delayed Consumption', *Economic Journal*, 97, pp. 666–84.

Loomes, Graham and Sugden, Robert (1982) 'Regret Theory: An Alternative Theory of Rational Choice Under Uncertainty', *Economic Journal*, 92, pp. 805–24.

Loomes, Graham, Starmer, Chris and Sugden, Robert (1988) 'Preference Reversals: Information-Processing Effect or Rational Non-Transitive Choice?', presented at *RES AUTE Conference*, Oxford, March 1988. Mimeo available, Dept. of Economics, University of York.

Loomes, Graham, Starmer, Chris and Sugden, Robert (1989) 'Preference

Reversal: Information Processing Effect or Rational Non-Transitive Choice?', *Economic Journal*, 99.

Lucas, R. E (1972) 'Expectations and the Neutrality of Money', *Journal of Economic Theory*, 4, pp. 103–24.

Luce, R. D. and Raiffa, H. (1957) *Games and Decisions* (New York: John Wiley).

Luxemburg, R. (1906 reprinted 1971) *The Mass Strike* (New York: Harper & Row).

Lyons, B. R. (1987a) 'Strategic Behaviour', in R. Clarke and A. J. McGuinness (eds) *Economics of the Firm* (Oxford: Basil Blackwell).

Lyons, B. R. (1987b) 'International Trade and Technology Policy', in *Economic Policy and Technological Performance* (Cambridge: Cambridge University Press).

Lyons, B. R. (1988) 'Barriers to Entry', in S. Davies and B. Lyons *et al.*, *Surveys in Industrial Organisation* (London: Longman).

MacCrimmon, Kenneth R. (1968) 'Descriptive and Normative Implications of the Decision-Theory Postulates', in Borch, C. H. and Mossin, J. (eds) *Risk and Uncertainty* (London: Macmillan).

MacCrimmon, Kenneth R. and Larsson, Stig (1979) 'Utility Theory: Axioms Versus Paradoxes', in Allais and Hagen (1979).

MacCrimmon, Kenneth R. and Wehrung, Donald A. (1986) *Taking Risks: The Management of Uncertainty* (New York: The Free Press).

MaCurdy, T. (1981) 'An Empirical Model of Labour Supply in a Life Cycle Setting', *Journal of Political Economy*, 89, pp. 1059–85.

Machina, Mark (1982) '"Expected Utility" Analysis Without the Independence Axiom', *Econometrica*, 50, pp. 277–323.

Machina, Mark J. (1983a) 'The Economic Theory of Individual Behavior Toward Risk: Theory, Evidence and New Directions', Stanford University Institute for Mathematical Studies in the Social Sciences Technical Report.

Machina, Mark J. (1983b) 'Generalized Expected Utility Analysis and the Nature of Observed Violations of the Independence Axiom', in Stigum and Wenstøp (1983).

Machina, Mark J. (1984) 'Temporal Risk and the Nature of Induced Preferences', *Journal of Economic Theory*, August, 33, pp. 199–231.

Madden, P. J. (1987) 'A Diagrammatic Introduction to Disequilibrium Macroeconomics', *Bulletin of Economic Research*, 39, pp. 121–49.

MacLeod, W. B. and Malcomson, J. M. (forthcoming) 'Implicit Contracts, Incentive Compatibility, and Involuntary Unemployment', *Econometrica*, 1989.

Malcomson, J. M. (1984) 'Work Incentives, Hierarchy, and Internal Labor Markets', *Journal of Political Economy*, 92, pp. 486–507.

Malcomson, J. M. (1986) 'Rank–Order Contracts for a Principal with Many Agents', *Review of Economic Studies*, 53, pp. 807–17.

Malcomson, J. M. and Spinnewyn, F. (1988) 'The Multiperiod Principal–Agent Problem', *Review of Economic Studies*, 55, pp. 391–408.

Malinvaud, E. (1977) *The Theory of Unemployment Reconsidered* (Oxford: Basil Blackwell).

Mansfield, Edwin (1968) *The Economics of Technological Change* (New York: W. W. Norton).

Markowitz, Harry (1952) 'The Utility of Wealth', *Journal of Political Economy*, April, 60, pp. 151–8.

Marschak, Jacob (1950) 'Rational Behavior, Uncertain Prospects, and Measurable Utility', *Econometrica*, April, 18, pp. 111–41, 'Errata', *Econometrica*, July 1950, 18, p. 312.

Marschak, T. and Selten, R. (1972) *General Equilibrium with Price Making Firms* (Lecture Notes in Economics and Mathematical Systems) (Berlin: Springer-Verlag).

Mas-Colell, Andreu (1974) 'An Equilibrium Existence Theorem Without Complete or Transitive Preferences', *Journal of Mathematical Economics*, December, 3, pp. 237–46.

Maskin, Eric (1979) 'Decision Making Under Ignorance with Implications for Social Choice', *Theory and Decision*, September, 11, pp. 319–37.

May, Kenneth O. (1954) 'Intransitivity, Utility, and the Aggregation of Preference Patterns', *Econometrica*, January, 22, pp. 1–13.

McCord, Marc and Neufville, Richard de (1983) 'Empirical Demonstration that Expected Utility Analysis Is Not Operational', in Stigum and Wenstøp (1983).

McCord, Marc and Neufville, Richard de (1984) 'Utility Dependence on Probability: An Empirical Demonstration', *Large Scale Systems*, February, 6, pp. 91–103.

McNeil, Barbara J., Pauker, Stephen G., Sox, Harold C., Jr. and Tversky, Amos (1982) 'On the Elicitation of Preferences for Alternative Therapies', *New England Journal of Medicine*, May, 306, pp. 1259–62.

Meeks, Gay (ed.) (1988) *Rationality, Self-Interest and Benevolence* (Cambridge: Cambridge University Press).

Mehran, F. (1976) 'Linear Measures of Income Inequality', *Econometrica*, 44, pp. 805–9.

Melman, Seymour (1983) *Profits without Production* (New York: Alfred Knopf).

Milgrom, P. and Roberts, J. (1982) 'Predation, Reputation and Entry Deterrence', *Journal of Economic Theory*, 27, pp. 280–312.

Milgrom, P. and Roberts, J. (1987) 'Informational Asymmetries, Strategic and Industrial Organisation', *American Economic Review*, 77, pp. 184–93.

Milne, Frank (1981) 'Induced Preferences and the Theory of the Consumer', *Journal of Economic Theory*, April, 24, pp. 205–17.

Mitchell, Wesley Clair (1913) *Business Cycles* (Berkeley: University of California Press).

Moriarty, Shane (ed.) (1986) *Laboratory Market Research* (Norman, Oklahoma: Center for Economic and Management Research, University of Oklahoma).

Morrison, Donald G. (1967) 'On the Consistency of Preferences in Allais' Paradox', *Behavioural Science*, 12, pp. 373–83.

Morton, Adam (1987) 'Hypercomparatives', typescript.

Moskowitz, Herbert (1974) 'Effects of Problem Representation and Feedback on Rational Behavior in Allais and Morlat-Type Problems', *Decision Sciences*, 5, pp. 225–42.

Mowen, John C. and Gentry, James W. (1980) 'Investigation of the Preference–Reversal Phenomenon in a New Product Introduction Task', *Journal of Applied Psychology*, December, 65, pp. 715–22.

Myrdal, Gunnar (1954) *The Political Element in the Development of Economic Thought* (Cambridge: Cambridge University Press).

Myrdal, Gunnar (1960) *Beyond the Welfare State* (New Haven: Yale University Press).

Myrdal, Gunnar (1973) *Against the Stream: Critical Essays on Economics* (New York: Pantheon Books).

Nalebuff, B. J. and Stiglitz, J. E. (1983) 'Prizes and Incentives: Towards a General Theory of Compensation and Competition', *Bell Journal of Economics*, 14, pp. 21–43.

Nash, J. F. (1950) 'The Bargaining Problem', *Econometrica*, 18, pp. 155–62.

Neven, D. (1985) 'Two Stage (Perfect) Equilibrium in Hotelling's Model', *Journal of Industrial Economics*, 33, pp. 317–26.

Newbery, David (1970) 'A Theorem on the Measurement of Inequality', *Journal of Economic Theory*, 2, pp. 264–6.

Nozick, Robert (1974) *Anarchy, State and Utopia* (Oxford: Blackwell).

Olson, M., Jr (1965) *The Logic of Collective Action* (Cambridge: Harvard University Press).

Parfit, Derek (1984) *Reasons and Persons* (Oxford: Oxford University Press).

Patinkin, D. (1965) *Money, Interest and Prices* (New York: Harper & Row) 2nd edn.

Pauly, M. V. (1974) 'Overinsurance and Public Provision of Insurance', *Quarterly Journal of Economics*, LXXXVII, pp. 44–62, 974.

Payne, John W. and Braunstein, Myron L. (1971) 'Preferences Among Gambles with Equal Underlying Distributions', *Journal of Experimental Psychology*, January, 87, pp. 13–18.

Pearce, D. G. (1985) 'Rationalizable Strategic Behaviour and the Problem of Perfection', *Econometrica*, 52, pp. 1029–50.

Phelps, E. (1968) 'Money Wage Dynamics and Labour Market Equilibrium', *Journal of Political Economy*, 76, pp. 687–711.

Phelps, E. (1970) *Microeconomic Foundations of Employment and Inflation Theory* (Basingstoke: Macmillan).

Phelps, E. and Taylor, J. B. (1977) 'Stabilizing Powers of Monetary Policy under Rational Expectations', *Journal of Political Economy*, 85, pp. 163–90.

Phlips, L. (1974) *Applied Consumption Analysis* (Amsterdam: North-Holland).

Piore, Michael and Sabel, Charles (1984) *The Second Industrial Divide* (New York: Basic Books).

Pissarides, C. A. (1985) 'Job Search and the Functioning of Labour Markets', in D. Carline, C. A. Pissarides, W. S. Siebert and P. J. Sloane (eds) *Labour Economics* (New York: Longman).

Plott, Charles (1979) 'The Application of Laboratory Experimental Methods in Public Choice', in C. S. Russell (ed.) *Collective Decision Making: Applications from Public Choice Theory* (Baltimore, MD: Johns Hopkins University Press for Resources for the Future), pp. 137–60.

Plott, Charles (1982) 'Industrial Organization Theory and Experimental Economics', *Journal of Economic Literature*, 20, pp. 1484–1527.

Plott, Charles (1986) 'Laboratory Experiments in Economics: The Implications of Posted-Price Institutions', *Science*, 232, pp. 732–8.

Pommerehne, Werner W., Schneider, Friedrich and Zweifel, Peter (1982) 'Economic Theory of Choice and the Preference Reversal Phenomenon: A Re-examination', *American Economic Review*, June, 72, pp. 569–74.

Porter, R. H. (1983) 'A Study of Cartel Stability: The Joint Executive Committee, 1880–1886', *Bell Journal of Economics*, 14, pp. 301–14.

Porter, R. H. (1985) 'On the Incidence and Duration of Price Wars', *Journal of Industrial Economics*, 33, pp. 415–26.

Pratt, John W. (1964) 'Risk Aversion in the Small and in the Large', *Econometrica*, January/April, 32, pp. 122–36.

Prescott, E. C. and Visscher, M. (1977) 'Sequential Location among Firms with Foresight', *Bell Journal of Economics*, 8, pp. 378–93.

Quiggin, John (1982) 'A Theory of Anticipated Utility', *Journal of Economic Behavior and Organization*, December, 3, pp. 323–43.

Radner, R. (1981) 'Monitoring Cooperative Agreements in a Repeated Principal–Agent Relationship', *Econometrica*, 49, pp. 1127–48.

Radner, R. (1985) 'Repeated Principal–Agent Games with Discounting', *Econometrica*, 53, pp. 1173–98.

Radner, R. (1986) 'Repeated Partnership Games with Imperfect Monitoring and No Discounting', *Review of Economic Studies*, 53, pp. 43–57.

Raiffa, Howard (1961) 'Risk, Ambiguity, and the Savage Axioms', *Quarterly Journal of Economics*, November, 75, pp. 690–4.

Raiffa, Howard (1968) *Decision Analysis: Introductory Lectures on Choice Under Uncertainty* (Reading, Mass.: Addison-Wesley).

Rees, R. (1985) 'Cheating in a Duopoly Supergame', *Journal of Industrial Economics*, 33, pp. 387–400.

Reich, Robert (1984) *The Next American Frontier* (New York: Penguin Books).

Reilly, Robert J. (1982) 'Preference Reversal: Further Evidence and Some Suggested Modifications of Experimental Design', *American Economic Review*, June, 72, pp. 576–84.

Riley, J. G. (1979) 'Testing the Educational Screening Hypothesis', *Journal of Political Economy*, 87, S227–S252.

Roemer, J. E. (1985) 'Rationalizing Revolutionary Ideology', *Econometrica*, 53, pp. 85–108.

Roemer, John E. (1986) 'Equality of Resources Implies Equality of Welfare', *Quarterly Journal of Economics*, 101, pp. 751–84.

Rogerson, W. P. (1985) 'The First-Order Approach to Principal–Agent Problems', *Econometrica*, 53, pp. 1357–67.

Rosenbaum, J. E. (1984) *Career Mobility In a Corporate Hierarchy* (London: Academic Press).

Roth, Alvin (1986) 'Laboratory Experimentation in Economics', *Economics and Philosophy*, 2, pp. 245–73.

Roth, Alvin (ed.) (1987) *Laboratory Experimentation in Economics: Six Points of View* (New York: Cambridge University Press).

Rothschild, Michael and Stiglitz, Joseph E. (1970) 'Increasing Risk: (I) A Definition', *Journal of Economic Theory*, September, 2, pp. 225–43.

Rothschild, Michael and Stiglitz, Joseph E. (1973). 'Some Further Results on the Measurement of Inequality', *Journal of Economic Theory*, 6, pp. 188–204.

Rothschild, M. and Stiglitz, J. (1976) 'Equilibrium in Competitive Insurance Markets: an Essay on the Economics of Imperfect Information', *Quarterly Journal of Economics*, 90(4), pp. 629–49.

Rubinstein, A. (1982) 'Perfect Equilibrium in a Bargaining Model', *Econometrica*, 50, pp. 97–109.

Rubinstein, A. and Yaari, M. E. (1983) 'Repeated Insurance Contracts and Moral Hazard', *Journal of Economic Theory*, 30, pp. 74–97.

Russo, J. Edward (1977) 'The Value of Unit Price Information', *Journal of Marketing Research*, May, 14, pp. 193–201.

Russo, J. Edward, Krieser, Gene, and Miyashita, Sally (1975) 'An Effective Display of Unit Price Information', *Journal of Marketing*, April, 39, pp. 11–19.

Samuels, Warren and Schmid, A. Allan (1981) *Law and Economics: An Institutional Perspective* (Boston: Martin Nijhoff).

Samuelson, Paul A. (1952) 'Probability, Utility and the Independence Axiom', *Econometrica*, 20, pp. 670–8.

Santomero, A. M. and Seater, J. J. (1978) 'The Inflation–Unemployment Trade-off: A Critique of the Literature', *Journal of Economic Literature*, 16, pp. 499–544.

Sapsford, D. and Tzannatos, Z. (1989) *Current Issues in Labour Economics* (London: Macmillan).

Savage, Leonard (1954) *The Foundations of Statistics* (New York: Wiley).

Schelling, T. C. (1956) 'An Essay on Bargaining', *American Economic Review*, 46, pp. 281–306.

Schelling, T. C. (1960) *The Strategy of Conflict* (Cambridge, Mass: Harvard University Press).

Schmalensee, R. (1984) 'Imperfect Information and the Equitability of Competitive Prices', *Quarterly Journal of Economics*, 99, 3, pp. 441–460.

Schmeidler, David (1986) 'Subjective Probability and Expected Utility Without Additivity', manuscript, Tel-Aviv University.

Schmid, A. Allan (1978) *Property, Power and Public Choice: An Inquiry Into Law and Economics* (New York: Praeger).

Schoemaker, Paul J. H. and Kunreuther, Howard (1979) 'An Experimental Study of Insurance Decisions', *Journal of Risk and Insurance*, December, 46.

Schumpeter, Joseph Alois (1926) *Theorie der Wirstschaftlichen Entwilung* (Munchen, Leipzig: Dunker & Humblot).

Schumpeter, Joseph Alois (1934) *The Theory of Economic Development* (Cambridge, Mass: Harvard University Press).

Schumpeter, Joseph Alois (1939) *Business Cycles* (New York & London: McGraw Hill).

Schumpeter, Joseph Alois (1942) *Capitalism, Socialism and Democracy* (New York: Harper and Bros).

Segal, Uzi (1984) 'Non-linear Decision Weights with the Independence Axiom', manuscript, University of California, Los Angeles, November.

Segal, Uzi (1987) 'The Ellsberg Paradox and Risk Aversion: An Anticipated Utility Approach', *International Economic Review*, February, 28, pp. 175–202.

Selten, R. (1965) 'Spieltheoretische Behandlung eines Oligopolmodells mit Nachfragetragheit', *Zeitschrift fur die gesamte Staatswissenschaft*, 121, pp. 301–24 and 667–89.

Selten, R. (1978) 'The Chain Store Paradise', *Theory and Decision*, 9, pp. 129–59.

Sen, A. K. (1967) 'Isolation, Assurance and the Social Rate of Discount', *Quarterly Journal of Economics*, 80, pp. 112–24.

Sen, Amartya (1973) *On Economic Inequality* (Oxford: Oxford University Press).

Sen, Amartya (1976) 'Poverty: An Ordinal Approach to Measurement', *Econometrica*, 44, pp. 219–31, reprinted in Sen (1982), pp. 373–87.

Sen, Amartya (1978) 'Ethical Measurement of Inequality: Some Difficulties', in Krelle and Shorrocks (1978), reprinted in Sen (1982), pp. 416–31.

Sen, Amartya (1980) 'Equality of What?', in *The Tanner Lectures on Human Values* (University of Utah Press and Cambridge University Press), reprinted in Sen (1982), pp. 353–69.

Sen, Amartya (1982) *Choice, Welfare and Measurement* (Oxford: Blackwell, and Boston, Mass.: MIT Press).

Sen, Amartya (1985) *Commodities and Capabilities* (Amsterdam: North-Holland).

Shafer, Wayne J. (1974) 'The Non-transitive Consumer, *Econometrica*, September, 42, pp. 913–19.

Shaked, A. and Sutton, J. (1982) 'Relaxing Price Competition Through Product Differentiation', *Review of Economic Studies*, 49, pp. 3–14.

Shaked, A. and Sutton, J. (1983) 'Natural Oligopolies', *Econometrica*, 51, pp. 1469–84.

Shaked, A. and Sutton, J. (1984) 'Natural Oligopolies and International Trade', in H. Kierzkowski (ed.) *Monopolistic Competition and International Trade* (Oxford: Oxford University Press).

Shaked, A. and Sutton, J. (1984) 'Involuntary Unemployment as a Perfect Equilibrium in a Bargaining Model', *Econometrica*, 52, pp. 1351–64.

Shaked, A. and Sutton, J. (1987) 'Multiproduct Firms and Market Structure', ICERD Working Paper, no. 154, London School of Economics.

Shaked, A. and Sutton, J. (1987) 'Product Differentiation and Industrial Structure', *Journal of Industrial Economics*, 36, pp. 131–46.

Shapiro, C. and Stiglitz, J. E. (1984) 'Equilibrium Unemployment as a Worker Discipline Device', *American Economic Review*, 74, pp. 433–44.

Shavell, S. (1979) 'On Moral Hazard and Insurance', *Quarterly Journal of Economics*, 93, 4, pp. 541–62.

Siebert, W. S., Bertrand, P. V. and Addison, J. T. (1985) 'The Political Model of Strikes: A New Twist', *Southern Journal of Economics*, August, pp. 23–33.

Silvestre, J. (1986) 'The Elements of Fixprice Micro Economics', in L. Samuelson (ed.) *Microeconomic Theory* (Boston: Kluwer & Nijhoff).

Simon, Herbert Alexander (1947) *Administrative Behavior: A Study of Decision Making Processes in Administrative Organization* (New York: Macmillan).

Slovic, Paul (1969) 'Manipulating the Attractiveness of a Gamble Without Changing its Expected Value', *Journal of Experimental Psychology*, January, 79, pp. 139–45.

Slovic, Paul (1975) 'Choice Between Equally Valued Alternatives', *Journal of Experimental Psychology: Human Perception and Performance*, August, 1, pp. 280–87.

Slovic, Paul, Fischhoff, Baruch, and Lichtenstein, Sarah (1982) 'Response Mode, Framing, and Information Processing Effects In Risk Assessment', in Robin Hogarth (ed.) *New Directions for Methodology of Social and Behavioral Science: Question Framing and Response Consistency* (San Francisco: Jossey-Bass).

Slovic, Paul and Lichtenstein, Sarah (1968) 'Relative Importance of Probabilities and Payoffs in Risk Taking', *Journal of Experimental Psychology*, November, Pt 2, 78, pp. 1–18.

Slovic, Paul and Lichtenstein, Sarah (1971) 'Comparison of Bayesian and Regression Approaches to the Study of Information Processing in Judgement', *Organizational Behavior and Human Performance*, November, 6, pp. 649–744.

Slovic, Paul and Lichtenstein, Sarah (1983) 'Preference Reversals: A Broader Perspective', *American Economic Review*, September, 73, pp. 596–605.

Slovic, Paul and Tversky, Amos (1974) 'Who Accepts Savage's Axiom?', *Behavioral Science*, November, 19, pp. 368–73.

Smith, Vernon (1979, 1982, 1985) *Research in Experimental Economics* (Connecticut: JAI Press), vols 1, 2 and 3.

Smith, Vernon (1985) 'Experimental Economics: Reply', *American Economic Review*, 75, pp. 265–72.

Sobel, J. and Takahashi, I. (1983) 'A Multi-stage Model of Bargaining', *Review of Economic Studies*, 50, pp. 411–26.

Solo, Robert A. (1967) *Economic Organizations and Social Systems* (Indianapolis: Bobbs Merrill).

Solo, Robert A. (1974) *The Political Authority and the Market System* (Cincinnati: South-Western Press).

Sonnenschein, Hugo F. (1971) 'Demand Theory Without Transitive Preferences, with Applications to the Theory of Competitive Equilibrium', in John S. Chipman, Leonid Hurwicz, Marcel K. Richter and Hugo F. Sonnenschein (eds) *Preferences, Utility and Demand* (New York: Harcourt Brace Jovanovich).

Spence, A. Michael and Zeckhauser, Richard J. (1971) 'Insurance, Information and Individual Action', *American Economic Review, Papers and Proceedings*, May, 61, pp. 380–7.

Spence, M. (1974) *Market Signalling* (Cambridge, Mass: Harvard University Press).

Starrett, D. (1973) 'Inefficiency and the Demand for "Money" in a Sequence Economy', *Review of Economic Studies*, 40, pp. 437–48.

Stigler, G. J. (1964) 'A Theory of Oligopoly', *Journal of Political Economy*, 72, pp. 44–61.

Stiglitz, J. E. (1975) 'The Theory of "Screening", Education, and the Distribution of Income', *American Economic Review*, 65, pp. 283–300.

Stigum, Bernt and Wenstøp, Fred (1988) *Foundations of Utility and Risk Theory with Applications* (Dordrecht, Holland: D. Reidel).

Sugden, Robert (1986) 'New Developments in the Theory of Choice Under Uncertainty', *Bulletin of Economic Research*, January, 38, pp. 1–24.

Sugden, R. (1987) *The Economics of Right, Cooperation and Welfare* (Oxford: Blackwell).

Sutton, J., Shaked, A. and Binmore, K. (1986) 'An Outside Option Experiment', *American Economic Review*, 76, pp. 57–63.

Sutton, J. (1986) 'Non-Cooperative Bargaining Theory: An Introduction', *Review of Economic Studies*, 53, pp. 709–24.

Svejnar, J. (1986) 'Bargaining Power, Fear of Disagreement, and Wage Settlements: Theory and Evidence from US Industry', *Econometrica*, 54, pp. 1955–78.

Symons, E. and Walker, I. (1988) 'Simulation Program for Indirect Taxation', IFS Working Paper 88/17.

Temkin, Larry (1987) 'Intransitivity and the Mere Addition Paradox', *Philosophy and Public Affairs*, 16, pp. 138–87.

Temkin, Larry (forthcoming) *Inequality*.

Thaler, Richard (1980) 'Toward a Positive Theory of Consumer Choice', *Journal of Economic Behavior and Organization*, March, 1, pp. 39–60.

Tracy, J. S. (1987) 'An Empirical Test of an Asymmetric Information Model of Strikes', *Journal of Labour Economics*, 5, pp. 149–73.

Tversky, Amos (1969) 'Intransitivity of Preferences', *Psychological Review*, January, 76, pp. 31–48.

Tversky, Amos (1975) 'A Critique of Expected Utility Theory: Descriptive and Normative Considerations', *Erkenntnis*, 9, pp. 163–73.

Tversky, Amos and Kahneman, Daniel (1971) 'Belief in the Law of Small Numbers', *Psychological Bulletin*, July, 2, pp. 105–10.

Tversky, Amos and Kahneman, Daniel (1974) 'Judgement under Uncertainty: Heuristics and Biases', *Science*, September, 185, pp. 1124–31.

Tversky, Amos and Kahneman, Daniel (1981) 'The Framing of Decisions and The Psychology of Choice', *Science*, January, 211, pp. 453–8.

Tversky, Amos and Kahneman, Daniel (1983) 'Extensional vs. Intuitive Reasoning: the Conjunction Fallacy in Probability Judgment', *Psychological Review*, October, 90, pp. 293–315.

Tversky, Amos and Kahneman, Daniel (1986) 'Rational Choice and the Framing of Decisions', *Journal of Business*, October, Pt 2, 4, pp. 251–78.

Varian, H. (1978) 'The Stability of a Disequilibrium IS–LM Model', in S. Strom and L. Werin (eds) *Topics in Disequilibrium Economics* (London: Macmillan).

Varian, H. (1978) *Microeconomic Analysis* (New York: W. W. Norton).

Varoufakis, Y. (1987) 'Optimisation and Strikes', Ph.D thesis, University of Essex.

Veblen, Thorstein (1899) *The Theory of the Leisure Class* (New York: Macmillan).

Veblen, Thorstein (1906) *The Theory of Business Enterprise* (New York: Charles Scribner's Sons).

Veblen, Thorstein (1921) *The Engineers and the Price System* (New York: Viking Press).

Veblen, Thorstein (1923) *Absentee Ownership and Business Enterprise in Modern Times* (New York: Viking Press).

Vickrey, William (1961) 'Counterspeculation, Auctions and Competitive Sealed Tenders', *Journal of Finance*, 16, pp. 8–37.

Viscusi, W. Kip (1985) 'Are Individuals Bayesian Decision Makers?', *American Economic Review, Papers and Proceedings*, May, 75, pp. 381–5.

von Neumann, John and Morgenstern, Oskar (1947) *Theory of Games and Economic Behavior* (Princeton: Princeton University Press, 1944) 2nd edn., 1947; 3rd edn., 1953.

Weber, Max (1950) *The Protestant Ethic and the Spirit of Capitalism* (New York: Scribner).

Weber, Max (1968) *Max Weber on Charisma and Institution Building*, edited by S. N. Eisenstadt (Chicago: University of Chicago Press).

Weber, Max (1978) *Economy and Society*, edited by Gunther Roth and Claus Wittich (Berkeley: University of California Press).

Wiggins, David (1985) 'Claims of Need', in Honderich (1985).

Williamson, O. E. (1987) *Antitrust Economics: Mergers, Contracting, and Strategic Behaviour* (Oxford: Basil Blackwell).

Yaari, Menahem (1969) 'Some Remarks on Measures of Risk Aversion and On their Uses', *Journal of Economic Theory*, October, 1, pp. 315–29.

Yaari, Menahem (1987a) 'The Dual Theory of Choice Under Risk', *Econometrica*, January, 1987, 55, pp. 95–115.

Yaari, Menahem E. (1987b) 'A Controversial Proposal Concerning Inequality Measurement', typescript.

Yitzhaki, S. (1983) 'On an Extension of the Gini Inequality Index', *International Economic Review*, 24, pp. 615–28.

Zeuthen, F. (1930) *Problems of Monopoly and Economic Warfare* (New York: Augustus M. Kelley reprint 1968).

Author Index

Subject Index